Christina Pabst

KATHA POLLITT, the author of *Virginity or Death!*
and *Learning to Drive,* is a poet, essayist, and columnist for *The Nation*. She has won many prizes
and awards for her work, including the National
Book Critics Circle Award for her first collection of
poems, *Antarctic Traveller,* and two National Magazine Awards—for Essays and Criticism, and Col-
umns and Commentary. She lives in New York City.

Additional Praise for *Pro*

"With Pollitt's characteristic wit and logic, *Pro* marshals science, history, medicine, religion, statistics, and stories of real women's lives—with all the 'tangled secret misfortunes' of families—to make a myth-busting argument that abortion is a social good. It's good for women. It's good for children. It's good for men. It's a normal fact of life and has been since ancient times. All of which might sound shocking, so rarely do we hear about abortion's benefits."   —Kate Manning, *Time*

"Pollitt does an excellent job of unpacking [the statistics] and showing the contradictions in our views, as well as the limits to what surveys can tell us about the decisions Americans make for themselves."   —Laurie Abraham, *Elle*

"[This] shouldn't be a radical message, but in an era when some feminists feel the need to defend the birth control pill by highlighting its use for reasons other than contraception, the very idea that we should insist that abortion is a good thing because it's good for women feels incredibly bold. . . . 'No one is pro-abortion' is a common refrain among liberals defending the right to choose. In the abstract, no, but if you need an abortion to live your life as you see fit, then pro-abortion is exactly what you are. Katha Pollitt has your back on this."   —*Ms.*

"A refreshing and comprehensive look at abortion rights . . . *Pro* is a passionate plea—and a book that is needed now more than ever."   —Michele Filgate, *Salon*

"Astute and convincing."   —*San Francisco Chronicle*

"Throughout *Pro*, Pollitt maintains a moral clarity. . . . Ultimately, Pollitt is arguing not just for reproductive rights but for reproductive justice, which places the right to mother, or not, within the global context of human rights and social and economic justice, inextricable from the fight for universal health insurance, immigration reform, and a host of social challenges. It's a holistic vision of a more just society that in her telling is at once utterly reasonable and heartbreakingly elusive."

—*Chicago Tribune*

"A lucid and passionate book."   —Jane Ciabattari, BBC.com

"[*Pro* is] a challenging, smart book, and it will change what you think about and talk about when the topic of abortion comes up."   —*Flavorwire*

"[A] powerful call to understand abortion not as some singular culture-war issue but as one part of a struggle for women to be able to live full, complete lives, and for the reproductive labor that is still done mostly by women to be understood as something that benefits all of society and is deserving of respect and (financial) support."   —*Refinery 29*

"Such an important book . . . Pollitt's fearlessness in exposing and dismissing the misogynist kernel at the center of the issue makes *Pro* the most fearlessly feminist book I've read in ages, a genuine work of bravery and scholarship and discourse. Am I gushing? You bet. You will be, too."   —*The Stranger*

"An impassioned, persuasive case for understanding [abortion] in its proper context . . . With wit and logic, Pollitt debunks the many myths surrounding abortion, and analyzes what abortion opponents really oppose: namely, women's growing sexual freedom and power. . . . With arguments that are both lucid and sensible, Pollitt successfully reframes the abortion debate to show that, 'in the end, abortion is an issue of fundamental human rights.'" —*Publishers Weekly* (starred review)

"In this powerful pro-choice treatise, Pollitt, the well-known feminist, poet, and award-winning columnist for *The Nation*, expertly lays out why she supports a woman's right to decide whether to end a pregnancy." —*Booklist* (starred review)

"A dramatic, persuasive argument for abortion . . . Bolstered by dramatic statistics ('excluding miscarriages, 21 percent of pregnancies end in abortion'), personal interviews, and historical references reaching as far back as ancient Greece and Egypt, Pollitt impressively makes her case while admitting that abortion clinics have become increasingly inaccessible and certain 'pronatalist pundits' are holding women's intimately private pregnancy decisions up for public scrutiny. . . . Pollitt's cogent opinion presents potent testimony on a woman's right to choose." —*Kirkus Reviews*

"Pro-choice advocates will find Pollitt's summation helpful in recruitment." —*Library Journal*

PRO

RECLAIMING ABORTION RIGHTS

KATHA POLLITT

PICADOR   NEW YORK

www.picadorusa.com
www.twitter.com/picadorusa • www.facebook.com/picadorusa
picadorbookroom.tumblr.com

Picador® is a U.S. registered trademark and is used by St. Martin's Press under license from Pan Books Limited.

For book club information, please visit www.facebook.com/picadorbookclub or e-mail marketing@picadorusa.com.

Grateful acknowledgment is made for permission to reprint lines from the following:

"The Wide and Varied World" by Ellen Bryant Voigt, copyright © 1987 by Ellen Bryant Voigt. Used by permission of Ellen Bryant Voigt.

Designed by Anna Gorovoy

The Library of Congress has cataloged the hardcover edition as follows:

Pollitt, Katha.
   Pro : reclaiming abortion rights / Katha Pollitt. — First edition.
      pages cm
   ISBN 978-0-312-62054-7 (hardcover)
   ISBN 978-1-250-05584-2 (e-book)
   1. Abortion—United States.   2. Abortion—United States—Public
opinion.   3. Abortion—Government policy—United States.   I. Title.
   HQ767.5.U5P65 2014
   363.460973—dc23

                                                    2014017553

Picador Paperback ISBN 978-1-250-07266-5

Picador books may be purchased for educational, business, or promotional use. For information on bulk purchases, please contact the Macmillan Corporate and Premium Sales Department at 1-800-221-7945, extension 5442, or write specialmarkets@macmillan.com.

First published by Picador

First Picador Paperback Edition: July 2015

10   9   8   7   6   5   4   3   2   1

In memory of Lynn Schneider
1950–2013
as promised

Outside, snow falls in the streets
and quiet hills, and seems, in the window,
framed by the room's continuous greenery,
to obliterate the wide and varied world.
We half-smile, half-nod to one another.
One returns to her magazine.
One shifts gently to the right arm
her sleeping newborn, unfurls the bud of its hand.
One of us takes her turn in the inner office
where she submits to the steel table
and removes from her body its stubborn wish.
We want what you want, only
we have to want it more.

—Ellen Bryant Voigt
"The Wide and Varied World"

CONTENTS

INTRODUCTION

I never had an abortion, but my mother did. She didn't tell me about it, but from what I pieced together after her death from a line in her FBI file, which my father, the old radical, had requested along with his own, it was in 1960, so like almost all abortions back then, it was illegal. The agent who kept her file wrote that she was in the care of a physician for gynecological problems that spring, which I like to think was his chivalrous way of protecting her from further investigation, but perhaps he too was in the dark and only put down what he knew. For a while I was angry at her, the way one is angry at the dead for keeping their secrets till it is too late to ask questions, and the way one can be angry at one's mother for having a life outside her child's ken. I thought she owed me this bit of woman-to-woman realism and honesty, instead of, or at least in addition to, tales of the nine marriage proposals she had received by the time she met my father, and falling in love with him at first sight, and eloping with him three months later when she had just turned twenty-one. Knowing about her abortion might have helped me. It might have given me a truer sense of life as a young, very romantic woman who had no idea what was what.

When I ask myself why I have been so preoccupied with abortion rights for so long, I wonder if learning about my mother's abortion—its illegality, the fact that she didn't tell my father, the unknowability of her reasons or her feelings or the experience itself—is part of the answer. I find myself wondering: Was whoever performed the procedure a real doctor? Was he kind to her? Respectful? Did he do his best not to cause pain? Did she take someone with her? I remember her talking with her friend Judy about how another woman they knew had "had a D&C," which was often a euphemism for abortion back then, so maybe her circle of women steered her to a good practitioner. Maybe her friend Judy sat in the waiting room, if there was a waiting room, and took her home in a taxi afterward and made her a cup of tea. I hope so. It would have been so wrong if my tender, fragile mother had had to go through that all by herself.

What did it mean that my mother had to break the law to end a pregnancy? It meant that America basically said to her, *It's the twentieth century, so we're going to let you vote and go to college, and have a family and a job—not a great job, not the one you wanted, because unfortunately that job is for men—and your own charge accounts at Bonwit's and Altman's and your own subscription to the Heritage Book Club, but underneath all that normal, forward-looking, mid-twentieth-century middle-class New York life is the secret underground life of women, and that you must manage outside the law. If you are injured or die or are trapped by the police, you'll only have yourself to blame, because the real reason you are here on Earth is to produce children, and you shirk that duty at your peril.* I wonder if my mother knew that her own grandmother died of an abortion after bearing nine children, back in Russia, during the First World War, or if her mother kept that family secret from her as she kept her secret from me.

Women's lives are different now—so much so we're in danger of forgetting how they used to be. Legalizing abortion didn't just save women from death and injury and fear of arrest, it didn't just make it possible for women to commit to education and work and free them from shotgun marriages and too many kids. It changed how women saw themselves: as mothers by choice, not fate. As long as abortion is available to her, even a woman who thinks it is tantamount to murder is making a choice when she keeps a pregnancy. She may feel like she has to have that baby—Jesus or her parents or her boyfriend is telling her she has to do it. But actually, she doesn't have to do it. She is choosing to have that baby. *Roe v. Wade* gave women a kind of existential freedom that is not always welcome—indeed, is sometimes quite painful—but that has become part of what women are.

One thing *Roe v. Wade* didn't do, though, was make abortion private.

Sometimes I look up from reading about the latest onslaught against abortion rights—while I've been writing this introduction, Louisiana passed laws like those that are forcing dozens of Texas clinics to close, Missouri legislators passed a seventy-two-hour waiting period requirement for its sole remaining clinic, and a Montana health center that performed abortions as part of a family practice was trashed beyond repair, allegedly by the son of a prominent local abortion opponent—and I think, How strange. Justice Harry Blackmun's majority opinion in *Roe v. Wade* was all about privacy, but the most private parts of a woman's body and the most private decisions she will ever make have never been more public. Everyone gets to weigh in. Even, according to the five conservative Catholic men on the Supreme Court, her employer. If the CEO of the Hobby Lobby crafts store chain, a secular business, decides that emergency contraception and IUDs are "abortifacients" and banned by God, he is entitled to keep them out of her health coverage—even though he's wrong about how these methods work. It's religion—facts don't matter, especially when the facts involve women's liberty.

Maybe Blackmun's mistake was thinking that a woman could claim privacy as a right in the first place. A man's home is his castle, but a woman's body has never been wholly her own. Historically, it's belonged to her nation, her community, her father, her family, her husband—in 1973, when *Roe* was decided, marital rape was legal in every state. Why shouldn't her body belong to a fertilized egg as well? And if that egg has a right to live and grow in her body, why shouldn't she be held legally responsible for its fate and be forced to have a cesarean if her doctor thinks it's best or be charged with a crime if she uses illegal drugs and delivers a stillborn or sick baby? Incidents like this have been happening all over the country for some time now. Denying women the right to end a pregnancy is the flip side of punishing women for conduct during pregnancy, and even if not punishing, monitoring. In the spring of 2014 a law was proposed in the Kansas state legislature that would require doctors to report every miscarriage, no matter how early in pregnancy.[1] You would almost think the people who have always opposed women's independence and full participation in society were still at it. They can't push women all the way back, but they can use women's bodies to keep them under surveillance and control.

That thought gives rise to a wish. Surely, I find myself daydreaming, there is something, some substance already in common use, that women could drink after sex or at the end of the month, that would keep them unpregnant with no one the wiser. Something you could buy at the supermarket, or maybe several things you could mix together, items so safe and so ordinary they could never be banned, that you could prepare in your own home, that would flush your uterus and leave it pink and shiny and empty without you ever needing to know if you were pregnant or about to be. A brew of Earl Grey, Lapsang Souchong, and ground cardamom, say. Or Coca-Cola with a teaspoon of Nescafé and a dusting of cayenne pepper. Things you might have on your shelves right now, just waiting for some clever person to put them together, some stay-at-home mother with a chemistry degree rattling around her kitchen late at night.

Something like the herbal concoctions Jamaica Kincaid remembers from her childhood:

> When I was a child, growing up on an island in the Caribbean, an island whose inhabitants were mostly descendants of people forcibly brought there from Africa, I noticed that from time to time my mother and her friends, all of them women, would gather together at some spot in our yard and talk and sip and drink some very dark hot drink that they had made from various leaves and bark of trees that they had gathered. Without them telling me anything directly, I came to understand that the potions they were drinking were meant to sweep their wombs clean of anything in it that would result in them being unable to manage the day-to-day working of their lives; that is, this clearing of their wombs was another form of house keeping.[2]

Think of it: no pharmacist refusing to fill your prescription for birth control or Plan B, no religious fanatics following you through the clinic parking lot screaming "Baby killer!" and taking down your license-plate number, hoping to raise your blood pressure so high that you won't be able to have your procedure that day, no need to notify your parents or get their permission. The whole elaborate panopticon that governs abortion today—gone. RU-486, the "French abortion pill," now better known as mifepristone, was supposed to accomplish that: Any doctor could prescribe it in his office and no one need be the wiser. A 1999 *New York Times Sunday Magazine* cover story called it "the little white bombshell" that "may well reconfigure the politics and perception of abortion," pushing abortion earlier and reintegrating it with regular medical practice. It's the age-old hope that a single technological or scientific advance will once and for all resolve a social issue, a fantasy that means forgetting that the new thing will be embedded in the existing system and involve the existing human beings. For a variety of reasons—difficulties obtaining the drug, laws that made medication abortions as heavily regulated as surgical ones, fear of abortion opponents—few doctors not already involved in abortion care took up the challenge of prescribing it. That women want early abortion, that many women prefer medication to surgery, that especially in rural areas it would be a lot simpler and cheaper and less stressful for women to get a prescription from their local OBGYN or GP than to travel long distances to a clinic, that it would be a good thing to free women from having to run a gauntlet of protesters—none of that mattered. What women want in their abortion care is simply not important.

"Trust Women" is a popular motto in the pro-choice movement. It sounds a little sentimental, doesn't it? Part of that old sisterhood-is-powerful feminism, it is fashionable to mock today. But "Trust Women" doesn't mean that every woman is wise or good or has magical intuitive powers. It means that no one else can make a better decision, because no one else is living her life, and since she will have to live with that decision, not you, and not the state legislature or the Supreme Court, chances are she is doing her best in a tight spot. Dr. George Tiller, who provided abortion care in Wichita, Kansas, and was one of a handful of doctors to perform abortions after twenty-four weeks, wore a "Trust Women" button. Unlike the vast majority of Americans, he did not assume that a woman seeking an abortion late in pregnancy was lazy or stupid or too busy having sex to have attended to matters early on. He did not assume that her body ceased to be her own because she was pregnant. Well, you see what trusting women got him: In 2009 he was gunned down in church by Scott Roeder, a far-right Christian anti-government anti-abortion activist, who thought he had the right to commit murder because, as he told a reporter, "preborn children's lives were in imminent danger."[3]

When *Roe v. Wade* was wending its way through the courts, and various states were reforming their abortion laws to permit abortion for rape, incest, fetal deformity and the like, the radical feminist activist Lucinda Cisler, head of New Yorkers for Repeal of Abortion Laws, warned against half measures that left women regulated by the state and the medical profession. She feared that qualifications of the essential right "would be extremely difficult to get judges and legislators to throw out later."[4] At one meeting, she held up a piece of paper representing the ideal abortion law: It was blank. Cisler saw *Roe v. Wade* as a defeat, and maybe she was on to something, because what seemed at the time to be small details have proven to be critical fault lines. The extraordinary deference paid to physicians and their judgment preserved the idea that the woman's desire to end a pregnancy was not enough in itself, it had to be approved by a respectable authority figure, at the time almost always a man. (*Roe* placed the medical profession under no burden to actually provide abortion care, and indeed few doctors and few hospitals want anything to do with it.) Furthermore, the acceptance of a near total ban on later abortion contained the germ of the idea that the fetus had rights that trumped those of the woman. It isn't hard to see how these small seeds blossomed into the whole infantilizing rigmarole we have today, which is all about disrespecting women's capacity to make an independent judgment about their pregnancies: parental notification and consent, judicial bypass, waiting periods, crisis pregnancy centers (CPCs), government-mandated scripts full of anti-abortion propaganda that doctors must read to patients, and so on. But Cisler was wrong in a way too: Had the Supreme Court agreed in 1973 that the proper abortion law was none at all, we would probably have ended up close to where we are today because of the power and determination of the anti-abortion movement and the qualms and hesitations and lack of engagement of most who are nominally pro-choice. It is just that hard to see women as belonging to themselves.

And yet, women keep trying. They put off the rent or the utilities to scrape together the $500 for a first-trimester abortion. They drive across whole states to get to a clinic and sleep in their cars because they can't afford a motel. They do not do this because they are careless sluts or because they hate babies or because they fail to see clearly what their alternatives are. They see the alternatives all too clearly. We live, as Ellen Willis wrote, in a society that is "actively hostile to women's ambitions for a better life. Under these conditions the unwillingly pregnant woman faces a terrifying loss of control over her fate." Abortion, wrote Willis, is an act of self-defense.[5]

Perhaps we don't see abortion that way because we don't think women have the right to a self. They are supposed to live for others. Qualities that are seen as normal and desirable in men—ambition, confidence, outspokenness—are perceived as selfish and aggressive in women, especially when they have children. Perhaps that is why women's privacy has so little purchase on the abortion debate: Only a self can have privacy.

And only a self can have equality. Many feminist legal scholars, including Justice Ruth Bader Ginsburg, have argued that the Supreme Court should have legalized abortion on grounds of equality rather than privacy.[6] Pregnancy and childbirth are not only physical and medical experiences, after all. They are also social experiences that, in modern America, just as when abortion was criminalized in the 1870s, serve to restrict women's ability to participate in society on equal footing with men. Would we be living in a different world today had Blackmun based abortion rights on the need to dismantle women's subordination? Or would the same people who don't accept women's privacy rights say, Well, if women can't be equal without abortion, they'll have to stay in their place?

As I write, reporters describe the return of illegal abortion in states where clinics have closed. In Texas, women in the Rio Grande Valley, now hundreds of miles from a clinic—no problem, said Judge Edith Jones of the Fifth Circuit, just drive fast—are going over the Mexican border to buy misoprostol, which causes miscarriage and is sold over the counter there as an anti-ulcer medication. Even where abortion is available, some women won't or can't go to a clinic: They're undocumented immigrants and fear arrest, they have no money, there's too much shame around abortion to risk being seen by someone who knows them. But now, with clinics disappearing, more and more women will have no choice but to turn to pills, as women do in Ireland and other countries where it is illegal for a woman to end a pregnancy. Some will end up in emergency rooms. Some will be injured. Some may die. This is what laws supposedly intended to protect women from "dangerous" clinics will have accomplished. This is what the so-called pro-life movement will have done for "life."

As I mentioned earlier, a single discovery or invention rarely lives up to its promise of deep social change. Even the birth-control pill, an immense advance over the clumsy and fallible methods that preceded it, has fallen short: Half of all pregnancies in the United States are accidental. Still, I imagine my mother, sitting at the kitchen table, in her pretty bathrobe with the blue and yellow flowers, on an ordinary day in 1960, cutting out articles from the *New York Times* as she loved to do. She lights a Benson & Hedges and sips her very dark hot drink while the sun pours in through the window facing the street.

I wrote this book because I wanted to put real women, women like my mother, back at the center of the way we talk about abortion. Abortion opponents have been very effective at shifting the focus of moral concern onto the contents of women's wombs—even an unimplanted fertilized egg is a baby now. Unless they are very brave, women who seek abortion have been pushed back into the shadows. It's one thing for a rape victim to speak up, or a woman with a wanted pregnancy that has turned into a medical catastrophe. But why can't a woman just say, This wasn't the right time for me? Or two children (or one, or none) are enough? Why must the woman apologize for not having a baby just because she happened to get pregnant? It's as if we think motherhood is the default setting for a woman's life from first period to menopause, and she needs a note from God not to say yes to every zygote that knocks on her door—even if, like most women who have abortions, including my mother, she already has children. There is deep contempt for women in that—and disregard for the seriousness of motherhood as well.

For many years, pundits dismissed the notion that abortion would ever be significantly restricted, and mocked as Chicken Littles pro-choicers who warned that both rights and access were at risk, and contraception, too. The conventional wisdom held the Republican Party would not risk waking the sleeping giant that is the middle-of-the-road more-or-less-pro-choice voter. Now we are seeing the Chicken Littles were right. Where is that giant? In some states, it is indeed stretching and standing up—Virginia is a blue state now because the Republicans in charge went too far, closing clinics, trying to mandate transvaginal ultrasounds, and so on. In others, the giant dozes on, immobilized by conflicting, not-very-well-thought-out notions about women, sex, family, race, government, and a general sense that America is going down the drain.

Clinic doctors, nurses, directors, and employees risk their lives to help women. Patient escorts, abortion-fund volunteers, bloggers, organizers, lawyers, and thousands of other activists work tirelessly to keep abortion legal, expand access, change the discourse, and sway the vote. But it's the millions of pro-choice Americans who are so far uninvolved (and still complacent) that will ultimately decide the fate of legal abortion in this country.

It's past time for the giant to rise.

A NOTE ON LANGUAGE

I have tried to avoid the terms "pro-life" and "pro-lifer." In general it makes sense to call people what they wish to be called and by which they are commonly recognized, but "pro-life" encodes too much propaganda for me: that a fertilized egg is a life in the same sense that a woman is, that it has a right to life as she does, that outlawing abortion saves lives, that abortion is the chief threat to "life" today, and that the movement to ban abortion is motivated solely by these concerns and not also by the wish to restrict sexual freedom, enforce sectarian religious views on a pluralistic society, and return women to traditional roles. It also suggests that those who support legal abortion are pro-death, which is absurd. Except when I am clearly referring to the organized political movement that calls itself "pro-life" I will use the neutral terms "opposition to abortion," "abortion opponents," "anti-abortion," and similar.

I've also tried to avoid using "fetus" to refer to every stage of human development in the womb. Unfortunately, there is no politically neutral general term that accurately covers the whole nine months, at least none that sounds like an English word ("conceptus"?), but "fetus" inaccurately suggests that late abortion is the norm. In fact, two-thirds of abortions take place at eight weeks or earlier, when the fetus is still an embryo. If all along abortion opponents had talked about "embryonic rights," and "the embryo's right to life" I wonder if they would have gotten as far as they have.

I will refer to supporters of abortion rights as "pro-choicers," because it is an accurate term for those who support women's right to decide for themselves whether to end a pregnancy or carry it to term.

ONE

RECLAIMING ABORTION

Abortion. We need to talk about it. I know, sometimes it seems as if we talk of little else, so perhaps I should say we need to talk about it differently. Not as something we all agree is a bad thing about which we shake our heads sadly and then debate its precise degree of badness, preening ourselves on our judiciousness and moral seriousness as we argue about this or that restriction on this or that kind of woman. We need to talk about ending a pregnancy as a common, even normal, event in the reproductive lives of women—and not just modern American women either, but women throughout history and all over the world, from ancient Egypt to medieval Catholic Europe, from today's sprawling cities to rural villages barely touched by modern ideas about women's roles and rights. Abortion takes place in Canada and Greece and France, where it is legal, performed by medical professionals, and covered by national health insurance, and also in Kenya, Nicaragua, and the Philippines, where it is a crime and a woman who terminates a pregnancy takes her life in her hands. According to anthropologists, abortion is found in virtually every society, going back at least 4,000 years. American women had great numbers of abortions throughout our history, when it was legal and when it was not. Consider this: At the beginning of the nineteenth century effective birth control barely existed and in the 1870s it was criminalized— even mailing an informational pamphlet about contraceptive devices was against the law and remained so until 1936.[1] Yet the average number of births per woman declined from around 7 in 1800 to around 3.5 in 1900 to just over 2 in 1930.[2] How do you think that happened?

We need to see abortion as an urgent practical decision that is just as moral as the decision to have a child—indeed, sometimes more moral. Pro-choicers often say no one is "pro-abortion," but what is so virtuous about adding another child to the ones you're already overwhelmed by? Why do we make young women feel guilty for wanting to feel ready for mother-hood before they have a baby? Isn't it a good thing that women think carefully about what it means to bring a child into this world—what, for example, it means to the children she already has? We tend to think of abortion as anti-child and anti-motherhood. In media iconography, it's the fetus versus the coat hanger: that is, abortion kills an "unborn baby," but ban-ning it makes women injure themselves. Actually, abortion is part of being a mother and of caring for children, because part of caring for children is knowing when it's not a good idea to bring them into the world.

We need to put abortion back into its context, which is the lives and bodies of women, but also the lives of men, and fami-lies, and the children those women already have or will have. Since nearly 1 in 5 American women end their childbearing years without having borne a child (compared with 1 in 10 in the 1970s), we need to acknowledge that motherhood is not for everyone; there are other ways of living a useful, happy life.[3]

We need to talk about abortion in its full human setting: sex and sexuality, love, violence, privilege, class, race, school and work, men, the scarcity of excellent, respectful reproductive health care, and of realistic, accurate information about sex and reproduction. We need to talk about why there are so many unplanned and unwanted pregnancies—which means we need to talk about birth control, but also about so much more than that: about poverty and violence and family troubles, about sexual shyness and shame and ignorance and the lack of power so many women experience in bed and in their relationships with men. Why *is* it such a huge big deal to ask a man to wear a condom? Or for a man to do so without being asked? Why do so many women not realize they are pregnant until they are fifteen or twenty or even twenty-five weeks along, and what does that say about the extraordinary degree of vigilance we demand women exercise over their reproductive systems? And speaking of that vigilance, what about the fact that some 16 percent of women, according to a Brown University study, have experienced reproductive coercion in at least one relationship— a male partner who used threats or violence to control a woman's contraception or pregnancy outcomes—with a remarkable 9 percent experiencing "birth control sabotage," a male partner who disposed of her pills, poked holes in condoms, or prevented her from getting contraception. One-third of the women reporting reproductive coercion also reported partner abuse in the same relationship.[4] Behind America's high rate of unintended pregnancy—almost half of all pregnancies—and high rates of abortion lies a world of hurt.

We need to talk about the scarcity of resources for single mothers and even for two-parent families, and the extraordinary, contradictory demands we make upon young girls to be simultaneously sexually alluring and withholding: hot virgins. We need to talk about blood and mess and periods and pregnancy and childbirth and what women go through to bring new life into the world and whether deep in our hearts we believe that those bodies mean women were put on Earth to serve and sacrifice and suffer in a way that men are not. Because when we talk about abortion as a bad thing, and worry that there's too much of it, sometimes we mean there's too much unwanted pregnancy and that women and men need more and better sex education and birth control, and sometimes we mean there's too much poverty, especially for children and their mothers, but a lot of the time we mean a woman should have a good cry, and then do the right thing and have the baby. She can always put it up for adoption, can't she, like Juno in the movie? And that is close to saying that a woman can have no needs, desires, purpose, or calling so compelling and so important that she should not set it aside in an instant, because of a stray sperm.

Abortion has been legal across the United States for more than four decades. More than a million abortions are performed every year—some 55 million since 1973, when *Roe v. Wade* became the law of the land. A few facts: By menopause, 3 in 10 American women will have terminated at least one pregnancy; about half of all US women who have an abortion have already had a prior abortion; excluding miscarriages, 21 percent of pregnancies end in abortion. Contrary to the popular stereotype of abortion-seeking women as promiscuous teenagers or child-hating professionals, around 6 in 10 women who have abortions are already mothers. And 7 in 10 are poor or low-income.[5] Abortion, in other words, is part of the fabric of American life, and yet it is arguably more stigmatized than it was when *Roe* was decided. Of the seven Supreme Court justices who made up the majority in *Roe*, five were nominated by a Republican president. These men were hardly radicals: Potter Stewart, nominated by President Eisenhower, had dissented in the court's 1965 landmark decision, *Griswold v. Connecticut*, which struck down that state's ban on the sale or use of contraceptives even by married couples; in two separate decisions he upheld prayer and Bible readings in public schools. Warren Burger, Richard Nixon's choice for Chief Justice, went on to rule in favor of laws criminalizing "sodomy" in *Bowers v. Hardwick* (1986) on the grounds that historically homosexuality had been viewed as heinous and wrong. What made these staid, gray-haired gentlemen permit abortion virtually on demand in the first six months of pregnancy?

To understand that, we have to see what those men saw. In the law, they were witnessing a rapid evolution toward increased personal freedom, and in particular increased freedom for women: These were the years when feminism was a true grassroots movement, one that achieved remarkable success in a very short time, knocking down hundreds of laws and regulations, challenging centuries of tradition and custom, and expanding women's rights and opportunities in almost every area of life. Ten million women were taking birth-control pills, and two-thirds of all Catholic women were using some form of contraception. Women were pouring into colleges and the workforce.[6] The year before the *Roe* decision, the Senate had passed the Equal Rights Amendment and sent it to the states for ratification.

In tandem with these huge social shifts, elite views were changing on abortion. Doctors had helped criminalize abortions after the Civil War as part of their effort to professionalize medicine by marginalizing midwives and lay healers. Now significant numbers of them saw abortion bans as a constraint on their right to care for their patients: Barring malpractice, there was no other circumstance in which a doctor had to defend his professional decisions as a matter of law. There had always been a little wiggle room in state abortion laws, because doctors were still permitted to perform them for "therapeutic" reasons—to save a woman's life, for example.[7] But what did that mean, exactly? An amicus curiae brief in *Roe* from the American College of Obstetricians and Gynecologists and several other medical groups observed that "a woman suffering from heart disease, diabetes or cancer whose pregnancy worsens the underlying pathology may be denied a medically indicated therapeutic abortion under the statute because death is not certain."[8] Meanwhile, the definition of "therapeutic" was being quietly expanded—for women with money, connections, and luck. Certain psychiatrists were willing to bend the rules by certifying abortion-seeking patients as mentally ill or suicidal (of course, you had to pay them for this service, and know how to find them in the first place). Beginning in the late 1940s, hospitals in many states set up abortion committees to which a woman seeking to terminate her pregnancy could appeal.[9] It was a humiliating process, which could involve multiple physical examinations and interrogations by unsympathetic doctors. For some women, the price of an abortion was sterilization. But it meant that some small fraction of middle-class white girls and women were able to obtain legal abortions, especially if they happened to be related to one of the doctors on the committee.

As a matter of public discussion, abortion was coming out of the shadows. In 1962, Sherri Chessen Finkbine was granted a legal abortion because she had taken Thalidomide, a sleeping medication her husband had brought back from a trip to Europe that, she belatedly discovered, had resulted in the births of thousands of babies with disastrous deformities. When the abortion was canceled after a newspaper article about her situation created an uproar, Finkbine publicly went to Sweden and terminated her pregnancy there. Her story was featured on the cover of *Life* magazine and helped break the silence around abortion.[10] But it did more than that. It presented an abortion-seeking woman as sympathetic, rational, and capable. Finkbine was not a college student or low-income single mother to be either pitied as a victim or scorned as a slut. She was a white, middle-class married mother of four, well known as Miss Sherri on the local version of *Romper Room*, a popular children's television show. In the early 1960s, epidemics of rubella, which is linked to birth defects, had the same effect: Americans had to listen to respectable white women unapologetically demanding the right to end their pregnancies. At the same time, Americans had to face the fact that illegal abortion was already common.

The more exceptions there were to the criminalization of abortion, the more glaringly unfair and hypocritical the whole system was seen to be. By the time *Roe* came to the court, well-off, savvy women could flock to New York or several other states where laws had been relaxed and get a safe, legal termination; poor women, trapped in states that banned abortion, bore the brunt of harm from illegal procedures. There was a racial angle, too: Not only did women of color, then as now, have far more abortions than whites in proportion to their numbers, they were much more likely to be injured or die in botched illegal procedures. According to the Centers for Disease Control and Prevention, from 1972 to 1974, the mortality rate due to illegal abortion for nonwhite women was 12 times that for white women.[11] The injustice of a patchwork system, in which a simple medical procedure could leave a woman dead or injured based purely on where it took place, was obvious.

Women were speaking up, too, about their abortions. In 1969 feminists invaded and disrupted the New York state legislature's "expert hearing" on abortion (the experts consisted of fourteen men and a nun). Women talked about ending their pregnancies in public speak-outs. In 1972 the first issue of Ms. magazine carried a statement headlined "We Have Had Abortions" that was signed by more than fifty prominent women, including Gloria Steinem, Nora Ephron, Billie Jean King, Lee Grant, and Lillian Hellman. In Chicago, the Jane Collective began by connecting women with an illegal provider and ended up performing abortions themselves. And if you assume the churches were united against abortion, think again: Beginning in 1967, the Clergy Consultation Service founded by the Rev. Howard R. Moody, a Baptist, along with Lawrence Lader, Arlene Carmen, and others, helped thousands of women across the country find their way to safe illegal abortions. In the years leading up to Roe, legalization of abortion under at least some circumstances was endorsed by the Union for Reform Judaism, the Southern Baptist Convention, the National Association of Evangelicals, the United Methodist Church, the Presbyterian Church USA, the Episcopal Church, and other mainstream denominations.

Because so much of this history has been forgotten—what, the Southern Baptists supported legalization?—we tend to see Roe as a bolt out of the blue. But to the Supreme Court—and to the public, a majority of which supported liberalization—the ruling ratified and expanded social changes that were already under way.[12] At the time, what its supporters saw as its chief effect was to transform an operation that was commonplace, criminal and sometimes extremely dangerous into an operation that was commonplace, legal, remarkably safe—and becoming ever safer: "Deaths from legal abortion declined fivefold between 1973 and 1985 (from 3.3 deaths to 0.4 deaths per 100,000 procedures)," reported the American Medical Association's Council on Scientific Affairs, reflecting increased physician education and skills, improvements in medical technology, and, notably, the earlier termination of pregnancy. The mortality rate for childbirth from 1979 to 1985 was more than ten times higher than that from abortion in the same period.[13]

Today the real-life harms *Roe* was intended to rectify have receded from memory. Few doctors remember the hospital wards filled with injured and infected women. The coat-hanger symbol seems as exotic as the rack and thumbscrew, a relic waved by gray-haired "radical feminists," even as anti-abortion advocates use rare examples of injury and death to paint all abortions as unsafe. They seized on the horrifying case of Dr. Kermit Gosnell, who ran a filthy Philadelphia "clinic" where a teenage girl administered anesthesia, a patient died and others were injured, fetuses were aborted well into the third trimester, and the ones who survived had their spines "snipped." You wouldn't know from their reporting that what Gosnell was doing was completely against the law; he was found guilty of three acts of first-degree murder on May 13, 2013.[14] Using deceptively edited secretly videoed encounters, abortion opponents tar all abortion clinics as inhumane "mills" staffed by callous, greedy people—transferring the century-old taint of the criminal "abortionist" to legitimate providers. Yet paradoxically, abortion opponents deny that when abortion was illegal it was both widespread and sometimes (though not always) dangerous. Look, they say, in 1960, Mary Steichen Calderone, medical director of Planned Parenthood, herself said there had been "only 260 deaths" in 1957. (They don't mention that she also said it was likely that there were one million abortions a year—almost as many as today, in a much smaller population—and this was in the supposedly staid and moral 1950s, before the sexual revolution or the women's movement.) Years ago I debated a leader of Massachusetts for Life who pooh-poohed the health risks of recriminalizing abortion: Thanks to suction machines and antibiotics (which illegal providers would all have access to) illegal procedures would be reasonably nonfatal. So there it is. Legal abortion: very dangerous. Illegal abortion: remarkably safe!

For many years after *Roe*, abortion opponents talked a lot about the need to overturn the decision, and worked hard to elect officials who would install anti-abortion justices on the Supreme Court. So far, they have not seen that dream realized. But they have been shockingly successful in making abortion hard to get in much of the nation. Between 2011 and 2013, states enacted 205 new restrictions—more than in the previous ten years: waiting periods, inaccurate scripts that doctors must read to patients (abortion causes breast cancer, mental illness, suicide), bans on state Medicaid payments, restrictions on insurance coverage, and parental notification and consent laws.[15] In Ohio, lawmakers have taken money from TANF, the welfare program that supports poor families, and given it to so-called crisis pregnancy centers (CPCs) whose mission is to discourage pregnant women from having abortions. (That's right: Embryos and fetuses deserve government support, not the actual, living children they may become.)[16] Twenty-seven states have passed laws forcing clinics into expensive and unnecessary renovations and burdening them with medical regulations intended to make them impossible to staff. Largely as a result, between 2011 and 2013 at least 73 clinics closed or stopped performing abortions.[17] When these laws have been challenged in court, judges have set aside some of them, but not all. The result: In 2000, according to the Guttmacher Institute, around one-third of American women of reproductive age lived in states hostile to abortion rights, one-third lived in states that supported abortion rights, and one-third lived in states with a middle position. As of 2011, more than half of women lived in hostile states.[18] Middle-ground states, such as North Carolina, Ohio, and Wisconsin, have moved in an anti-choice direction. Only twenty-three states could be said to have a strong commitment to abortion rights. In 2013, only one state, California, made abortion easier to obtain.

What this means is that although abortion has been legal for four full decades, for many women in America it might as well not be. It is inaccessible—too far away, too expensive to pay for out of pocket, and too encumbered by restrictions and regulations and humiliations, many of which might not seem to be one of those "undue burdens" the Supreme Court has ruled are impermissible curbs on a woman's ability to terminate a pregnancy, but which, taken together, do place abortion out of reach. It would be nice to believe that no woman is deterred from an act so crucial to her future by having to wait a mere twenty-four hours between state-mandated counseling and the actual procedure, but what if the waiting period means two long round trips from your rural home to a distant city while trying to juggle work and child care, and because the clinic has to fly in a doctor from out of state, the twenty-four hours actually means a week, and that puts the woman into the second trimester but the clinic only does abortions through twelve weeks? What about the teenage girls who must tell their parents in order to get an abortion and can't bear to do so until it's too late? (Thirty-eight states currently require parental involvement in a minor's decision to have an abortion.) What about low-income women who live in one of the thirty-three states without Medicaid abortion coverage? What if, while she is putting together the $500 for a first-trimester abortion, a low-income woman goes over into the second trimester, and now the abortion costs $1,000? It is as if a woman has a right to vote, but the polling place is across the state and casting a ballot costs two weeks' pay, and as if she has a right to be a Jew or a Muslim or a Buddhist, but her place of worship is a four-hour bus ride away, and before she can go to services she has to listen to a fundamentalist Christian sermon warning her that if she doesn't accept Jesus as her personal savior she's going straight to hell. We would never accept the kinds of restrictions on our other constitutional rights that we have allowed to hamper the right to end a pregnancy.

How has this happened?

One answer is that the Republican Party, home base of the organized anti-abortion-rights movement, has won a lot of elections. The midterm elections in 2010 were crucial: The GOP won the House of Representatives and, even more important, in twenty states it had "trifectas"—control of both statehouses and the governorship. By 2013 it had twenty-four. Democrats, by contrast had only fourteen. (It's important to note that not all Democratic politicians are pro-choice, especially in red states.

In 2014, Louisiana's bill that requires doctors at abortion clinics to have hospital admitting privileges, a measure that could close three out of the state's five clinics, was written by a Democrat, Katrina Jackson.)

But there's a deeper, more troubling answer. The self-described pro-life movement may not represent a numerical majority—only 7 to 20 percent of Americans tell pollsters they want to ban abortion—but what it lacks in numbers it makes up for in intensity, dedication, cohesion, and savvy. It is the closest thing we have right now to a mass social movement. It works in multiple ways at once—through its own organizations, electoral politics, abstinence-only sex education in the public schools, the Catholic and fundamentalist/evangelical churches, public protests like the annual March for Life in Washington, DC, and "sidewalk counseling" in front of clinics. It reaches all the way from a terrorist fringe that it regularly disowns but that has very effectively discouraged doctors from performing abortions to popular radio and TV haranguers like Bill O'Reilly and Rush Limbaugh to respectable journals like *National Review* and the *Weekly Standard*. Indeed, it is hard to think of American conservatism today without its opposition to abortion. You would never know that Ayn Rand and Barry Goldwater were pro-choice, and that in 1967, the governor of California, Ronald Reagan, signed what was then the most liberal abortion law in the nation. Some of this hostility to abortion is surely for political reasons: Right-wing Christians vote. But the fact that opposition to abortion is de rigueur even for mainstream Republicans like Mitt Romney shows the movement's power.

The anti-abortion movement has made abortion a lot harder to get in many states, but even more important, it has reframed the issue. It has placed the zygote/embryo/fetus at the moral center, while relegating women and their rights to the periphery. Over time, it has altered the way we talk about abortion and the way many people feel about it, even if they remain pro-choice. It has made abortion seem risky, when in fact it is remarkably safe—twelve to fourteen times safer than the alternative, which is continued pregnancy and childbirth.[19] It has made people think the abortion of viable fetuses happens all the time when in fact it is illegal in most states except for serious medical reasons, and happens very rarely: According to the Guttmacher Institute, only 1.5 percent of abortions occur after twenty weeks' gestation.[20] (The Supreme Court has said twenty-four weeks is the threshold of viability.) It has made practices that are virtually unknown in the United States, like sex-selective abortions, seem routine and clinics like Dr. Gosnell's seem typical.

Most of all, abortion opponents have made ending a pregnancy shameful, even for women who don't believe a fertilized egg or a lentil-sized embryo is a child. It is hard now to believe, or even remember, that for a brief moment in the 1970s (let alone when abortion was an illegal but common practice), it was permissible not to consider your abortion a personal tragedy and failure. You were not automatically a callous, superficial person if you felt nothing but relief that you were no longer pregnant, and you were not a monster if you said so.

Nowadays, we take it for granted that having an abortion is a sorrowful, troubling, even traumatic experience, involving much ambivalence and emotional struggle, even though studies and surveys consistently tell us it usually is not.[21] Even pro-choicers use negative language: Hillary Clinton called abortion "a sad, even tragic choice to many, many women."[22] True as far as it goes, but you'll notice she didn't add, "and for many others, a blessing and a lifesaver." For decades, the Democratic Party mantra has been "safe, legal, and rare," with the accent on the rare. Among hard-core opponents, the language is completely over the top: Abortion is a Holocaust, providers are Nazis, the womb is the most dangerous place on Earth for a child, the Democratic Party is the Party of Death.

As long as abortion has been legal, pro-choice activists have complained that abortion opponents have stolen the language of morality and used it to twist public opinion. Who can be against "life," after all? Or responsibility, family, babies, motherhood? But it's not just opponents who paint abortion as awful and tormented. Pro-choicers do so too.

We may roll our eyes when abortion opponents contrast the anguish of abortion with the joys of unwanted babies, and the selfishness of women who end their pregnancies with the nobility of women who keep theirs whatever the difficulty, but over time it seeps in. So defensive has the pro-choice community become since the 1970s, when activists proudly defended "abortion on demand and without apology," that in 2013 Planned Parenthood announced that it was moving away from the term "pro-choice," which was itself a bit of a euphemism: Choose what? In mass-media messaging you're likely to hear about "defending *Roe*," even though only 62 percent of Americans (and only 44 percent of those under thirty) know what *Roe* is.[23] When abortion opponents at the Susan G. Komen Foundation canceled its grants in 2012, Planned Parenthood's response emphasized that "More than 90 percent of Planned Parenthood health care is preventive, including lifesaving cancer screenings, birth control, prevention and treatment of STDs, breast health services, Pap tests, and sexual health education and information."[24] True, this cautious approach won the day—Komen was forced to restore the grants, and the anti-choice faction left the organization. But was there no room for Planned Parenthood to add, "Yes, we perform abortions, and we are proud to offer that service to women who make the decision not to bear a child at that time, because abortion is a normal part of health care"?

It's not just our leaders and spokespeople at major organizations who unwittingly participate in what's been rather uneuphoniously called the "awfulization" of abortion. Anywhere you look or listen, you find pro-choicers falling over themselves to use words like "thorny," "vexed," "complex," and "difficult." How often have you heard abortion described as "the hardest decision" or "the most painful choice" a woman ever makes, as if every single woman who gets pregnant by accident seriously considers having a baby, only a few weeks earlier the furthest thing from her mind and for very good reason? Or more accurately, as if every accidentally pregnant woman really *should* seriously consider having that baby—and if she doesn't at least claim she thought long and hard about it and only reluctantly and sadly realized it was impossible, she's a bad woman who thinks only of her own pleasure and convenience.

Until quite recently, arguments against abortion openly focused on sexual morality. Abortion was wrong for the same reasons birth control was wrong: It let unmarried women escape detection and punishment for having sex outside marriage, it let wives have small families instead of the big ones God meant them to have, it encouraged people to see sex as an end in itself, and it gave women too much power in matters of reproduction and too much freedom from their proper domestic role. In mid-to-late nineteenth-century America, the state-by-state banning of abortion was connected with fears of the growing independence and social power of middle-class white women, and in particular with the fear that native-born white Protestants were being "outbred" by immigrants. It's not an accident that those were the same years Anthony Comstock was busy banning birth control and even dissemination of information about it.

Those old social and economic arguments are still being made today, but they carry much less weight with the public. It is hard to sell contemporary adults on the notion that sex for pleasure and intimacy is a bad thing even within marriage, and that having lots of children is a white woman's patriotic duty. That's why today the official focus is on "life": the argument that from "the moment of conception," long before she even suspects she's pregnant—in fact, before she actually *is* pregnant as standard medicine defines it—a woman is carrying a human being who has, like other human beings, a right not to be killed.

Do abortion opponents really believe that a fertilized egg or a pea-sized shrimplike embryo is a child? True believers surely must. After all, American life is full of things large numbers of people consider coarse and callous and wrong, but nobody shoots up porn studios or burns down gambling casinos or physically waylays men seeking to enter massage parlors. The investment bankers who caused the worldwide financial collapse may be hated by millions, but they don't need to go to work in bulletproof vests.

The anti-abortion movement, however, is not just about "the unborn." It is also a protest against women's growing freedom and power, including their sexual freedom and power. That is why it is based in churches with explicitly limited roles and inferior status for women—not just the famously patriarchal Catholic Church but the Southern Baptists and other fundamentalist/evangelical Protestant denominations where women are barred from leadership and the submission of wives to their husbands is an official tenet. The anti-abortion movement is a crucial chunk of the base of the Republican Party, which in recent years has opposed just about every legislative proposal that would benefit women: the Violence Against Women Act, the Lilly Ledbetter Act (which merely restored long-standing equal pay protections overturned by the Supreme Court), the Paycheck Fairness Act, and the international Convention on the Elimination of All Forms of Discrimination against Women (CEDAW), which almost every country in the world has signed. Despite its extremism, the anti-abortion movement has been able to capitalize on widespread ambivalence about feminism and social change.

Legal abortion presents the issue of women's emancipation in particularly stark form. It takes a woman's body out of the public realm and puts her, not men and not children, at the center of her own life. It is thus not just a matter of women's physical health but a deep challenge to traditional views of women. Abortion did not always have this meaning: As long as women were firmly ensconced in the family as wives and mothers with few rights and little social power, abortion was legal or tolerated as a way to save unmarried daughters from shame, limit family size, and protect exhausted mothers from the rigors of yet more pregnancies and births. It was part of women's messy private business, like periods and miscarriages and giving birth, things men were well advised to leave alone. But once middle-class white women began to emancipate themselves and get involved in public and political life, even if only to join a women's club or take on charity projects, abortion took on its modern meaning of self-determination and independence and active decision-making. Those are bedrock American values for men, but not for women, who are supposed to be self-sacrificing, other-oriented, maternal, and dependent. Even though most women who have abortions go on to have children (if they are not already mothers, as we've seen the majority are), legal abortion challenges the social meaning of womanhood, and that makes a lot of people uneasy, even forty-odd years after *Roe*.

This anxiety explains why opinions about abortion have changed so little since *Roe*, even as Americans have become more liberal and more tolerant on many other issues. Abortion exemplifies a much deeper and more radical social change. Same-sex marriage and gays and lesbians in the military are causes that seek to bring more people *into* beloved bedrock conservative institutions, not to abolish them or even to change them. All the high-tech ways of creating a baby are still basically aimed at letting infertile people make a family like the rest of us. That's why abortion opponents have never been able to get people riled up over the discarding of unused preembryos—children!—created in vitro for fertility procedures: It's all for a good cause. But granting women total power over their wombs? It's not enough that they have the right to remain single, to divorce, to earn a decent living, to own property, to keep their names, to have all the crazy sex they can find, or good lord, accuse their own husbands of rape? "They can have the baby, they can kill the baby, they can do whatever they want," says my friend the writer Deirdre English. "Women aren't supposed to have that much power." Never mind that in real life, women who have abortions include some of the least powerful women in America—low-income single mothers, working-class students trying to get to college or stay there, teenage girls, women trying to extricate themselves from abusive relationships. Forget too that most of the time, women do involve their man, and girls their parents, in the decision to terminate a pregnancy. In the collective imagination, women who have abortions are privileged, licentious, or both, and ready access to abortion means women run wild, take over, and all hell breaks loose.

In this book I make many arguments, but let me mention three. First, the concept of personhood, as applied to the zygote, blastocyst, embryo, and, at least until late in pregnancy, fetus, makes no sense: It's an incoherent, covertly religious idea that falls apart if you look at it closely. Few people actually believe it, as is shown by the exceptions they are willing to make. Second, the absolutist argument that abortion is murder is a mask by which people opposed to the sexual revolution and women's advancement obscure their real motives and agenda: turning back the clock to an idealized, oversimplified past when sex was confined within marriage, men were the breadwinners and heads of families, Christianity was America's not-quite-official religion, and society was firmly ordered. Third, since critiquing what came before does not necessarily help us move forward, I want to help reframe the way we think about abortion. There are definitely short-term advantages to stressing the anguish some women feel when facing the need to end a pregnancy, but in the long run presenting that as a general truth will hurt the pro-choice cause: It comes close to demanding that women accept grief, shame, and stigma as the price of ending a pregnancy. I want us to start thinking of abortion as a positive social good and saying this out loud. The anti-abortion movement has been far too successful at painting abortion as bad for women. I want to argue, to the contrary, that it is an essential option for women—not just ones in dramatic, terrible, body-and-soul-destroying situations, but all women—and thus benefits society as a whole.

Twenty years ago, abortion opponents portrayed women who sought abortions as frivolous and unfeeling: the girl who wanted to fit into a prom dress, the woman who didn't want to miss her planned European vacation. (There was a class angle to these apocryphal stories: It was always a trip to Europe, never camping in the Ozarks.) Those characterizations didn't go over well: They made abortion opponents look misogynistic and mean. Today, abortion opponents blame everybody *but* the woman—parents, boyfriend, husband, "the abortion industry," Democrats, the "throwaway culture" of modern life—and present themselves as the woman's friend, defending her from physical and psychological harm. Somehow the "Abortion Holocaust" takes place without her active participation: She's one of those good Germans who didn't know what was going on.

The new message is cast as concern for women themselves: Even if your abortion does not kill you right away, down the road lurk breast cancer, infertility, depression, drug addiction, failed relationships, and suicide. The woman is "abortion's other victim." As one Feminist for Life put it to me, how can it not harm a woman to kill her baby? The whole burgeoning network of CPCs relies on a paternalistic view of women seeking abortion as childlike, ignorant, and confused. It's worked well: There are now 2,500 such centers in the United States.[25] As of 2013, thirteen states fund them directly (and many more through "Choose Life" license plates and similar programs). In 2011, Texas increased funding for CPCs while cutting family planning money by two-thirds. The money came straight out of the budget for women's health. In Virginia, an investigation by NARAL Pro-Choice America found that the state's Department of Health refers low-income women to a list of CPCs where they can receive a free ultrasound before having an abortion.[26] It does not matter that CPCs have been repeatedly exposed as presenting themselves as abortion clinics to lure in the unsuspecting, that they proselytize Christianity, or that they tell women lies: that abortion will harm them in all sorts of ways, that birth-control pills are "abortifacients" and condoms don't prevent sexually transmitted diseases.

I don't expect to convince many abortion opponents to see my point of view. But I do want to speak to the so-called "muddled middle," those millions of Americans—more than half—who don't want to ban abortion, exactly, but don't want it to be widely available, either.[27] This is the view that is echoed and reinforced endlessly in the mainstream media. Many commentators and pundits take a position of "permit but discourage" or maybe a better way to put it in their own case is "permit but deplore." They want abortion to be legal, at least in the early weeks, but they want to make clear it's a bad thing and there's way too much of it—not because our high rates of abortion indicate that women aren't getting good sexual information and good birth control or lack power in their relationships with men, or because poverty and lack of support are making women terminate wanted pregnancies, but because abortion, in and of itself, is morally troubling. It's a seductive position for people who make their living by staking out intellectual positions that resist, or appear to resist, tired pieties. Defying both camps lets one feel sensitive and judicious and mature, alert to moral complexities, above the vulgar slogan war—a plague on both your houses! "Here's an uninhibited insult that the professional 'life' and 'choice' agitators can listen to for free," wrote

Washington Post columnist Dana Milbank in 2012: "If these groups cared as much about the issue as they claim, and didn't have such strong financial incentives to avoid consensus and compromise, they'd cancel the carnivals and get to work on the one thing everybody agrees would be worthwhile—reducing unwanted pregnancies."[28] Right, Planned Parenthood, stop keeping contraception away from people. In a much-reprinted 1995 essay, Naomi Wolf chalked abortion up to lazy sluttish-ness ("It was such good Chardonnay") and urged women who ended their pregnancies to feel guilt and to mourn their fe-tuses; she even claimed that emergency contraception is a form of abortion (it's not).[29] Andrew Sullivan, another reluctant semi-pro-choicer, thinks "abortion is always and everywhere a moral tragedy."[30] Always? Everywhere? The safest position for a member of the commentariat seems to be: You can have your abortion as long as you feel really, really bad about it.

I'm not going to take that route here.

Terminating a pregnancy is always a woman's right and of-ten a deeply moral decision. It is not evil, even a necessary evil. You might make a different decision from a particular woman who chooses not to continue a pregnancy, and you might think your decision is morally superior—but beside the fact that you don't actually know what you would do faced with those exact same circumstances (how many people have said abortion should be legal but they would never have one, and who then end up having one?), your judgment about a woman's deci-sion is not relevant to the legal status of abortion as a whole, any more than someone giving a speech you consider foolish reflects on the First Amendment, or someone voting for a cor-rupt candidate raises questions about suffrage. A right includes the freedom to use it in ways others find distressing or even wrong. Your judgment of that woman is not even an interesting fact about yourself. There are many things other people do that you think you would never do (especially if there is, in fact, no possibility that you will ever be called upon to decide, as is the case with men and abortion). That tells us you have a certain idea about yourself, that's all.

Abortion is often seen as a bad thing for society, a sign of hedonism, materialism, and hyperindividualism. I argue that, on the contrary, access to legal abortion is a good thing for society and helping a woman obtain one is a good deed. Instead of shaming women for ending a pregnancy, we should acknowledge their realism and self-knowledge. We should accept that it's good for everyone if women have only the children they want and can raise well. Society benefits when women can commit to education and work and dreams without having at the back of their mind a concern that maybe it's all provisional, because at any moment an accidental pregnancy could derail them for life. It's good for children to be wanted, and to come into this life when their parents are ready for them. It's good for people to be able to have sexual experiences and know that birth-control failure need not be the last word. It would not make us a better country if more girls and women were nudged and bullied and cajoled and humiliated and frightened into bearing children they are ill-equipped to raise, even if more men could somehow be lassoed into marrying or supporting them. It would simply mean more lost hope, more bad marriages and family misery, more poverty and struggle for women, their partners, and their kids. Don't we have way too much of all that already?

Honestly, given how rarely we talk about abortion in a social context, you would think that all those women who have them were living on their own individual desert islands. But of course, the opposite is true. In addition to the 1 in 3 women who will have at least one abortion during their fertile years, there are at least as many men and women, and probably a lot more than that, who've helped them with money, transportation, information, emotional support, child care: husbands and boyfriends, parents and other relatives, friends and coworkers, therapists . . . even, sometimes, clergy. I've taken two friends to the clinic. Both kept their abortions secret from their extremely religious families, who to this day have no idea, but I was not the only person who helped them. Their boyfriends had been part of the decision and helped pay; in one case, other friends showed up after work to sympathize and share tea and takeout. (Abortion opponents tell women their relationships will fall apart if they have an abortion, but both of these women went on to marry the men they were with and to have kids—one a son, the other four daughters.) Multiply that situation by well over a million abortions a year, and maybe half the people in the country have not only been aware that someone they knew was planning an abortion, but played an active part in moving the process along. The involvement of others is particularly the case with later abortions; in fact, since the later an abortion is, the more expensive it is, the more travel is involved and the longer the recovery time, the very abortions that are the most despised and disapproved of are likely to be the ones that require the most help from others. There are few women, after all, who can come up with several thousand dollars on their own.

Abortion, in other words, does not happen on the edge of society, community, and family. It is enmeshed in the way we live, it requires the cooperation of many people beyond the woman herself. But that is not the way we talk about it, as something pervasive in American life, without which, indeed, that life would be radically different, and worse. We talk about it as if the pregnant woman exists in social isolation. The man who has impregnated her is useless, if indeed he has not already abandoned her; she has no friends; her family would disown her if they knew, or she is too ashamed to tell them. All alone, she is making a radical existential decision to terminate a pregnancy. Of course, there are women for whom this is true—some women are very private, some have no support system at all. But as a typical picture it's less a reflection of reality than of the way mainstream America prefers to see abortion: as a lonely, individual act chosen by a desperate woman making a fearsome decision in the dark. Abortion opponents use this picture to pose as this beleaguered, confused woman's helper: Shouldn't she have to think it over at a CPC and be made to consider the gravity of her choice by looking at a sonogram or listening to a fetal heartbeat or hearing a description of fetal development and all the awful things that could go wrong with the procedure? Shouldn't she know that she is increasing her risk of suicide and cancer, never mind that the studies actually don't show that?

Pro-choicers are so intent on resisting the image of the confused woman, preserving the woman's moral autonomy, honoring the courage of those who do indeed have no one to help them, and reminding the world of how truly extreme are some women's circumstances, that they inadvertently deemphasize the supportive role of others in the abortion decision. For them, too, the woman tends to be a solitary figure. That allows abortion opponents to fill in the blanks of her social world with negative stereotypes: the boyfriend who threatens to leave if she keeps the pregnancy; the parents who threaten to throw her out of the house if she has a baby; the callous friends who just want to party on; the brusque and unfeeling doctor at the money-grubbing "abortion mill"; the pimp.

Forty years of apologetic rhetoric, forty years of searching for arguments that will support legal abortion while never, ever implying that it is an easy decision or a good thing—for women, men, children, families, society—have left the pro-choice movement making the same limited, defensive arguments again and again. We hear endlessly about rape victims, incest victims, women at risk of death and injury, women carrying fetuses with rare fatal conditions—and make no mistake, those girls and women exist and their rights need to be defended, because the laws now being passed in many states will harm them greatly. But we don't hear much about the vast majority of women who choose abortion, who are basically trying to get their life on track or keep it there.

Women like Jan F, who responded to a request for abortion stories I ran in my column in *The Nation* and posted on Facebook and Twitter:

43 years ago, I had an abortion. Not for a single nanosecond have I ever regretted it. I was 23, a new college grad from Wisconsin, and was planning on a career using my dual foreign language degree, in the Big Apple where such opportunities abounded. My white Midwest boyfriend came out to visit for a weekend and before we broke up, had the sex that conceived. *Roe v. Wade* was not law then, but the *Village Voice* had a contact number. I made an appointment to travel to England for my weekend off and met another gal from Chicago in similar circumstances. I told the boyfriend that it would cost about $900 but he never contacted me again. I was able to pursue my career, and using all my savings for that one preventative action was the best money I ever spent.

Or Cinny, whose husband left her with three small children, and who had two abortions, flying to New York, where abortion was legal before *Roe*:

> For me the issue has always been quality of life. As a single mother with three young children, I knew I couldn't take care of more babies, so twice I made the decision to abort. I felt comfortable with the decision then, and I've never had regrets.

I realize that my perspective is going to sound insufficiently nuanced to those who pride themselves on being judicious and balanced and above the fray. In American political discourse, the safest place to be is in the middle, lamenting "extremes on both sides." The woman, the fetus—can't they just get along? Isn't there some combination of rules and regulations and birth control and women not being drunken tramps that will just make this whole tedious business go away? And while we wait for that to happen, let's wring our hands to show how moral and thoughtful we are, not forgetting to mention "new" developments like ultrasound that supposedly have changed everything.

That attitude is definitely the one to take if you want to be seen as ethically serious four decades after *Roe*. But what does that approach do, really, but let us feel superior, up on Pundit Mountain, to all those messy women down there in the steamy valley, trying to make a reasonable life for themselves as best they can? We talk about respecting life. But what if we tried respecting them?

In every other area of life, we praise careful consideration, intentionality, and weighing of options. We don't decide whom to marry, what kind of work to do, where to live by simply acquiescing to chance and calling it fate. We don't turn those decisions over to others—certainly not to state legislators or judges. Other societies may practice arranged marriages, but in America we like to make our own mistakes. We would never accept that we should be forced into particular jobs because society wanted more people to do that work—we don't even have a military draft anymore.

Motherhood is the last area in which the qualities we usually value—rationality, independent thinking, consulting our own best interests, planning for a better, more prosperous future, and dare I say it, pursuing happiness and dreams—are condemned as frivolity and selfishness. We certainly don't expect a man who accidentally impregnates a woman to drop everything and accept a life of difficulties and dimmed hopes in order to co-parent a baby. No college for you, young man— maybe you can pick up some courses later, when your child is in school. If a woman wants to put a baby up for adoption, we don't badger and humiliate the biological father into taking the child to keep it connected to its family of origin. We don't even legally require a man who impregnates a woman to support her financially through pregnancy and delivery, although lack of money is one reason women give for choosing abortion, and stress during pregnancy is a significant cause of miscarriage and premature delivery.[31] As for child support, few single mothers can expect the father of their child to pay anything remotely like half the true costs of raising it to adulthood, even if he is financially able to do so. We don't like the idea that a man might be severely constrained for life by a single ejaculation. He has places to go and things to do. That a woman's life may be stunted by unwanted childbearing is not so troubling. Childbearing, after all, is what women are for.

The common wisdom is that the battle lines on abortion have long been fixed. There is a huge temptation to say ho-hum, especially among the vaguely liberal, or to pull out of one's hat the magic solution, the compromise that will make this embarrassing, tiresome subject go away forever. Even I sometimes wonder if we have reached a permanent stalemate—except that you can't really call it a stalemate when the momentum is so clearly on the side of greater restrictions. Certainly abortion qualifies as one of those subjects about which people have not only their own opinions but their own facts. Still, I hope that by laying out the logic—or rather, the illogic—of the anti-choice position, and proposing an alternative way of looking at abortion, I might persuade a few people who think they are in the middle to realize that they in fact support legal abortion "on demand," and indeed, have always done so, but didn't realize it.

TWO

WHAT DO AMERICANS THINK ABOUT ABORTION?

Perhaps you think your opinions about abortion are pretty straightforward. You know what boxes to check off on a survey, and if a pollster asks you what you think, you'll speak your mind. But how clear, really, is your understanding of abortion and your reasoning about what you believe? What if your opinions contradict each other? What if you don't really believe what you think you do?

If you are like most Americans, you don't want abortion to be banned. You don't want the United States to be like El Salvador, where abortion is completely illegal and women suspected of having had abortions are shackled to hospital beds, invasively examined by police gynecologists, and sometimes packed off to prison.[1] Or Nicaragua, where women have died because obstetricians were afraid of the legal consequences of terminating a catastrophic pregnancy. You don't want to force barely pubescent incest victims to give birth, as in Mexico, much less compel a teenager to give birth to—and breastfeed— an anencephalic baby who has no hope of survival, as in Peru. You certainly don't want any woman to suffer and die like Savita Halappanavar in Ireland. In November 2012, this thirty-one-year-old Indian dentist, carrying a much-wanted pregnancy, went to University Hospital Galway with back pain that turned out to be a miscarriage in process. For three days, she and her husband pleaded with hospital doctors to remove the dying seventeen-week-old fetus, only to be told that as long as its heart was still beating, no abortion could take place. "This is a Catholic country," her husband says one doctor told him.[2] By the time the fetal heartbeat had stopped, it was too late: Savita died of septicemia and organ failure. These incidents are the kinds of things that happen in countries where abortion is illegal.

Indeed, if you're like most Americans, you're not at all sure you want the government making intimate decisions for women, especially in extreme circumstances like these. Fear of government overreach is one of the most important reasons why even Americans morally opposed to abortion don't support strict abortion bans.[3] In scarlet-red South Dakota, voters rejected a total abortion ban in 2006, while telling pollsters that they would have approved it had an exception been included for rape and incest. But when a ban with those exceptions was put on the ballot two years later, voters rejected that version too. Given time to think it through and talk to one another, to consider all the tangled secret misfortunes that take place in families, and all the medical complexities of pregnancy, the majority of voters chose not to give the government total power over something so personal. Besides, by then there was only one abortion clinic left in the whole state and it only performed abortions a limited number of days per week.[4] It was hard to argue that there was an epidemic of casual baby killing in the Mount Rushmore State. Even more tellingly, in 2013, Albuquerque voters decisively rejected a local measure that would have banned abortion after twenty weeks and shut down one of the two clinics in the state that offer such abortions, and one of only three or four clinics in the whole country that perform abortions in the third trimester.[5] These are precisely the abortions that only a small minority of Americans say they believe should be legal. Polls are one thing; voting, another.

However, if you are like most Americans, you disapprove of "abortion on demand"—that is, women being able to access abortion freely. (Could it be the phrasing? "Demand" is such an angry, second-wave-feminist word—*I want an abortion and I want it now!* Maybe polls should ask about "abortion on request.") You don't have a lot of empathy for women who get pregnant from voluntary sex, especially if they've been careless about protection (in other words, women who "use abortion as birth control"), and just don't want to have a baby. Gallup's average of multiple polls from assorted organizations since 1996 yields these findings (the percentage is those who approve of permitting abortion for the reason stated):

Life of the woman 84%
Physical health of the woman 83%
Rape or incest 79%
Mental health of the woman 64%
Baby would be mentally impaired 53%
Baby would be physically impaired 51%
Would force teenager to drop out of school 42%

Woman/family can't afford the baby 39%
Woman/family want no more children 39%
Couple does not want to marry 35%
Fertility selection (when fertility process creates multiple
    embryos) 29%
Would interfere with woman's career 25%[6]

There's a clear distinction here between reasons that are medical and/or involve obvious coercion and those that have to do simply with women's own needs and desires and circumstances— what Gallup rather dismissively refers to as "lifestyle choice."

Note, though, that 1 in 6 Americans told pollsters a woman should die rather than terminate her pregnancy, and about the same said she should suffer any physical injury short of death. (That figure would include former vice-presidential candidate Rep. Paul Ryan, who famously described the health exception as "a loophole big enough to drive a Mack truck through it.") More than 1 in 3 regarded the woman's sanity as irrelevant, according to these findings. These respondents would presumably find too permissive Ireland's new abortion law, passed in the wake of Savita Halappanavar's death, which permits abortion only to save the woman's life, but includes the risk of suicide as a possible factor.

The National Opinion Research Center, which has been tracking the public's views on abortion since 1972, shows a similar divide, although its numbers are a bit different. It estimates that only 7.2 percent of the population opposes abortion for any reason whatsoever, rising to 8.1 percent if they oppose legal abortion for six of the seven reasons offered in the survey. Interestingly, 31 percent are totally pro-choice.[7] (Other polls have different findings. In a 2013 Quinnipiac poll 16 percent said abortion should be "illegal in all cases."[8] In a CBS poll, 21 percent of respondents said abortion should "not be permitted.")[9]

What does this mean in real life? In 2011, the most recent year for which we have figures, 1.06 million women had an abortion.[10] Going by earlier surveys, about 1 percent of those abortions were due to rape, less than half a percent were due to incest, while 7 percent of women cited health concerns for themselves or the fetus.[11] In theory, then, you disapprove of more than 9 in 10 abortions. So sorry, fifteen-year-old girls who got drunk at a party, single mothers with all the kids they can handle and no money, mothers preoccupied with taking care of disabled children, students with just one more year to a degree, battered women, women who have lost their job or finally just landed a decent one, and forty-five-year-olds who have already raised their kids to adulthood, to say nothing of women who just don't feel ready to be a mother, or maybe even don't ever want to be a mother. A woman forgets her pill? No fancy-schmancy "career" for her. Only thirteen? If she's old enough to have sex, she's old enough to have a baby. (Most gynecologists would disagree about that.)

Well, maybe your position sounds a bit callous to you, put like that. Maybe, if you thought a bit harder about it—or if it were your daughter or your girlfriend or your wife—you'd give some of those women and girls a pass. But I don't see a whole lot of consistency in your thinking. If you really mean what you tell pollsters, your respect for "life" is entirely conditional. It depends not on any quality of the embryo or fetus—you're willing to dispose of it if the reason meets your approval—but on your judgment of the pregnant woman. If she had voluntary sex, even with her husband, that's all that matters: not who she is, or what will become of her. This is why feminists believe that people who want to force women to give birth see pregnancy as punishment for sex. They're right. It's not about the embryo/fetus. It's about her.

I also wonder how you imagine your preferences would be enacted. Do you want to shut down all the clinics and bring back the hospital committees, which decided whether a woman was abortion-worthy in the years before *Roe*? As I mentioned earlier, those committees were notoriously cruel, capricious, and class-biased. Besides, they did not settle the abortion issue at all. They proved to be a step toward legalization. So too were early efforts at reform, in which various states permitted abortion for much the sort of reasons you approve. Once you say yes to some women, it's hard to say no to others.

How do you define a rape victim, for instance? Only ones who promptly reported their rape to the police? Only ones whom the police believed? Only ones whose rapists were caught and confessed their guilt? What happens when the accused rapist claims the sex was consensual, as so many of them do? Then too, legally, girls under their state's age of consent are victims of statutory rape. That teen who so many think was old enough to bear a child because she was old enough to have sex actually, in law, probably wasn't old enough to have sex. So if you believe rape victims should be permitted to terminate their pregnancies, do you believe that all teens under sixteen, and, in some states, all teens under eighteen, should be allowed to end their pregnancies? If they are poor, should their abortions be covered by Medicaid? (The Hyde Amendment, which bars the federal government from covering abortion through Medicaid, makes exceptions for rape, as do the bans on Medicaid for abortion enacted in thirty-three states.) I'm guessing you don't think so, because seeing underage girls as victims of statutory rape conflicts with the dominant narrative about them, which is that they are eager little sexpots who are asking for trouble. The other exceptions pose similar difficulties. Who decides when a woman's clinical depression is severe enough to justify her appeal for a termination? How serious a risk to her eyesight does the high blood pressure caused by her pregnancy have to be? What fetal abnormalities count?

Even permitting abortion "to save the woman's life" is not so simple. In 1998, Michelle Lee, a medically fragile patient on the waiting list for a heart transplant, was denied an abortion at Louisiana State University Medical Center because hospital policy required that the risk of death from continuing her pregnancy be greater than 50 percent.[12] (Abortion advocates ended up paying for an ambulance to transfer Lee to a Texas hospital that agreed to perform the abortion.) In 2013, Tamesha Means was sent home twice from Mercy Health Partners in Muskegon, Michigan, after her water broke when she was eighteen weeks pregnant. According to the lawsuit filed on her behalf by the ACLU, although she was in terrible pain, her health was at serious risk, and her fetus was doomed, the hospital, following its Catholic directives, did not tell her that terminating the pregnancy was an option. It was only when she returned a third time, with an infection, and began to miscarry even as the hospital was preparing to send her home yet again, that the hospital treated her miscarriage.[13] In a similar situation, Savita Halappanavar died. How much risk is risky enough?

Here is another question: Are you prepared for the invasions of privacy and the ramped-up law enforcement that will be required to put teeth into your distinctions? Libertarians, for example, abhor government intrusions and surveillance, and want to reduce the government to its most minimal level. Yet quite a few of them—Paul Ryan and Rand Paul, for example—want to see abortion criminalized, a measure that would require government to expand enormously in ways they find intolerable in other areas of life. Banning abortion, or restricting it to a few reasons, would not end demand, after all: A million women a year would still be seeking to end their pregnancies. That is a lot of crime to be prevented, monitored, investigated, prosecuted, and don't forget, punished. Would you be comfortable putting women on trial for ending a six-week pregnancy by taking a pill they buy on the Internet or bring back from Mexico or get from a friend? What about that friend? How about jailing a beloved obstetrician who quietly helps out his patients? Or the boyfriend or sister or aunt who provides money or transportation? Do you want to see miscarriages investigated as possible abortion attempts? If you are serious about outlawing nine out of ten abortions, you need to think about what that would entail.

I am beginning to suspect that your position is not all that carefully considered. You are just expressing your dislike of abortion and the women who have them, and you're not really thinking about the real-world implications. Much has been made of polls showing that increasing numbers of Americans describe themselves as pro-life. At the same time, almost two-thirds of those polled say they agree with "*Roe v. Wade,* which established a woman's right to an abortion." In fact, that position—the pro-choice position—increased slightly at the same time that people became less willing to describe themselves as pro-choice. There's a message in here about the inadequacy of labels and polling questions to capture what people really think: 35 percent of people who describe themselves as pro-life also support a woman's right to choose abortion, and a lot of people who think abortion is wrong in most cases also think it should be legal in most cases. A 1996 University of Virginia poll found that 38 percent of respondents agree that abortion is "murder, as bad as killing a person already born." Since 84 percent in that poll approved of abortion when the woman's life or health is at stake, an awful lot of people who believe abortion is murder apparently believe it's all right to murder an innocent person to save someone else's life or health. Really? I doubt these people would say it was all right for me to kill someone to take their kidney, even if I would die without it. And what to make of the 10 percent who told the same pollsters that abortion is murder but "not as bad as killing a person already born." What kind of murder is that?[14]

Answers like these suggest that many of you are caught between your wish to make a strong moral statement and your sense that abortion is complicated in all sorts of ways, because the relationship of a pregnant woman to the developing embryo/fetus is not like other relationships, whether mother and baby or murderer and victim. Of those who say abortion is wrong even if the woman's life is at stake, how many literally mean that if their daughter or their wife or their friend had a heart too weak to sustain a pregnancy, like Michelle Lee, she should just die, and how many think, Well, it's wrong—killing is always wrong—but sometimes you have to do it anyway in self-defense? (This might be a good place to mention that Mitt Romney's son Tagg signed a contract with a surrogate mother that gave her the right to abort for health reasons and him and his wife the right to decide on abortion should the fetus prove "physiologically, genetically or chromosomally abnormal."[15]) Some abortion opponents simply deny that pregnancy can ever be life-threatening. Illinois congressman Joe Walsh, for example, claimed in a 2012 debate with his Democratic opponent, Tammy Duckworth, that "with modern technology and science," abortion is never necessary to protect a woman's life or health. "You can't find one instance."[16] In Ireland, some abortion opponents refused to accept that Savita Halappanavar died of septicemia. Perhaps she had a rare Indian blood disease?

When people say they think abortion should be illegal except under narrow circumstances, how literally do they mean "illegal"? Illegal as in arrests and trials and prison, or illegal as in littering and jaywalking, which usually get no more than a glare from a policeman? We've seen that even people in one of the staunchest anti-abortion states didn't vote for the ban they said they supported. Does that mean they believe murder should be legal? In a much-mentioned video, a reporter for AtCenterNetwork.com asked demonstrators holding up bloody-fetus posters at a clinic what they thought the penalty should be for women who had abortions when and if the procedure was banned.[17] None of them had ever thought about it. Politicians who mention criminal penalties for women soon learn their mistake. In his first presidential debate, in 1988, George H. W. Bush said, "I'm for the sanctity of life, and once that illegality is established, then we can come to grips with the penalty side, and of course there's got to be some penalties to enforce the law, whatever they may be." After the debate, Bush's campaign chairman, James A. Baker III, walked it back: Providers should be prosecuted, but women were "additional victims," not criminals.[18]

Regardless of your views on the law, though, polls do suggest you think most abortion is immoral—although it's less clear whether you mean immoral like infanticide or immoral like marital infidelity or even immoral like some sexual practice that harms no one but which you happen to find disturbing.

Immoral as in, I want to berate you for getting into this mess and then I'll drive you to the clinic? Or immoral as in, Now that you're in this mess, you have to have that baby?

Polls also suggest you think abortion is too easy to get—especially after the first trimester, when support for legal abortion goes way down (first trimester, 61 percent; second, 27 percent; third, 14 percent).[19] As I write, abortion opponents are focusing on whittling down the time limit on legal abortion—from twenty-four weeks, roughly the threshold of viability, to twenty weeks or even less. In polls you approve of the twenty-week ban. At the same time, you also support measures intended to slow down and encumber women seeking abortion—waiting periods, parental notification and consent laws and "informed consent" laws that make doctors read scripts intended to dissuade the patient from choosing abortion.[20] (A few years ago, Guttmacher Institute researchers found that in twenty-three states these scripts contain loaded language and blatant falsehoods.)[21] According to Pew Research, you even support forcing wives to notify their husbands—never mind that the Supreme Court struck spousal notification down in 1992 as giving husbands too much power, especially abusive ones.[22] Do you support those restrictions because you want women to feel the weight of what they are choosing to do or because you want to discourage them from making the choice? Because you don't believe these restrictions are very onerous—what's so hard about waiting twenty-four hours? Can't everyone come up with $500 if they really need to?—or because you hope they will be so onerous women won't be able to overcome them? Clearly anti-abortion activists want it to be the latter. One leader recently admitted that the purpose of restrictions was simply to make abortions too expensive and too difficult for women to get them. "Require the woman to see an ultrasound, or require two trips to the clinic," Michael J. New, an adjunct scholar at the anti-choice Charlotte Lozier Institute, told the 2012 Values Voters Summit.[23] "That raises the costs; that stops the abortion from happening. You can lengthen the waiting period. Don't be like the other states that do 24, 48, 72 hours. Do it for nine months—that'll stop abortions in your state. I guarantee it."[24]

What if the people who support restrictions knew that their chief effect was to push abortions later into the pregnancy, not only raising the cost and the physical and emotional toll on the woman but increasing the number of abortions that the public finds particularly disturbing? In one survey, 58 percent of women reported that they would have liked to have had their abortion earlier, which is quite a statement when you consider that almost 9 in 10 abortions take place in the first twelve weeks. The chief reason for delay was the difficulty of making arrangements.[25]

It's hard to tell why people hold the positions they do, because opinion polls don't usually measure how much they know. Perhaps they would respond differently if they were given more information. Would you support banning abortion after twenty weeks if the pollster reminded you that the twenty-week sonogram is when many serious fetal problems are diagnosed? In one poll, only 62 percent of respondents could correctly identify what issue *Roe v. Wade* was about. Even those who have some understanding of a law often disagree about its meaning, so we don't know what people mean when they say they do or don't approve of *Roe v. Wade*. What do they think it says? Abortion opponents claim *Roe* guarantees legal abortion more or less at will through all nine months of pregnancy because, while it permits states to ban it during the last trimester, it mandates an exception for the life and health of the mother—that supposedly interstate-highway-broad exception mentioned by Paul Ryan. This is what abortion opponents are referring to when they say *Roe* permits abortion the day before birth. In *The Party of Death*, the conservative writer Ramesh Ponnuru claims most people don't know about the health exception: They think *Roe* makes it impossible to get a third-trimester abortion except to save the woman's life.[26] Would more people support *Roe* if they knew how hard it is to obtain a late-second-trimester abortion in most of the country, let alone a third-trimester one? At present, only four doctors are known to perform abortions in the last three months of pregnancy.[27] If people knew how few abortions are performed after twenty-four weeks, and how serious are the problems that lead women to seek them out, would more of them support *Roe*? Or would more people reject *Roe* if they knew about the health exception, because, like Paul Ryan, they think "health" is just an excuse? We don't know.

Then too, polls rarely describe the kind of complicated real-life situations women with an unwanted pregnancy face. (Anita is raising her autistic son alone with no child support from his father; Nikki can only afford college because she won an athletic scholarship, which she will lose if she stays pregnant; forty-two-year-old Jennifer raised two sons and thought she was in menopause—now she's four months pregnant, while working full-time and caring for her own mother; Lily and her boyfriend, Sam, have only been together for three months and neither of them feels remotely ready for parenthood.) It's one thing to say in a general sort of way that a woman should have the baby even if she can't afford it. But what about Linda, who has a low-wage job, an unemployed husband, and a toddler?

What about Danielle, who sleeps with her two-year-old son on her sister's pullout sofa? What should Linda and Danielle do? Do those who say a woman should have the baby even if she has no money assume there's help out there for her, the way so many believe anyone who really wants to work can find a job? Do they think poor people shouldn't have sex, even if they're married, so tough luck if the condom breaks? Or that no woman should have sex unless she is prepared to have a baby nine months later? That is the logic, after all, of the rape and incest exception: She can kill her baby if she was forced into intercourse, but not if she volunteered. It would be good to know, too, how much time and care people devote to thinking about the questions when they answer a poll about abortion. Are they really considering their answers or are they giving the answers they think a good person or a believing Christian would give, the way people tell surveys they exercise and eat healthy food when really they spend their free time playing Candy Crush while plowing through big bags of chips?

Wishful or truthful, offhand or firmly held, ill-informed or knowledgeable, this mélange of opinions, intuitions, hesitations, and judgments, elicited by oversimplified or ambiguous poll questions, is what characterizes a bit more than half the American population—what's been called the "muddled middle." You. There's nothing wrong with having complicated views, or even confused views. In ordinary life, people's opinions are often vague and contradictory. But while you in the muddled middle dither and worry and fret and vent—yes abortion should be legal, sort of, but it's wrong, sort of, and it shouldn't be too easy, and it shouldn't be too late, and the woman needs to think about it more, but also not wait too long, and most of all she should not be such an irresponsible slut—a radical movement against abortion rights has gathered enormous speed. As we've seen, this movement represents only a small minority. Many more take the total pro-choice position—25 percent in Gallup.[28] And 31 percent in the NORC survey.[29] And many don't care:

"Do you think the issue of abortion is a critical issue facing the country, one among many important issues, or not that important compared to other issues?"

		01/13	08/09	03/06
Critical	%	18	15	28
One of many important issues	%	27	33	38
Not that important	%	53	48	32
Unsure/ Refused	%	2	3	2

(Pew Research Center)[30]

So why is the anti-abortion movement doing so well when so few people support its goal, which is the criminalization of all abortion? Most Americans, even most Catholics, don't share the extreme religiosity that animates the movement. One answer: Abortion opponents make up in passion what they lack in numbers. In the most recent iteration of the poll above, for example, 38 percent of abortion opponents said the issue was "critical" to them, but only 9 percent of pro-choicers said so.[31] Another answer: The anti-abortion movement has effectively exploited the inchoate negative feelings people have about abortions—the women who have them, the doctors who provide them, the clinics where they take place, the permissive sexual mores that they believe lies behind them—in order to pass what may seem like reasonable restrictions taken individually if you don't look at them too closely or know what they really involve or consider their likely effects. Consider, for example, the widespread feeling that abortion after the first trimester is a bad thing. Fine. Most pregnant women feel the same way. That's why 88 percent of abortions take place before the twelfth week, and only 1.5 percent take place after the twentieth week.[32] But one reason women end up going over into the second trimester is that they couldn't come up with the money sooner. And why is that? A lot of you in the muddled middle support the Hyde Amendment and other funding restrictions. The anti-choice movement has put these two situations in different mental silos, as if they were unrelated: Government funding is bad, and later abortions are also bad. But they work together: If it's harder to get a first-trimester abortion, more women will have second-trimester abortions. And some women—20 percent of poor women who want to end a pregnancy, according to one survey—won't be able to pull the money together in time.[33] Is that what you want? The poorest women, the ones with so little support from friends or family or partners that they could not beg or borrow a few hundred dollars, have babies they don't want and can't afford?

Another example: In the wake of the enormous publicity surrounding the Texas state legislature's passing of a ban on abortion after twenty weeks in the summer of 2013, polls show it had majority or plurality support. Five months is plenty of time to make up your mind, right? So what do you think should happen when your cousin Suzanne learns at her twenty-week ultrasound that she is carrying a fetus missing most of its brain? Should Suzanne have to wait and watch her baby die? (It's not an idle question: In nine states twenty-week bans have no exception for serious fetal impairments.)[34] And what should happen when Emily, your daughter's tenth-grade classmate, refuses to believe she's pregnant because she only had sex once and douched with Pepsi afterward, and her parents, who you've always thought were kind of strange, don't notice until she's twenty-one weeks along? We wring our hands over the too-early motherhood that is the fate of child brides in the developing world. Must Emily go through childbirth because she had sex with her boyfriend the last night of summer camp instead of because she was married off to some gnarled old man with a beard?

But wait a minute—why do we even ask people to judge different reasons for having an abortion? Pollsters, legislators, and judges don't invite people to weigh in on reasons for exercising other personal rights, to get married, say, or to have a baby. Not every reason is necessarily so wonderful: getting married for money or status or to get away from home, having a baby to please your parents, save your marriage, feel important, produce an heir to the throne. We seem content to let people reproduce for whatever reason they like, even if we gossip about their poor judgment with our friends and, some of us, resent them if they are poor. Similarly, we seem able to separate our support for a legal right from our feelings about the ways people exercise it: The fact that people write racist tracts and blame hurricanes on gays and lesbians doesn't make us think we need to rewrite the First Amendment.

And what about the Second Amendment? If abortion is different because it's about life and death, so too, potentially, are guns, yet we seem positively loath to examine people's reasons for wanting to own them. Any old wave in the direction of an explanation is good enough—"they're fun," "they're part of our tradition down here," "I'm a collector." And unlike abortion, guns kill more than 32,000 actually existing people every year.[35] Gun enthusiasts love the self-defense argument: You need to carry a gun, preferably at all times, in church or school or Starbucks, because the world is a dangerous place. Stand your ground! Even as abortion becomes more and more restricted, gun rights expand—not even the Sandy Hook Elementary School massacre was able to turn the nation toward significant restrictions on the right to bear arms—lots and lots of arms. Is this because the gun culture is predominantly male and we don't judge men's choices as much? If it's their right, end of story?

Maybe abortion is different not because it's uniquely grave but because it's about *women*. It's one of the few decisions that by law only a woman makes as long as she is of age, and that means everyone can pile on. America invites us to judge women, even rape victims, in a way rarely applied to men. Popular culture is a kind of training in how to scrutinize, analyze, and moralize even women's smallest, most trivial choices and qualities: what they eat, what they wear, how they look, how they talk. Is that a baby bump on that celeb, or has she—oh no!—gained weight? Reality shows are a kind of judgment spectacle, in which a mostly female audience is invited to feel superior to assorted exhibitionists behaving badly: Look at Snooki, drunk again! Shows like *16 and Pregnant* and *Teen Mom* extend the reach of judgment to girls, legally still children, who naively agree to have their intimate lives, terrible decisions, and endless "drama" splashed all over television and the tabloids. Interestingly, men mostly get a pass: perhaps because, unlike women, who are quick to call one another sluts, gold-diggers, and bad mothers, men tend to absolve one another when it comes to sex and relationships, and look around for a woman to blame: bros before hos. You would never think, comparing the coverage of Lindsay Lohan or Paris Hilton to that of Charlie Sheen, that he was the one arrested numerous times for a serious crime—assaulting women.

Perhaps if pollsters invited people to judge the reasons behind other important life decisions, they would uncover a national penchant to slather censorious disapproval over all of them. In fact, in the rare cases where pollsters do ask, they often come up with fairly shocking findings, such as that 46 percent of Mississippi Republicans think interracial marriage should be illegal.[36] Mostly, though, we don't let an individual's personal reasons affect what the law should be. There used to be only a few grounds for divorce, and a judge had to assess the relevant facts and assign blame. Now divorce is no-fault. If you want to place your baby for adoption, you don't have to have a reason other people approve of; in fact, you don't need to give a reason at all. Legally, indeed, we don't even ask it of abortion: Unlike the law in some other countries, in the United States the right to abortion doesn't depend on the woman's reasons until the third trimester—although some states are passing laws against abortion for reasons of sex selection or "racial bias," whatever that means.

Socially, though, the reason is all-important. That is part of what people mean when they talk about abortion not being a black-and-white issue, but one of shades of gray. And that is interesting, because women's reasons are not, officially, what the organized opposition to abortion is about. Officially, the opposition sees abortion entirely in black and white: It's not about the woman's promiscuity or irresponsibility, the weakness of her judgment, her lack of moral fiber. It's about the right to life of the zygote/embryo/fetus. To devoted members of the right-to-life movement, abortion is just as wrong if a woman terminates a pregnancy because her baby will be born with Tay-Sachs disease as if she wants to sail around the world or smoke crack. And it is just as wrong if she ends her pregnancy at six days or six weeks or thirty-six weeks, because what's in her womb is a person from the moment sperm meets egg.

If you in the muddled middle really thought about that idea, you'd realize how little sense it makes.

THREE

WHAT IS A PERSON?

The bedrock argument of the anti-abortion movement is that intentionally ending new life at any point after conception is murder, or close to it. A fertilized egg is as much a person as Pope Francis. Not a potential person, but a person at that very moment. People who try to be "fair to both sides" tend to wave away this conviction because it sounds so bizarre, but it is essential to the anti-abortion position. Because they oppose all abortion as morally wrong and want to ban it, abortion opponents can't allow that some abortions are less evil than others— for example, that terminating a pregnancy at six weeks, when the embryo is the size of a pea, is qualitatively different from having one of those mythical day-before-birth abortions on a whim. The conservative Christian owners of the Hobby Lobby chain and the Conestoga Wood furniture company want to exclude IUDs and certain kinds of emergency contraception from the insurance coverage they must offer under the Affordable Care Act because they believe these are "abortifacients"—that is, that they prevent implantation of fertilized eggs. (The latest studies suggest they do not work this way, with the exception of the copper T IUD when inserted within five days of unprotected sex. Unfortunately, this is the most effective form of emergency contraception.)[1] As this book was in production, the Supreme Court ruled in their favor, and seems poised to permit any CEO to bar coverage of any method of contraception to which he has a religious objection.

This absolutist view is held by only a small percentage of the population, but it is the position of powerful political institutions: the Catholic Church, which owns one-sixth of all American hospitals, the Southern Baptist Convention and other fundamentalist/evangelical Protestant denominations, and the Republican Party.[2] Since 1984, the Republican Party platform has called for a constitutional ban on abortion with no mention of an exception to save the woman's life. ("We assert the sanctity of human life and affirm that the unborn child has a fundamental individual right to life which cannot be infringed. We support a human life amendment to the Constitution and endorse legislation to make clear that the Fourteenth Amendment's protections apply to unborn children.")[3] For some reason, commentators rarely take this plank in the party platform seriously. Oh, those wacky party platforms, nobody even reads them! Well, maybe they should. Of the nine Republicans running in the 2012 presidential primaries, only Mitt Romney and Jon Huntsman, both anti-abortion, declined to sign a pledge promising to support state and federal laws that would uphold "the unalienable personhood of every American, from the moment of conception until natural death" and appoint only judges and other officials who held that view.

If abortion opponents were to accept abortions for reasons

that majorities find acceptable—in cases of rape or severe fetal defect or to preserve the woman's physical or mental health—they might gain support from those who want to see abortion greatly restricted but not banned entirely. Some anti-abortion commentators, writing for a general audience, seem to realize the movement's official position is too extreme, even for themselves. Fire-breathing Ann Coulter has written that she supports legal abortion in the case of rape, and blamed Todd Akin and Richard Mourdock ("these two idiots") for derailing Mitt Romney's otherwise excellent chance of winning the White House by insisting that abortion be illegal even then.[4] But no pro-life leader, and no pro-life organization, supports permitting abortion for rape on principle, as opposed to a tactical concession. In fact, the wave of laws passed in the last few years include many that lack exceptions for rape, fetal defect, or any but the gravest threats to the woman's health, which somehow her doctors are supposed to predict with complete certainty. Movement leaders, and much of the rank and file, too, correctly perceive that such concessions would open the door to others.

Once you admit that embryonic or fetal life can be sacrificed for one reason, you're admitting that it is not equivalent to a born person, so why stop there? Moreover, once the door is opened a crack—say, by permitting suicidality to count as a risk to the woman's life, as in Ireland's new law—desperate women will try to push through and sympathetic people in authority may do their best to help them. The potential for wiggle room is one reason abortion opponents tend to deny that abortion is ever necessary, even to save a woman's life. Instead of making moral distinctions among reasons, they start with third-trimester abortions, which most people find distressing and even shocking (and which are extremely rare), and reason backwards. If it's wrong at nine months, why not at eight, or seven or three or one week or one hour? Even implantation—the very definition of pregnancy in standard medicine—is too late. Why does this tiny being, already a whole week old, acquire a right to life only when it moves from the fallopian tube to the womb? You might as well say you acquire human rights by moving from Brooklyn to Queens.

Abortion opponents use words like "the unborn" and "preborn" to claim the essential sameness of the fertilized egg and the fetus the day before birth. Similarly, they use "human life," "life," "human being," and "person" interchangeably as if they were all the same. But they are different. Obviously a fertilized egg is human—it isn't feline or canine—and it is alive and it is a being in the sense that it exists. So is an embryo, and so is a fetus. But are they human beings in the ordinary meaning of the term? Are they persons?

What is a person? It's not so easy to say. The philosopher Joel Feinberg uses the term "common-sense person" to mean one who thinks, feels, communicates, has more-or-less human features, and so on.[5] Many of the qualities that are part of being a common-sense person can be taken away, and yet that human being is still said to be a person. Take physical shape: A man or woman could be grotesquely misshapen, missing all four limbs, or entirely covered with hair, or green, and that would not make him or her less a person. Take consciousness— the capacity to think, feel, speak, perceive, respond, possess a personality (note the word), be self-aware. Even people with the most serious mental disabilities can do some of those things to some extent and qualify as a person in the moral sense—that is, imbued with full human rights. In fact, even if I am in a permanent vegetative state, most people would still regard me as a person: After all, I still have a residual social place—I am a relative, a citizen, a patient in the hospital, I still own whatever property I owned when I was conscious, and (some might insist) may still have some faint mental activity going on. Conversely, if I am lost on a desert island all alone and have no social place, I still have consciousness and am therefore still a person. (But if a coconut hits me on the head and I fall into a permanent vegetative state, I may not be a person for long.)

If some combination of those qualities is what makes a person, it is hard to see how a fertilized egg qualifies as one. It has no brain, no blood, no head, organs, or limbs; it cannot think, feel, perceive, or communicate. It has no character traits or relationships and it occupies no social space. It is the size of the period at the end of this sentence. Before it implants in the uterine wall, and usually for quite a while after that, the woman in whose body it exists does not even know it is there. In fact, about half of all fertilized eggs fail to implant and are simply washed out of her body with her menstrual flow.[6] If fertilized eggs are persons, God is remarkably careless about them. They are potential persons, yes, but that is not the same thing as actually being one, any more than my being a potential seventy-year-old means I am one now.

Many people, including many Catholics, believe that the official Catholic position is that the fertilized egg acquires a soul at "the moment of conception." (Actually, there is no moment; fertilization is a process that takes up to twenty-four hours.)[7] In fact, the official position on ensoulment is that we don't know for sure when it happens. The Church's total ban on destroying even the unimplanted fertilized egg is a precaution against the possibility of taking an ensouled life. Better to "err on the side of life" than risk even the remotest, unlikeliest death of an ensouled creature—other than that of the woman, that is.

In 1869, Pope Pius IX issued a bull (*Apostolicae Sedis Moderationi*) declaring that the punishment for abortion at any stage of pregnancy would be the same as for murder: excommunication. It was not always so. Before the nineteenth century there were numerous respectable Catholic positions about the status of the embryo and fetus, and thus a multiplicity of positions about abortion. Up until that point, the theologian Christine Gudorf writes, "The dominant, but not the only, *theological* position was adopted from Aristotle and championed by Thomas Aquinas, who counted ensoulment of the fetus as occurring 40–80 days after conception, depending on the sex of the fetus. The dominant *pastoral* position—obviously because it was more practical and obvious—was that ensoulment occurred at quickening, when the fetus could first be felt moving in the mother's womb, usually early the fifth month. Before ensoulment the fetus was not understood as a person."[8]

Leaving aside how anyone in Aquinas's day would know the sex of, say, a two-month-old embryo and thus whether it was souled (boy) or unsouled (girl), and why, despite this lack of information, Aquinas, like Aristotle before him, still felt it important to imprint the inferiority of the female on even this unseen speck of life, what matters here is that abortion, though seen as a sin, along with contraception, masturbation, and other ways of thwarting procreation, was not always seen as murder.

Today abortion opponents often speak the language of science and human rights as well as theology, or instead of it. We do not need the concept of ensoulment, argue the conservative Catholic political theorists and prominent abortion opponents Robert George and Christopher Tollefsen in *Embryo: A De-*

fense of Human Life. "We can know from science what the embryo is."[9] It is "a complete, albeit developmentally immature, human being" that deserves "full moral respect."[10] Religion has nothing to do with it: "Human-embryo ethics is, in this regard, no different from the ethics of our treatment of minorities or dependents. Human beings are capable of understanding, through reason, that it is morally wrong and unjust to discriminate against someone because he is of a different race or has a different ethnic heritage. And we are capable of understanding that it is wrong and unjust to discriminate against someone because of his age, size, state of development, location, or condition of dependency."[11] Because a fertilized egg or embryo has a complete set of chromosomes, and because it may develop into a baby, abortion is a form of discrimination against "a very young child."[12] A woman who terminates a pregnancy because she can't bear the thought of having a fifth or sixth child is practicing something akin to racism, or anti-immigrant politics, discriminating against the embryo because of who it is and its "location"—that is, her womb. She herself has no special interest in her own body, no connection to it that is more intimate and more demanding than anyone else's.

And yet, DNA-as-person functions very much like the concept of ensoulment. Like the soul, DNA stands for the quintessential self, the real you, when in fact you are far more than a set of chromosomes. Abortion opponents like to quote a line from Dr. Seuss's *Horton Hears a Who*: "A person's a person no matter how small." (This is much to the displeasure of Dr. Seuss's wife, who says her husband did not want his characters used for political purposes.)[13] But the Whos were not fertilized Who eggs. They were funny-looking Seussian grown-ups who talked and sang and had a town of their own. The question isn't whether small persons are persons. It's whether fertilized eggs and embryos and fetuses qualify as small persons.

It is as if abortion opponents imagine that the "moment of conception" creates a homunculus—the tiny man that seventeenth-century scientists imagined they could see when they looked at semen through the first microscopes. The homunculus was entirely produced by the male partner in reproduction. All it needed was a nice warm womb to help it get bigger. As Todd Akin put it in a speech to Congress opposing stem-cell research:

> Now, an embryo may seem like some scientific or laboratory term, but in fact the embryo contains the unique information that defines a person. All you add is food and climate control, and some time, and the embryo becomes you or me.[14]

An embryo is a person; a woman is a place, a kind of comfy survivalist bunker—food, climate control, some time.

This view of the pregnant woman as merely a convenient growing medium for a completely independent embryo sounds off-key today. Virginia state senator Steve Martin became a national laughingstock when he wrote on his Facebook page, "Once a child does exist in your womb, I'm not going to assume a right to kill it just because the child's host (some refer to them as mothers) doesn't want it." (In the wake of the publicity, he changed "host" to "the bearer of the child," which sounds as if pregnancy meant carrying a baby about on a platter.) But the image goes back at least as far as ancient Greece. In Aeschylus' *Eumenides*, Apollo defends Orestes, on trial for murdering his mother, who has murdered his father:

The mother is not the begetter of the child begotten, as
they call it—merely the nurse of the new-sown embryo.
The male who mounts is the begetter. The woman keeps
the offspring as a hostess for a guest, if no god harms it.[15]

In this ancient version, the woman is variously a flowerpot,
a baby nurse, a hostess offering her uterus like a spare room, or
possibly a hostess minding a package for a traveler. Her effort,
her needs, the dangers and pains and injuries of pregnancy and
childbirth are all erased—and this was in an era when death in
childbirth was a common occurrence. Apollo goes on to under-
line the unimportance of the woman to reproduction by noting that a male could bring forth a child without a mother—look
at Athena, born of Zeus's forehead, "not reared at all by a nurse
in the dark of the womb."[16] Indeed, he says, "no goddess could
give birth to" such a marvelous being.[17] (Not surprisingly, Athena
agrees. Breaking the tie, she rules for Orestes on the grounds
that she had no mother and is her father's daughter: "I honor
the male sex wholeheartedly.")[18]

The same idea is at work in metaphors of male semen fertil-
izing the female womb—he is the seed, she is the soil, he is the
active principle, she is the place where the activity occurs, he is
the landowner, she is the land. It is hard to overstate how far
back in history this imagery goes. The ancient Egyptian "Instructions of the Vizier Ptahhotep," written around 2400 BCE,
describes a wife as "a fertile field for her lord."[19] Three thousand years later, the same idea shows up in the Koran: "Your
women are your fields, so go into your fields whichever way you
like."[20] The very words "semen" and "sperm" mean seed, and
"fertile" and "infertile" were used only of women till our own
day, since infertility was generally thought to be their fault.

("Barren," another field word used only of women, seems to have been retired from the lexicon.) Sometimes the field did seem to have a mind of its own, but that wasn't a good thing: "Why do you sow where the field is eager to destroy the fruit?" the fourth-century saint John Chrysostom wrote, attacking "medicines of sterility," that is, herbal contraception, as even "worse than murder."[21] The metaphor of woman as a man's field persists into our own time. Ellen Willis quotes Ken Kesey on why abortion is wrong even in cases of rape: "You don't plow under the corn because the seed was planted with a neighbor's shovel."[22]

Today we know that there is no such thing as a homunculus—a fertilized egg is the work of both sexes and it looks nothing like a child, although abortion opponents often call it one. But the tiny man lives on as a mental image: the fertilized egg as a complete person that just happens to have only one cell. Even once it has traveled down the fallopian tube and attaches to the uterine wall (a process which does not happen until six to twelve days after fertilization) and becomes technically known as a blastocyst, it has only 70 to 100 cells. It is not until this stage, implantation, that medical science says pregnancy begins—because medical science sees pregnancy as the changes a woman's body undergoes to produce a baby, not as a notional, theoretical mini-child that no one knows is there. But the blastocyst is still not a person, if that word means anything at all. Yes, its DNA is unique to the individual-to-be, but it is not the same as that individual. Your DNA is not you. It is more like the basic instructions for you. DNA is to a person as a blueprint is to a house. As with houses, moreover, the instructions are only an outline. All sorts of particular conditions, from your mother's hormonal mix and stress levels during pregnancy to parental love, diet, and intellectual stimulation afterward, help determine how your genes are expressed, or not expressed. If we could clone Mozart today, he might be brilliant or he might be a charming slacker, but he would not be Wolfgang Amadeus Mozart. For that, eighteenth-century Austria—and that most demanding of all stage fathers, Leopold Mozart—would be required.

So problematic indeed is the notion that a fertilized egg or embryo or even a pre-viable fetus is a person that the legal scholar Ronald Dworkin argued in *Life's Dominion* that few people really believe it, even if they insist they do:

> The scalding rhetoric of the "pro-life" movement seems to propose the derivative claim that a fetus is from the moment of its conception a full moral person with rights and interests equal in importance to those of any other member of the moral community. But very few people—even those who belong to the most vehemently anti-abortion groups—actually believe that, whatever they say.[23]

Dworkin does not dwell on the 7 to 20 percent of Americans who tell pollsters they would ban abortion completely or on the fact that such bans are law in some thirty-three countries, mostly in the developing world.[24] Instead he notes that even many people who say the zygote/embryo/fetus is a person with full human rights believe that abortion is permissible—tragic and troubling, but permissible—to save the pregnant woman's life. If they truly regarded it as a person, they could not permit that any more than they would permit a doctor to kill one of his patients to give another a new heart, even if that first patient was seriously injured and unlikely to recover.

Dworkin notes that many who believe in fetal personhood will reluctantly allow that abortion should be legal not only when the woman's life is threatened but in other extreme circumstances as well—when a woman conceives from rape or incest, or would be seriously injured by carrying to term and delivering, or when it will result in a baby with such severe problems it will quickly die. That some who say the fetus is a person from the moment of conception make these exceptions leads Dworkin to think they don't really mean what they say. In truth, he argues, most people who say they believe in fetal personhood really mean that human life is sacred, inviolable, of very great value: "They believe that a fetus is a living, growing human creature and that it is intrinsically a bad thing, a kind of cosmic shame, when human life at any stage is deliberately extinguished."[25]

Perhaps if people who claim zygotes are persons had to spend a week arguing with Ronald Dworkin, they would collapse in exhaustion and admit that a fertilized egg is not the same as a five-year-old. Perhaps they would admit that they, too, would be more upset by a fire that killed four hundred workers in a factory or young people in a club—or even, who knows, four hundred horses at a horse farm—than at a fire in a fertility clinic that destroyed four hundred frozen embryos. Imagine such a clinic fire, and a firefighter who ignored the screams of workers and patients and dashed about collecting embryos instead on the grounds that they were children, and even more helpless than the trapped adults. Maybe even those who say they believe fertilized eggs are persons would admit that this firefighter was taking his convictions too far. (But maybe not: Imagining a choice between one five-year-old girl and ten embryos, George and Tollefsen argue that "if Jones happens to be the mother or father or grandparent of the embryos, Jones might well choose to rescue them, and most people would not regard this as immoral."[26] One definition of fanaticism: when you imagine, on no evidence, that "most people" share your most outlandish convictions.)

Life's Dominion is a brilliant book, but in the two decades since its publication, the notion that "the unborn" are persons from conception on has grown only more influential. It is the most common and most powerful argument against legal abortion, the basis upon which opponents claim to be pro-*life*. It's not the only argument they make. They often talk about abortion as being bad for society: By removing the fear of unwanted pregnancy it encourages premarital sex and thus weakens the family; it cheapens all sex, even within marriage, by disconnecting it from reproduction; it encourages people to be selfish and materialistic, causes women to stray from their true calling as mothers, frees men from responsibility, and so on. But such arguments will not persuade outsiders who do not share this view of women, sex, and family life: They are, after all, the same arguments made against birth control, and birth control is very popular. Rick Santorum was widely mocked when he spoke of "the dangers of contraception in this country": "It's not okay. It's a license to do things in the sexual realm that is counter to how things are supposed to be."[27]

By contrast, "Life begins at conception" sounds like a simple scientific fact: When sperm meets egg, a new life is started. It allows opponents to skirt the social and political issues that abortion raises: whether for example women can flourish as individuals, let alone be equal to men, if they have to bear children at the drop of a hat, and whether the fact that criminalizing abortion falls most heavily and most cruelly on low-income women is an argument against it. All they have to do is keep saying "baby."

DOESN'T ULTRASOUND PROVE THERE'S A BABY IN THERE?

In his vice-presidential debate with Joe Biden in 2012, GOP candidate Paul Ryan said:

> Now, you want to ask basically why I'm pro-life? It's not simply because of my Catholic faith. That's a factor, of course. But it's also because of reason and science. You know, I think about ten and a half years ago, my wife Janna and I went to Mercy Hospital in Janesville, where I was born, for our seven-week ultrasound for our firstborn child, and we saw that heartbeat. Our little baby was in the shape of a bean. And to this day, we have nicknamed our firstborn child, Liza, "Bean." Now I believe that life begins at conception.[28]

Ryan was expressing what many parents-to-be feel when the doctor shows them that first grainy, gray picture on the ultrasound-machine screen. For people looking forward to having a baby, as my daughter's father and I were, it's a thrilling moment. Suddenly, it's all so immediate, so concrete: That shadowy blur is going to be your Olivia, your Ben. In a happy ritual that would have seemed like science fiction only a few decades ago, couples e-mail ultrasound photos around to friends and family, post them on Facebook, stick them up on the refrigerator. Seeing the photo can be part of the bonding process, the imaginative work of seeing yourself as a parent, of making it all real: *I'm going to have a baby!* I felt that way, even though the picture was really just a gray blur, like those photos that supposedly show the Loch Ness Monster. (Women who are having abortions sometimes want an ultrasound printout to keep—life is complicated.)

Ryan wasn't just describing his excitement as a father-to-be, however. He was claiming that seeing the sonogram and hearing the embryo's heartbeat proved to him, through "reason and science," that "life begins at conception." (Not to nitpick, but why does hearing the heartbeat prove anything about the fertilized egg, which has no heartbeat?)

It's true that reason and science can tell us a lot about fetal development. But they can't explain why a bean-sized embryo, a being with no consciousness and no self-interests, has a right to use a woman's body, no matter what the cost to the woman. As Ryan himself acknowledged, he was "pro-life" long before he saw that sonogram (and I stayed pro-choice after seeing mine). The ultrasound confirmed what he already believed. By themselves, in fact, reason and science might seem to suggest the opposite of what Ryan believes: that an embryo, which cannot think or feel or have self-awareness, does not meet the definition of a person.

The fact that ultrasound has profoundly altered the abortion debate is a journalistic and political truism. "The sonograms and the being able to view the unborn child has created a positive thing for the pro-life movement and has created a difficulty for the pro-choice movement," Susan B. Anthony List president Marjorie Dannenfelser told Diane Rehm on NPR in 2013, but the claim goes back many years.[29]

"No technology has had as much impact on the abortion debate as ultrasound," wrote *New York Times* reporter Sheryl Gay Stolberg, in a 1998 piece marking the twenty-fifth anniversary of *Roe v. Wade*. Stolberg describes the effect of ultrasound on one pregnant woman:

"I'm pro-choice," Leslie Singman says. "Always was and always will be." Mrs. Singman, a 35-year-old saleswoman from Potomac, Md., grew up believing that no child should be an unwanted child. She sends money to the National Abortion and Reproductive Rights Action League, and never thought to question her views—until she got pregnant and saw her daughter on the ultrasound screen: There, in fuzzy black and white, floating in her mother's womb at 16 weeks' gestation, was the tiny but perfectly formed fetus that would become Leah Shayne Singman. "I could see fingers and toes and the shape of her head and the body," Mrs. Singman says. "I could see bones in her hands, a hand waving at me. It made me think that there is definitely a life growing there."[30]

Did this four-months-pregnant woman really not think there was "definitely a life growing there" before she saw it on a screen? Not getting her period, morning sickness, tender breasts, odd cravings, a swelling belly, perhaps even feeling the fetus move didn't do it for her as they have for women for thousands of years? Maybe not. Perhaps ultrasound pictures have indeed changed the way women experience their pregnancy, by making a private, internal experience public and visual. It was the woman herself, and only she, who experienced "quickening"—the first movements of the fetus that were the traditional proof that a baby was on the way—but the pregnant woman is in the same relation to an ultrasound picture as anyone else: She has no privileged knowledge. At the same time, those fuzzy, high-tech smudges carry a big emotional charge: Leslie Singman imagined her baby was waving to her. It may well be true that ultrasound images have made later abortions more disquieting—not that people were keen on those abortions before. But given the ubiquitous practice of ultrasound during pregnancy, you would expect opposition to abortion to have ramped up if that was the effect ultrasound had, and that has not been the case. Just about every pro-choice woman who has had a baby in the last three or four decades has seen a sonogram, and so have their partners. Leslie Singman herself was careful to say she was still pro-choice. Most of the 1 in 3 American women who will have had at least one abortion by menopause will have also seen a sonogram, given that 6 in 10 women who have abortions have already carried a pregnancy to term. Indeed, given that the main purpose of ultrasound is to diagnose fetal abnormalities, it's a technology that has probably increased the number of abortions that take place for medical reasons.

"Brittany," a young African American woman whom I interviewed for this book, went back and forth on having an abortion as she tried to put together the money. She finally decided against it after she saw a sonogram at seventeen weeks. By the time I met Brittany, her son was a three-year-old ball of energy and joy. But Brittany is hardly a pro-life poster girl. Not only does she still support abortion rights, she works as a counselor in an abortion clinic. (I met her at a regional meeting of independent abortion providers.) And the sonogram was not the only factor in her decision: She told me she was only able to have her son as a young single woman just starting out in life because of the support of her close and loving family. If she got pregnant again anytime soon, she would definitely consider abortion.

As of May 2014, twenty-three states had passed laws regulating ultrasound scans before abortion.[31] Three states require the provider to describe and show the image to the woman and the rest require the provider to offer to show it to her. After a huge outcry condemning the practice as "medical rape," Virginia decided not to mandate ultrasound by transvaginal probe, but in Texas, this requirement was quietly passed.[32] Some states also require that the woman listen to the fetal heartbeat. The rationale is that women deserve to have this "information," but if the concern were to give women all the facts they need to make an informed decision, there would not be an Arizona law protecting doctors who intentionally withhold from pregnant women information about fetal abnormalities.[33] Nor would the Virginia state legislature have passed, and Governor McAuliffe signed, a bill with a "conscience clause" that permits genetic counselors to withhold information they believe will lead a woman to choose abortion.[34] The purpose of forcing women to have ultrasounds, whether they are medically necessary or not, and forcing doctors to describe the fetus and show them the image, is to make women feel even worse—*Bad Mommy! Look at this baby you want to kill!*

Ultrasound laws serve another important purpose too, which has gotten less attention: They ratchet up the costs and complications of abortion. By mandating waiting periods between ultrasound and abortion (ostensibly to give the woman time to change her mind), they make getting an abortion more expensive and time-consuming.[35] And by requiring that ultrasounds be performed by a doctor, and by the same doctor who would perform the abortion, they complicate the already-difficult logistics of abortion provision, especially for clinics which must bring in doctors from out of state. Interestingly, no state requires that ultrasound be performed by a doctor for general purposes. My own ultrasound was performed by a hospital technician. In anti-abortion crisis pregnancy centers, ultrasounds are usually performed by volunteers with no medical training at all.[36]

Abortion opponents claim that many women change their minds when shown a sonogram of their embryos and fetuses before their abortion. "So why do abortion providers avoid showing ultrasound images to women?" asks Lifenews.com. "Perhaps this is because up to 78% of women who see an ultrasound of their babies choose not to have abortions."[37] A footnote leads one to a 2011 *Time* article about the results of a 2008 Focus on the Family study on the effect of hearing the fetal heartbeat, a study cited by Michele Bachmann but subsequently retracted by the organization: "We don't have any 'studies,' and we don't publish any percentages like that," a Focus on the Family official acknowledged.[38] Lifenews.com was still citing this nonexistent fact in 2013. Conservative pundit Rachel Campos-Duffy, wife of Rep. Sean Duffy (R-WI), claimed the true number of changed minds was "upwards of 90%" and the Family Research Council cited "one pregnancy resource center director in Baton Rouge who claimed that an astonishing 'Ninety-eight percent of women who have ultrasounds choose to carry to term.'"[39] One wonders how any abortion clinic stays in business.

Politifact investigated Campos-Duffy's claim and found it to be false, although, based on one study, it also found that "some women" did change their mind after seeing a sonogram. Other studies, also cited by Politifact, find that women stick to their abortion decision.[40] A 2014 study in *Obstetrics & Gynecology*, the largest to date, looked at the records of 15,575 patients at one Los Angeles clinic. It found that of the 42.5 percent of abortion patients who voluntarily looked at the ultrasound, 98.4 percent stuck to their decision to end the pregnancy. Of the 1.6 who changed their minds, all were part of the 7.4 percent of patients who were already ambivalent.[41] For that small number of women, being given the choice to see the sonogram may have tipped the balance, as it did for Brittany. (Choosing to view the ultrasound may have helped firm the decision of the women who went through with abortions too—maybe some were relieved it looked so much less like a baby than they had expected.) But the fact that a few ambivalent women voluntarily looked at the ultrasound and decided against abortion is not an argument for forcing ultrasound viewing on all women, most of whom choose not to look.

Perhaps the more important goal, though, is to sway the public. Images of the fetus in the womb have long been used for this purpose, most dramatically in Dr. Bernard Nathanson's 1984 film *The Silent Scream*, which purports to show an agonized twelve-week-old fetus mutely struggling against an in-process abortion. But fetal imagery can be misleading: In *The Silent Scream*, an embryo the size of a lime is made to look as large as a toddler. And sonograms distort reality in another, more subtle way: You can only take a picture of the embryo/fetus if you erase the body of the pregnant woman. As with the famous optical illusion of the duck-rabbit, you can't see them both at the same time. In a sonogram the fetus is the subject, the woman is the background; the case for its personhood is made by turning her into gray-and-white wallpaper.

PERSONHOOD AMENDMENTS

Since 2007, a highly organized movement has attempted to pass ballot initiatives adding "personhood amendments" to state constitutions in more than a dozen states.[42] These typically declare, "The terms people and person shall apply to every human being at any state of development."

So far, personhood amendments have universally failed at the ballot box, even in Mississippi, where voters rejected one, Proposition 26, in 2011.[43] This loss was widely hailed as a major pro-choice victory: If voters in one of the nation's most conservative and most religious states wouldn't pass it, who would? Significantly though, the arguments that turned the tide were not about a woman's right to end a pregnancy, or to use emergency contraception. They were more focused on the possible dangers posed by the measure to fertility treatments, stem-cell research, and hormonal contraception. Would fertility specialists be prosecuted for in-vitro procedures that destroyed embryos? Would the IUD and the Pill become illegal? Would miscarriages be investigated as possible crimes? Even conservative voters hesitated to add to their state constitution an amendment that could have so many unforeseen and strange consequences, however logically they followed from the personhood premise.

The man behind the personhood amendment movement, Keith Mason of Personhood USA (he met his wife while both were protesting outside an abortion clinic), could easily have reassured voters that his proposed law would have no effect on these benign practices. Instead, he seemed to go out of his way to suggest that indeed, it might. "Certainly women, my wife included, would want to know if the pills they're taking would kill a unique human individual," he told NPR.[44] If a woman continued taking the Pill, despite this "knowledge," could she be prosecuted for murdering some untold number of "unique human individuals"? Or at least for creating a hazard, like someone who leaves dangerous old farm equipment where the neighborhood kids can get into it? Assuming that Keith Mason is sincere, he is definitely one person who believes the fertilized egg is a person, and accepts the consequences of that belief.

(It's worth noting that Personhood USA is an explicitly Christian organization, whose primary mission "is to serve Jesus by being an advocate for those who cannot speak for themselves, the pre-born child.")[45]

Despite all the warnings of dire medical, legal, and social consequences to the citizenry, 4 in 10 Mississippi voters approved the amendment—the highest percentage of a state electorate so far. (Interestingly, African Americans opposed it by a wide margin, despite the large numbers who are devoted Christians.) It was endorsed by both candidates for governor; the Republican, Lt. Gov. Phil Bryant, was co-chair of Yes on 26.[46] His campaign gave out free pro-26 bumper stickers and pulled out all the rhetorical stops: He evoked the Holocaust (fertilized eggs were like Jews "being marched into the oven" because of "the people who were in charge of the government at that time") and described the vote as "a battle of good or evil."[47] In other words, a loss for 26 would mean "Satan wins." Bryant's opponent, the Democratic mayor of Hattiesburg, Johnny DuPree, Mississippi's first black gubernatorial candidate since Reconstruction, said he would vote for Prop 26, despite his worries that it would ban abortion for rape victims and contraception. Pressed by the victim of a particularly brutal rape, DuPree acknowledged that his daughter had had an ectopic pregnancy and used IVF to conceive her child and finally said, "I'm starting to see that there are issues . . . I've said I'm going to vote yes and it's too late to go back on it now. It'd destroy me politically."[48] It's not every day that a politician is so frank, but DuPree may have been right. No major state politician of either party was willing to publicly call for the proposition to be voted down. This is a state, after all, in which back in 2003 the Democratic candidate for lieutenant governor, Barbara Blackmon, suggested that she and her Republican opponent, Amy Tuck, each sign affidavits affirming that she had never had an abortion. (This was a not-so-subtle way of planting in voters' heads the suspicion that Tuck had indeed had one. Tuck signed and won.)

Bryant won the governor's mansion, but a personhood amendment failed to obtain enough signatures to be placed on the ballot in 2015. Meanwhile, the North Dakota state legislature passed, and the governor signed, a personhood amendment to the state constitution that will go before the voters in 2014. There are no exceptions for rape, incest, or the life or health of the woman. How could there be? "No exceptions" is what fetal personhood *means*.

The extremism of personhood amendments is why some major anti-abortion organizations such as National Right to Life, Americans United for Life, and the Eagle Forum oppose them.[49] For one thing, they are almost certain to be declared unconstitutional by the courts, and risk giving the Supreme Court a chance to further enshrine *Roe v. Wade* as the law of the land. It is hard to imagine a Supreme Court declaring that the Constitution allows states to ban abortion to save a woman's life. Even Justice William Rehnquist, in his dissent from *Roe*, acknowledged that would go too far. Moreover, the anti-abortion movement is doing very well with a piecemeal approach, attacking abortion rights and access from multiple angles: Ban abortions after twenty weeks on the theory, which most research rejects, that it's at this point that the fetus can feel pain; force clinics to close through burdensome regulations and requirements; impose restrictions that raise the cost to patients and push them past the point at which area clinics can perform abortions. The personhood amendment was too much for Mississippi voters—but as of this writing, the state's sole remaining abortion clinic is open only because a federal judge has granted a preliminary injunction against a 2012 law requiring its doctors to have admitting privileges at a local hospital, none of which will grant them. And Governor Bryant isn't giving up. In his 2014 state of the state address, he said, "On this unfortunate anniversary of *Roe v. Wade*, my goal is to end abortion in Mississippi."[50]

Personhood amendments are not only a dubious legal strategy; they show the movement's extremist face at a time when it is attempting to emphasize incremental restrictions ostensibly aimed at protecting women. But their failure at the ballot box is not necessarily bad news for abortion opponents. They make other proposals look moderate by comparison. If the most outspoken and energetic opponents want to outlaw abortion entirely, along with the Pill, the IUD, in-vitro fertilization, and embryonic stem-cell research, the middle-of-the-road, reasonable compromise position becomes: Let's make abortion really hard to get, broaden "conscience clauses" and allow employers generous exemptions from the birth-control provisions of the Affordable Care Act, permit in-vitro fertilization—more babies!—and not think too much about embryonic stem-cell research, because even though it kills pre-embryos, someday we ourselves might benefit from it. Before you know it, pro-choicers are spending their energy debating how much risk to a pregnant woman's life or health or sanity is too much, and whether laws that have the effect of shutting down the majority of a state's clinics are really intended to protect women's health, and making the case for birth-control coverage based on the wonderful things the Pill does for ovarian cysts and acne.[51]

TAKING FETAL PERSONHOOD SERIOUSLY

Perhaps you are thinking this is all rather arcane. What do un-implanted fertilized eggs have to do with real abortions, the ones that trouble so many? Surely Dworkin is right to wonder if many people can really believe that an entity of at most a few dozen cells is a child. Or is he wrong? We know that some people do think that: The anti-abortion movement also opposes fertility treatments and stem-cell research that result in the destruction of embryos. Nadya Suleman, the "Octomom," explained that she had herself implanted with all eight embryos she had had frozen on a previous occasion because "those are my children."[52] There are women who have themselves implanted with the abandoned leftover frozen embryos of others—they are known as "snowflake babies"—and see this as a form of adoption, like taking in an abandoned child. "For me," comments "Tvelians" on the Catholic News Agency Web site, "it is a clear-cut moral issue. An embryo and an infant do not differ in kind, only in degree of development. Therefore, a child in foster care and an embryo in a test-tube are morally equivalent, with the only distinction being that the latter is at a greater risk of destruction without adoption."

Evangelical Protestants are big supporters of embryo adoption. In 2006, when George W. Bush vetoed legislation increasing funding for stem-cell research, he was surrounded by "snowflake children"—a photo op that *Time* columnist Joe Klein said made him "want to throw up. It is so transparently political and cynical." But interestingly, the Catholic Church is still making up its mind. *Dignitas Personae*, a 2008 instruction from the Vatican, maintains that there is "no morally licit" solution.[53] On the one hand, both the production of the embryo and its "adoption" involve banned artificial reproduction techniques. On the other, the embryos will eventually die if not implanted. So, it would seem, "embryonic life," which for the Church outweighs the lives of women, does not automatically outweigh *every* consideration: It does not necessarily outweigh, for example, the Church's own strictures against assisted reproduction.

Even by the generous and unverified account of Nightlight Christian Adoptions, which has done the most to popularize the practice, embryo adoption is not a big success: Nightlight claims a few thousand babies have been born to embryo adopters since the first one in 1998. According to *Time*, about a thousand transfer cycles took place in 2011, with more than a third resulting in at least one birth.[54] Given that there are around 500,000 embryos stored in fertility clinics, the *Washington Times* was surely indulging in wishful thinking when it said embryo adoption was "the rage."[55] Although since 2002 an "embryo adoption awareness" program has received between $980,000 and $4.2 million in federal funding annually, there is no mass outreach campaign on the part of right-to-life organizations to find uterine homes for these unfortunate waifs.[56] If they're serious, shouldn't abortion opponents be demanding that the government treat these embryos just like other children whose parents cannot or will not care for them? Foster parents, after all, are paid stipends and expenses. Why not a national program to pay women to be implanted with these forlorn and helpless creatures? Indeed, since abortion opponents believe women should give birth even if the pregnancy is unwanted and conception was involuntary, should they not be issuing stern demands that women who oppose abortion demonstrate their belief in "life" by hosting orphan embryos regardless of their personal wishes or circumstances? If there are no extenuating circumstances for a woman seeking abortion, why is embryo adoption something only the most willing of the willing undertake? The interest of the embryo is the same. What's different is that in the case of abortion the embryo is in a woman and not in a freezer. And it is in the woman because she had sex. Sooner or later, the case against abortion rights always comes down to sex. Sex and women.

Despite the many words I've just spent on it, the question of fetal personhood is crucial to the anti-abortion position but not to the abortion-rights position. Even if we all decided to define personhood to include fertilized eggs and embryos and fetuses, they would not have the right to use a woman's body against her will and at whatever cost to herself. Persons are not entitled to use one another like that: Even if I am the only person in the world who can save my child by donating a kidney, the decision is still mine to make. For the anti-abortion argument to work, abortion opponents must take a further step. They have to argue that when a woman has sex she is contracting to carry any resultant pregnancy to term, no matter what. But who says sex implies this contract and that it can never be qualified or broken? With whom does the woman make this contract? The not-yet-existent fertilized egg? The man with her in bed? Nature? God? And who says there is a contract in the first place? And why does this contract to give life at the expense of one's own body place no demands on the man? And why does it end at birth? The notion of sex as a contract is just another way of asserting that women shouldn't be sexual beings—even with their husbands—except on those rare occasions when they wish to conceive a child.

Let's look again at the professed belief that personhood begins at the moment of conception. What would it mean to take this view seriously? First of all, overturning *Roe v. Wade* would be a cowardly, halfhearted goal: What, each state is going to decide for itself whether or not women can murder their unborn babies? We would never allow that to be the case with born children. Sick of caring for your teething toddler? Move to New York (or Maine, or Oregon) and drown it, it's your right! Protecting the zygote/embryo/fetus requires national legislation, such as the Human Life Amendment to the Constitution. Otherwise, women in states where abortion is banned will flock to states where it is legal, as they did after New York legalized abortion in 1970.[57]

No, abortion would have to be illegal even in those tragic cases where large majorities, including some people who call themselves pro-life, would permit it. Embryonic stem-cell research would have to be outlawed, along with many kinds of fertility treatment. And although the best research shows that birth-control pills, the IUD, and emergency contraception do not prevent implantation of a fertilized egg, you can expect to be fighting that issue for the rest of your life.

Since a woman usually becomes aware of pregnancy after she misses a period, or maybe two, there is a fairly long stretch of time in which, if she has been sexually active, she doesn't know she's hosting an embryo. Some women don't realize they are pregnant for months; they mistake "spotting" for their regular period, or usually have irregular periods anyway; they don't experience common symptoms of pregnancy like morning sickness, or they misinterpret them (I should go on a diet, I've gained fifteen pounds). Thus, if the government really wanted to protect these vulnerable tiny people, it should regard pregnancy as the default position for every female between menarche and menopause. It would have to look at thousands of rules and regulations and evaluate them for possible danger to these unknown zygotes and embryos.

If that sounds bizarre, it shouldn't. In 2006, the Centers for Disease Control and Prevention (CDC) issued guidelines suggesting that all fertile girls and women practice "preconception care": They should treat themselves—and be treated by healthcare providers—as, in the pungent phrase of the *Washington Post*, "pre-pregnant, regardless of whether or not they plan to get pregnant soon."[58]

> Among other things, this means all women between first menstrual period and menopause should take folic acid supplements, refrain from smoking, maintain a healthy weight and keep chronic conditions such as asthma and diabetes under control. . . . While most of these recommendations are well known to women who are pregnant or seeking to get pregnant, experts say it's important that women follow this advice throughout their reproductive lives, because about half of pregnancies are unplanned and so much damage can be done to a fetus between conception and the time the pregnancy is confirmed.[59]

Study coauthor Janis Biermann even advised women to avoid cat feces—not only must a single woman avoid "high-risk sex," she can't even have a cat to console her lonely nights.[60] Needless to say, no comparable list was set out for the fathers of these future embryonic surprises (don't expose a woman to your cigarette smoke or a sexually transmitted infection, keep that litter box squeaky clean, start saving now for child-support payments).

This picture of girls and women summoned to lives of clean

living and watchful moderation for thirty years or more on the tiny chance that at any given moment they might be accidentally pregnant (with an embryo the CDC seems to assume they will carry to term) may sound like something out of *The Handmaid's Tale*, but it was the product of consultation with important and highly respected organizations, including the American College of Obstetricians and Gynecologists and the March of Dimes. Instead of urging doctors to treat their patients as if they were already pregnant or about to become so, why didn't the CDC use the occasion to zero in on accidental pregnancy?[61] For example, by urging doctors to educate patients about the many different methods of birth control, instead of just one or two, help them find one they were happy with, stress the importance of continuous protection if one switched from one method to another, and make themselves available on short notice to patients who need to change methods. If, as Jane Brody reported in the *New York Times*, lots of women drop contraception because they think their doctors have told them they can't get pregnant, when in fact they are of normal fertility (about 90 percent chance of pregnancy over two years of regular unprotected intercourse), wouldn't it make more sense for the CDC to figure out what doctors are telling their patients that gets so misinterpreted?[62] The fact that the CDC thought in terms of protecting accidental fertilized eggs from women, and not protecting women from accidental fertilized eggs shows how shallow still is the idea of women truly being in control of their fertility. Pregnancy to the CDC is something that happens *to* them, for which, ideally, they should be ready.

If you really believe in personhood from the moment of conception, logically you should believe that fertile women should be legally barred from work that poses a danger, however slight, to any zygote or embryo they might be harboring, just as you would support requiring parents to put their children in a car seat, even though the chance of an accident is relatively slim. But in 1991 the Supreme Court ruled otherwise in *Automobile Workers v. Johnson Controls*: It held that employers could not bar fertile women from work that posed actual or potential risks of causing birth defects. That decision was an important victory for working women—if the ruling had gone the other way, fertile women could have been barred from a wide range of jobs, including those where the danger was just a pretext to keep them out. (Don't like it? Sue!) A true believer in fetal personhood would be fighting for that verdict to be overturned.

It would also be legally incumbent on pregnant women to follow their doctor's advice. If your doctor says you need to take it easy, and you carry on with your physically demanding job or with chasing your toddler, you are surely guilty of something, just as if you left your baby at home alone and it fell out of its crib. At present, it is mainly women in the later stages of pregnancy who face those attitudes. Women have been forced to have cesarean sections against their will, and have been prosecuted if they rejected their doctor's advice and delivered babies who were born dead or died.[63] Hundreds of women around the country have been jailed on charges that their drug use resulted in a stillborn baby or a baby who tested positive for drugs.[64] "Feticide laws," intended to protect pregnant women from assault by hostile male partners, are being used against women themselves—even when no harm has resulted to the fetus.

In Iowa in 2010, Christine Taylor, mother of two, fell down

the stairs, and while in the hospital to make sure the fetus was all right, confessed to a nurse that she had considered adoption or abortion because her husband had left her when she became pregnant this time, and she worried about raising three kids alone. The nurse called the police. In the end Taylor was not charged—but only because she was still in her second trimester and the state "feticide law" covered only the third.[65] In Indiana, Bei Bei Shuai was charged with murder and attempted feticide on the grounds that the rat poison she took to commit suicide while pregnant killed her newborn daughter.[66] Interestingly, Shuai tried to kill herself after her boyfriend, the father of the baby, announced that he was married and was returning to his family. For Shuai, Taylor, and many other women prosecuted or threatened with prosecution because of their behavior during pregnancy, the fact that her male partner abandoned her and their child-to-be is of no legal interest. Producing that healthy, live baby is all on her.

A true believer would not only applaud all these prosecutions—as many do—but to be logically consistent, they should also want to vastly expand the range of these laws to cover even the earliest miscarriages, and the loss of embryos and fetuses due to such legal activities as drinking, smoking, failing to control diabetes, and exposing oneself to domestic violence and stress. Every miscarriage would have to be investigated as a possible crime—not just because it might really have been an illegal abortion but because it might be the result of something the woman did. And perhaps this is the place to point out that around 10 to 20 percent of known pregnancies end in miscarriage.[67] Why is miscarriage of so little interest to the movement that calls itself "pro-life"? Where are the calls from the American Life League and Operation Rescue for a national crusade against miscarriage? For vast sums to be spent on figuring out how to prevent it? In fact, some crisis pregnancy centers try to dissuade pregnant women from terminating their pregnancies by telling them to hold on a while, they might have a miscarriage—problem solved. That does not suggest that the personhood of the fetus is uppermost in their minds, because from the fetal point of view, a miscarriage—medically referred to as a spontaneous abortion—is just as deadly as an intentional termination.

Actually, fetal personhood itself is a misnomer. Under its aegis, the fetus is actually a kind of superperson—it can compel things no born baby can. It can take command of its mother-to-be's health and life, for example. There is no other circumstance in which parents are required to lend their actual physical bodies to preserve their offspring, or in which any person in general is required to do that for another person. Parents, of course, have many responsibilities toward their children that they do not have toward others, but those obligations stop at their own skin.

Thus parents are not required to donate blood to their child—much less a kidney or other vital organ—even if they are the only match available and the child will die without it. Of course, we are free to think a parent who would refuse to make this sacrifice is a monster; most parents would rejoice that they could save their child's life by giving up a part of their own body. Maybe some readers will think that a law compelling parents to donate blood or organs to their kids would be a good idea. But we will never see parents forced by law into a hospital, to be tied down, anesthetized, and deprived of a kidney. Surely there is a question of sex discrimination when laws against abortion require women to lend their bodies to fertilized eggs for nine months, not to mention childbirth, but men are never required to give so much as a pint of blood to their born child.

Once you spell out all the logical consequences, the idea that zygotes, embryos, and fetuses are persons collapses. Intuitively, most people seem to get that there is something wrong with it: That explains why half the people in America say they believe abortion is murder, but only around 1 percent say that abortion is the most important issue facing the country.[68] It explains why politicians who vote against abortion rights, like John McCain, give pro-choice answers when asked awkward questions about what they would do if their daughter became pregnant from rape.[69] It explains why even Mississippi voters did not want to see fertility clinics closed, despite the carnage their procedures visit upon fertilized eggs.

To say that zygotes, embryos, and fetuses are not persons doesn't mean they have no value, especially as the pregnancy progresses and the fetus becomes able to survive on its own. Dworkin was right about that. *Roe* in effect acknowledged as much by giving the fetus limited rights around the time of viability. It wasn't exactly a person, but it was close enough that it could only be destroyed to protect the pregnant woman. If you want to say that the "unborn" have some kind of special worth, you do not need to torture the concept of personhood to do so. They can matter for other reasons that might vary from one individual to another and be hard to put into words, but involve a basic sense of human connectedness. In Judaism, after all, a fetus becomes a person when it takes its first breath. When anti-abortion Christians cite the Old Testament, they ignore thousands of years of rabbinical interpretation. But that doesn't mean Jews don't ask a pregnant woman how the baby is doing, or never refer to her as a mother, and it doesn't mean they have abortions the day before birth.

Abortion opponents are trapped by their reliance on person-hood, a concept that forces them into impossible positions and arid arguments that few believe and fewer live by. And if they themselves don't follow their own logic, why should anyone else?

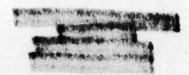

FOUR

ARE WOMEN PEOPLE?

What if we started with women? After all, they are right here. You do not need to give someone an ultrasound to know that a woman is present; no one doubts that she can think or perceive or suffer pain. What is the moral status of women? How much right to life do women have? How much personhood? What about *their* souls?

Plenty of people think they don't know any women who've had abortions. They are probably wrong about that. The stigma of abortion is so great that women are very careful about whom they tell. The sociologist Sarah Cowan, who studies secret-keeping, found that women were much more likely to tell others about their miscarriages than about their abortions, and when they did confide in people about their abortions, they only told ones they thought would not be censorious, who also avoided telling people who would disapprove. That sounds obvious enough, but the implications may not be: Cowan found that abortion opponents underestimate the prevalence of abortion in their community and thereby miss out on personal connections that might make them more tolerant.[1]

Even pro-choicers don't necessarily bring their own experiences into abortion conversations—they are too private, and too likely to be used against them. I remember a dinner party years ago, at which one of the guests rather belligerently announced that he believed abortion was murder. Then he announced that his wife had had one. His wife, the murderer, stared at her coq au vin and said nothing. Twenty years later I'm still wondering: What was she thinking? And why didn't I ask her? I too just stared at my plate.

It's so much easier to focus on the fetus. It has no personality, no history, no motives to be scrutinized. It demands so little of anyone but the woman who is bearing it. In much of the philosophical debate about abortion, that woman barely exists. Robert George and Christopher Tollefsen cleverly cast their book *Embryo* as a brief against stem-cell research and in-vitro fertilization, although abortion is surely their larger target. They scarcely mention women at all. Even Ronald Dworkin and Laurence Tribe, whose books support abortion rights, are mainly concerned with the status of the fetus. The circumstances and motives of women who end their pregnancies get only a nod or two.

If you start from the fetus, however, it's hard to get back to the women who've had those 55 million abortions since *Roe*, let alone the ones who had illegal abortions before it, and are still doing so in great numbers around the world. You end up debating essentially unresolvable points: If we can all agree that a fetus is a fully formed baby at birth, what about the day before birth, a week before viability, or when it can feel pain or when it has a heartbeat or when it is implanted or at the very moment of conception? For abortion opponents, there is no logical stopping place, because fetal development is a continuous process, the unfolding of inherent capacities. Just as, in order to make the fetus visible the woman's body must be rendered invisible, so the interests of the fetus (if something that does not think or perceive or have self-awareness can be said to have interests) erase those of the woman.

What is graduating from high school or not feeling "ready" to mother a child or the fact that you are living in your car compared with the very existence of this tiny helpless creature? Abortion becomes a one-sided contest between responsibility and fecklessness, life and lifestyle, innocence and experience, which is to say innocence versus guilt. No one describes pregnant women as tiny or helpless—they are huge and powerful, they could kill a baby!—much less innocent. But fetuses are always innocent, even more innocent than babies, who scream and fuss and are full of needs and rage—"like a fiend hid in a cloud," as William Blake put it—and a fetus is way more innocent than a woman, even a rape victim, because what was she doing in that dress, in that place?

So let us consider women. Today we're told women can do anything and be anything (well maybe not if they're black or Latina or poor, but still). If they don't run the world, as a notorious *New York Times* magazine cover story had it, it's because they don't want to—they'd rather "opt out" of ambitious careers and channel their energies into raising children. But there is an underside to this uplifting story. In order to get anywhere in life—to get a good education, a graduate or professional degree, a job, a better job—a heterosexual American woman today, unless she is a nun, spends around thirty years trying to control her fertility. This is not easy. Every method of birth control has drawbacks: The Pill has side effects for some women, the IUD is expensive and can be painful to insert, condoms require forethought and a willing, skillful partner, and so on. Moreover every single method has a failure rate, even with perfect use, and perfect use for thirty years is improbable: People are only human. The hassle of birth control is one reason female sterilization is the second most popular method of birth control in the United States. But even sterilization has a failure rate.[2]

Millions of women go through all this, month after month—visits to doctor or clinic, out-of-pocket expenses, side effects, switching methods and pill prescriptions, trips to the pharmacy, keeping track of their cycle, following the news about the latest research—because having a child is such a serious matter, with such a profound effect on every aspect of a woman's life. It is a major physical event, and an even bigger emotional and social event. It affects her access to education, her lifelong earnings, all her relationships, and her ability to fulfill her dreams and live the life she thinks is best for her.

But strangely, unwanted or ill-timed pregnancy is something society treats as if it were a small thing, even as pundits and politicians wring their hands over teen pregnancy and single motherhood. When we put up obstacles to reproductive care (the doctor can see you next month, the free clinic is hours away, the pharmacy doesn't stock Plan B), and to the most effective forms of contraception, we are saying it's not so bad to get pregnant when you don't want to be. Or sure, it's bad, but you should have thought of that before you had sex.

What can that mean except that women's sexuality is what really defines them, not their brains and gifts and individuality and character, and certainly not their wishes or their ambitions or their will? If we allow women's lives to be derailed by a single sperm, if bearing and raising children is something she should be ready to do at any moment, we must not think women matter too much to begin with. What matters is that they had sex.

Judgments about women's sexuality permeate the discussion of abortion, much of which is about trying to distinguish good women from bad ones. Even raped women are suspect. How could we be sure she was really and truly a victim? Todd Akin famously thought pregnancy was proof that no "legitimate rape" had occurred, because "the female body has ways to try to shut that whole thing down."[3] But South Dakota state senator Bill Napoli imagined with some vividness a case in which a rape victim not only got pregnant but merited a legal abortion:

> A real-life description to me would be a rape victim, brutally raped, savaged. The girl was a virgin. She was religious. She planned on saving her virginity until she was married. She was brutalized and raped, sodomized as bad as you can possibly make it, and is impregnated. I mean, that girl could be so messed up, physically and psychologically, that carrying that child could very well threaten her life.[4]

A pregnant rape victim who wasn't so chaste or so religious? She'll get over it.

The obsession with women's virtue infuses the abortion debate even for some who want it to be legal. Is she promiscuous? On drugs? Does she want an abortion out of genuine hardship or is she taking the easy way out? If she were a serious responsible person, the thinking goes, she wouldn't have gotten pregnant

(*Haven't these people ever heard of condoms?*). So having an abortion becomes an evasion of the responsibility to be prudent and continent. Yet it is precisely because having a baby determines so much about a woman's life, and because women take maternal responsibilities so seriously, that they have abortions. Instead of acknowledging that a woman ending a pregnancy usually has a good sense of what she can offer a child—which is why she didn't get pregnant intentionally in the first place—we do our best to make her feel like a bad person.

Old-school abortion opponents going back to the early days of Christianity lambasted the abortion-seeking woman as selfish and immoral. She knew her own mind, all right, and it was full of evil. That view is still easy to find, but the smarter abortion opponents have largely moved away from it. Instead, they promote a paternalistic view of the woman as gullible, impulsive, and childlike. She's coerced by others, is too upset to think straight, doesn't understand what's at stake—but because abortion violates her essential nature as a woman, her mental and emotional health will suffer, and when she realizes that she killed her baby (which may take decades) she will be devastated by sorrow and remorse, so abortion must be restricted, and ultimately banned, for her own protection. The annual March for Life in Washington, DC, regularly features tearful women who stand in front of the Supreme Court Building and read from laminated cards accounts of their journey from abortion and despair to repentance and redemption through a return to the Catholic Church. While the surface narrative is one of guilt (*I killed my baby; I'll never really get over it*), the latent one blames others: the drug-dealing boyfriend who pushed her into it, the doctor or friend who told her it's just a clump of cells. Deep down, she never wanted to do it.

How common is abortion regret? Study after study has found that having an abortion is not psychologically harmful: Any sadness it yields is usually transitory. Many women feel only relief.[5] But despite the lack of evidence for it, the myth of widespread abortion regret is powerful. Indeed, in 2007 Supreme Court Justice Anthony Kennedy used it in his decision in *Gonzales v. Carhart*, which upheld the Partial-Birth Abortion Ban Act: "It seems unexceptionable to conclude some women come to regret their choice to abort the infant life they once created and sustained." And when such a woman discovers the gruesome nature of "partial-birth abortion" it is "self-evident" that she will feel "grief more anguished and sorrow more profound."[6] This was, not coincidentally, the first time the court had upheld an abortion restriction that lacked the *Roe*-mandated exception for the woman's health. A doctor's judgment about what procedure is safest for his patient mattered less than Justice Kennedy's wish to protect some unknown number of women from feelings he imputes to them.

Do *some* women suffer because they wish they had kept their pregnancies? Of course. People make mistakes, sometimes tragic ones. They also can come to believe something was a bad decision when, in fact, they had no alternative or would choose the same thing again in the same circumstances. Then too, if you have an abortion and your life goes wrong afterward, you can form a causal connection when things were really a lot murkier than that. But why should the sad feelings of some constrain the choices of millions? Why are we even talking about feelings at all in the context of what the law should be? After all, second-guessing, self-blame, and regret are hardly limited to abortion. Who doesn't regret some choices? But nobody would ban marriage because almost half end in divorce, and no one would ban cosmetic surgery because some patients wish they had their old faces back. If it were not so taboo to admit it, we might even find that some women regretted *not* having abortions—but you won't find the Supreme Court using that possibility to shut down maternity wards. Letting women who regret their abortions stand for all women is another way of saying that women *should* regret their abortions, because abortion is wrong and against women's nature.

Regret is also a way of saying a woman could have done something different, that having an accidental baby would not have been a major problem, that the abortion was merely a matter of "convenience." It seems odd to describe any part of having a child—pregnancy, childbirth, breastfeeding, sleepless nights, eighteen years (at least!) of intensive caregiving and expense with all sorts of consequences in every area of your life—as merely inconvenient. Having to pick up your dry cleaning when you're in a hurry, finding yourself in the slowest checkout lane at the supermarket—*that's* inconvenient.

The picture of abortion as a casual decision with little at stake, as something a woman falls into or is pushed into, renders incomprehensible why women go to such lengths to find one. Consider: She has to find a hefty sum of money, and except in a few major cities arrange travel, child care, time off from work or school. She may have to walk through a throng of picketers, stay overnight to fulfill a waiting period, listen to government-mandated anti-abortion propaganda intended to frighten her into changing her mind. She may have to overcome the disapproval of family or friends, as well as self-hatred and shame and her fears of the procedure itself. "Just TODAY," Margaret Johnston, a clinic administrator in upstate New York, wrote on a private listserv for independent abortion providers, "a patient was told by her friend that they put a coat hanger with a light on the end of it up you, and then pull the baby out 'piece by piece.'" "We've had women ask if the clinics are clean," another list member wrote, "if the providers are 'real' doctors, who believe with absolute certainty that they will get cancer, become infertile, etc, that they will ABSOLUTELY burn in hell for doing this." Far from being frivolous or easily bullied, a woman seeking an abortion in America today has to be practical, determined, resourceful, and brave. She ends her pregnancy even if it means burning in hell.

At the heart of opposition to legal abortion is an anti-feminist, anti-modern view of relations between the sexes: Women are (or should be) maternal and domestic, men are (or should be) energetic breadwinners, and sex is a powerful, dangerous force that must be narrowly channeled, with parents controlling girls to keep them virgins and women refusing men sex in order to corral them into early marriage with babies soon to follow. This is the basic arrangement promoted by abstinence-only sex education, and by the Christian virginity cult of father-daughter purity balls and the Silver Ring Thing. It isn't a view that is openly expressed much anymore in liberal, urban circles; in fact it is so rarely expressed that *New York Times* Catholic conservative columnist Ross Douthat, frequent advocate of what he calls "moral traditionalism," can seem clever and original merely by dressing up with stylish allusions this antiquated and rather brutal vision of life. In "The Daughter Theory," for example, he argues that social conservatism protects women from charming cads like the eponymous hero of Adelle Waldman's novel *The Love Affairs of Nathaniel P.*:

> He provokes [unhappiness in women] by taking advantage of a social landscape in which sex has been decoupled from marriage but biology hasn't been abolished, which means

women still operate on a shorter time horizon for crucial life choices—marriage, kids—than do men. In this landscape, what Nate wants—sex, and the validation that comes with being wanted—he reliably gets. But what his lovers want, increasingly, as their cohort grows older—a more permanent commitment—he can afford to persistently withhold, feeling guilty but not *that* guilty about doing so.[7]

This concern-trolling of educated women led astray by feminism ignores that women have benefited hugely from the social changes Douthat laments—in fact, they drove those changes. As economists Claudia Goldin and Lawrence Katz lay out in great detail, the minute the Pill became available to teenage and college-age women they abandoned the old model of early marriage and childbearing practically overnight.[8] (In the 1950s and 1960s, half of all women were married by twenty-one, many having dropped out of school to wed; teen motherhood was actually much more common than it is today.) The Pill let women commit to education and work without giving up sex; they could have larger ambitions and longer-range career plans. Between 1970 and 1990, for example, the Pill accounted for nearly three-quarters of the increase in the number of women who became doctors and lawyers. (Abortion is the less-discussed element in this story of progress for women, but it surely plays a role. Indeed, Caitlin Knowles Myers argues that legalized abortion did more than the Pill to drive these changes.)[9] Nothing in life is without complications (men like Nathaniel P., for example). But on the whole, having one's twenties to learn and achieve and become an independent, self-supporting adult has meant good things for women, including the greater likelihood of making a happy marriage. Douthat's nostalgic view implies that his female college classmates and colleagues at the *Times* would be happier as undereducated wives and mothers with maybe a part-time job once the kids are in school, and the country would be better off if men ran even more of it. Really?

That view ignores too the many cruelties that propped up the old sexual system, the vicious social retribution visited upon the girl who fell by the wayside and for whom a shotgun marriage (or an illegal abortion) could not be arranged: being expelled from school, ostracized by family and friends, sent off to a maternity home and forced to give up her baby for adoption. The pain caused by those old morals, vividly depicted in Ann Fessler's *The Girls Who Went Away*, Rickie Solinger's *Wake Up Little Susie* and countless personal essays and memoirs, permeates the quest middle-aged women undertake today for the children they had to give up, and of those children for their lost birth mothers.

Nonetheless, with this narrative social conservatives do offer a coherent idea about how life should be lived, and one to which our culture still pays plenty of homage. Fear of girls gone wild helps explain the popularity of parental notification and consent laws on abortion. It explains why parents are reluctant to have their middle-school-age daughters vaccinated against the sexually transmitted human papilloma virus (HPV)—why put ideas into their heads? And it explains why emergency contraception was kept prescription-only in America years after it had been made widely available all over the world. Adolescents would "form sex-based cults," said one high George W. Bush appointee to the FDA.[10] Older men would force their underage girlfriends to take it. Women would use it for "birth control." (At $50 a pop there can't be many women who use it regularly, but let's say there are some who do, perhaps even some affluent teenage girls. So what? It's not one of the more effective birth-control methods, but it's a safe and harmless drug.) Despite President Obama's promise to use good science to set policy, his first secretary of Health and Human Services, Kathleen Sebelius, rejected the unanimous recommendation of her own expert panel and refused to put it over the counter for young teens. She had to be forced by a judge to make one brand, Plan B One-Step, non-prescription for all ages.[11] Even today, many pharmacies insist that age restrictions are still in force and refuse to sell Plan B to teenagers.

IT'S ABOUT SEX

Too often, the pro-choice movement focuses its arguments on limiting the damage caused by repressive laws while avoiding direct confrontation with the sexual mores behind those laws. On young people having sex, pro-choicers too say abstinence is best, with contraception as the fallback: the seat belts keeping the passengers safe in the runaway car. On parental notification and consent, which is more popular among rank-and-file pro-choicers than the official positions of pro-choice organizations would suggest, the focus is on the danger of violence to girls in abusive and incestuous families, and on government intrusion into families (a popular conservative talking point), not on the injustice of permitting parents—any parents—to force their daughters to give birth. On women using the Pill, pro-choicers underplay sex as pleasure, and rarely present sexual freedom as a good thing in and of itself. No wonder pro-choicers sound evasive when they start talking about acne or painful periods as typical reasons for taking the Pill: No one believes that these side benefits are the reason why well over

10 million women are using it. How refreshing it would be if pro-choice leaders would come right out and say, *Of course* the Pill is about sex. Of course it has allowed women a wide range of sexual experiences and sexual partners—and better sex, too. Think what it was like when couples had to worry about pregnancy every time they made love! For thousands of years human beings have tried to separate sex from reproduction, using everything from crocodile dung to boric-acid douches, and we've finally figured it out. Thank you, Margaret Sanger.

The pro-choice movement needs to present a positive message about what birth control has done, not just for women's physical health but for sex, love, marriage, and family life. Cristina Page's pithy book, *How the Pro-Choice Movement Saved America*, gets it just right: The ability to determine the timing and number of children undergirds the modern ideal of egalitarian, intimate marriages based on love, companionship, and mutual sexual delight. It makes for marriages that are less rigidly role-bound and more democratic—and better for children, who get more parental attention and more resources. (I know this sounds rosier than many a marriage, but I did say it was the ideal.) Since birth control is far from perfect, legal abortion is essential to this way of life. Why not say that out loud?

The reluctance to say sex is a good thing and an important and enjoyable part of ordinary life for almost everyone (unless they are very unlucky) lets abortion opponents characterize it as a strange, rare event that carries an implicit contract to have a baby nine months later. It also lets them promote a double standard: Sex may be part of life for men—wink, wink—but it's damaging and sullying to women unless it is hedged about with religion, law, and fatherly blessings. That constant production of shame and disapproval has a lot to do with our astronomical unplanned pregnancy rate: Nonmarital sex is shameful and wrong, at best a mistake, at worst a sin, so you shouldn't prepare for it; just let yourself be swept away. Shame pushes abortions later too: If a woman is to blame for sex, even if she is raped, she'd best not focus on it or tell anyone about it or deal with the fact that she hasn't had her period in months. Indeed, best if she can persuade herself it wasn't really sex at all. According to one study, 1 in 200 teenage girls believes she got pregnant while still a virgin.[12]

The way we distribute contraception reinforces the view that there's something unusual about having a sex life. It's too medicalized, as if a woman still needs a doctor's permission to have sex without risking pregnancy. According to the American Congress of Obstetricians and Gynecologists (ACOG) and the US Preventative Services Task Force, there is no medical reason for a gynecological exam to get a prescription for the Pill, with an annual repeat in order to renew it.[13] This matters, because many girls and young women find the prospect of a doctor rummaging around inside them frightening and so they put off getting contraception. In fact, according to ACOG, birth-control pills shouldn't require a prescription at all.[14] The reason often cited to justify keeping the Pill prescription-only is that the need to renew it gets women into the doctor's office for an annual checkup and Pap smear. But not only is that paternalistic—are men hauled in for checkups as the price of their Viagra prescription renewal?—it makes it harder for women to stay on the Pill continuously. What if you need a refill now, and you can't get to the doctor till next month or the month after that? What if you are traveling out of the country, or lose your pills? Doctors should focus on how to facilitate patients taking their pills without a break—being able to buy a year's supply at once would help—not on how to use women's need for contraception to get them into the office.

Why does it sound radical to call for the Pill to be nonprescription and for emergency contraception to be on drugstore and grocery shelves like aspirin and toothpaste, and cheap enough for women not to think twice about using it every time they have a birth-control mishap? It's because we're in the wrong frame, the social-conservative one, in which it feels natural for women's sexuality (but not men's) to be monitored and regulated and worried about. And yet, the end result is the opposite of what most of us would say we want: religious zealots controlling sex education, doctors and pharmacists and legislators putting up barriers to women's ability to control their fertility, women taking chances with their birth control, or dropping it entirely, and playing pregnancy roulette because acquiring emergency contraception is too difficult and too expensive when you calculate, perhaps wrongly, that the chances of impregnation are low.

These commonsense ideas sound radical also because women are not at the center of our thinking, even about issues so basic to their lives as control over their own fertility. Right now, in the United States, women, in their full humanity, are so far from the heart of politics and social policy and our everyday way of life, we don't even see it. From seat belts designed for the larger male frame (if I didn't slip the chest strap behind me, I'd be strangled in a crash) to medicines tested only on men (even lab rats are mostly male) to our ideas about what qualities a leader should have (tallness, a deep voice, relaxed but authoritative gestures and speech patterns), men are the norm and women have to make do. If you think I'm exaggerating, how come you never find long lines outside the men's room at the theater, as if the time one half of humanity needs to pee is the proper amount, and the time the other half needs is just some willful foible? Our way of life was designed by men, for men, along the precepts of an earlier day—sometimes a much earlier day indeed—and hasn't changed as much as we like to think. Most crucially, the workforce is half female, but the world of work is still organized around the ideal of the unencumbered always-available employee. Which sex would that be, I wonder? The sex with a wife at home.

In thirty-one states, a rapist who impregnates his victim can sue for child custody or visitation.[15] (Current efforts to change this are a rare example of cooperation between pro-choicers and abortion opponents.) Indeed, the whole way our society deals with rape is based on suspicion that the victim is lying about consensual sex or in some way "asked for it." It's he said/she said, even when there are bruises and vaginal tears (maybe she liked it that way?). And then there is the unending stream of ridiculous sexist verdicts. The Iowa Supreme Court, which upheld the right of a married dentist to fire his assistant because his wife thought her attractiveness threatened his marriage.[16] The New York judge who approved the firing of a bank employee because her beauty was too distracting.[17] Distracting to whom? You can dismiss these items as anecdata, but they make a picture about who is important, whose needs and desires are primary, who is holding the lens through which society perceives its life.

PRONATALISM: THE BACKLASH AGAINST WOMEN'S EMANCIPATION

Abortion opponents are right about one thing: For a woman, reproductive rights are the key to every other freedom. They correctly perceive that birth control and abortion are about much more than women's health: They are what enable women to have at least a chance of shaping their lives. And that's not good, in their opinion, because women—if they are white—should be having babies. As a disheveled drunk in the subway said to me when I was heavily pregnant with my daughter, "You're doing the right thing!" (Has a drunken stranger ever in the history of the world said that to a man pushing a stroller?) If a pregnant woman is married, middle-class and white, America smiles beamily upon her (if she is single, poor, and black or brown, not so much: Then she is setting herself up to freeload off the taxpayer). Women are constantly told that motherhood is part of their essential makeup; it's what they really want, deep down, above all else. But if that is true, how come they need to be constantly reminded of what, theoretically, their entire being is driving them to do? If it were all that natural, they'd be doing it already. And why is it so important to others that a woman fulfill this part of her supposed nature, instead of some other part? It's hard to escape the thought that pronatalism—the promotion of a higher birth rate—isn't really about what women need or want at all. It's about everyone *but* her.

There's a steady drumbeat of conservative punditry warning of all the terrible things that will happen if women don't have enough babies. There won't be enough children to fuel consumer spending, enough workers to support Social Security, enough clever young people to invent things, enough Americans to best the Chinese in the race for world domination. "The widespread practice of abortion culled an entire generation's worth of babies that otherwise might have been born," laments Jonathan Last in *What to Expect When No One's Expecting* (no one? No one at all?).[18] Without plenty of young people, the right-wing writer David Goldman frets, war will become impossible: "A people without progeny will not accept a single military casualty."[19]

Parents unwilling to sacrifice their children in one of our many pointless wars? That *would* be terrible.

A lot of this literature is vaguely (or openly) racist. It's white women—often euphemistically called middle-class women, educated women, and high-IQ women—who are letting down the country (or the continent—Europe, where "demographic winter" holds frozen sway, plays a big role in this discussion). And since these women have the most ability to manage their fertility as they see fit, not surprisingly, pronatalism overlaps with arguments against sexual freedom, feminism, single motherhood, legal abortion, and contraception. The ultraconservative World Congress of Families regularly bemoans the decline of the "natural family"—one husband, one wife, lots of kids—and connects it to the decline of the West and the coming triumph of Islam.

Blatantly nationalist appeals of this sort are not likely to get very far. Few women are going to have babies to beat the Muslims or keep Social Security solvent, any more than they listened to Theodore Roosevelt in 1905 when he inveighed against birth control as "viciousness, coldness, shallow-heartedness, self-indulgence" that would lead straight to "race suicide"—that is, national ruin through population decline, especially among whites of Anglo-Saxon descent:

> If the average family in which there are children contained but two children the nation as a whole would decrease in population so rapidly that in two or three generations it would very deservedly be on the point of extinction, so that the people who had acted on this base and selfish doctrine would be giving place to others with braver and more robust ideals.[20]

Incredibly, Roosevelt's arguments are the same ones made by pronatalists today: America is on the path to nowhere because of contraception and abortion, divorce, hedonism, careers for women, investing resources in a few children rather than a flock or—horrors, having no children and investing resources in something else. "I would have had to move back in with my parents and work for minimum wage in a flower shop," one friend of mine who had just opened her own horticultural business said of what her life would become if she'd kept her pregnancy and had a baby in her mid-twenties. She wouldn't get much sympathy from pronatalists for her "elitist" preference for interesting, well-paying work and an apartment of her own. People doing what they want. *Women* doing what they want. Nothing good will come of that.

In western Europe, pronatalism is part of the reasoning behind strong government support for families, but in the United States, pronatalists rarely propose the sort of robust social benefits that might make it easier for those who want more kids to have them: free tuition for parents returning to college, paid parental leave, free child care and after-school programs, subsidized housing, outright payments to families. Massive investments of that sort in the context of a much more egalitarian society have helped raise the fertility rate (a little) in France and Sweden.[21] By contrast, the countries with the lowest fertility rates are the ones that cling to patriarchal ways and refuse to accommodate working mothers—Japan, Italy, Spain, Greece— even if, like Germany, they have an advanced welfare state. Pronatalists should be advocating support for working mothers, acceptance of single motherhood, and the gender equality that is one of the bases of Swedish society instead of banging on about tax breaks and marriage and the family-fortifying effects of old-time religion. The fact that pronatalism is so firmly allied with the Republican platform of social and economic conservatism rather than with social-democratic welfare policies and women's rights shows what it's really all about: pushing women back into the home and re-creating the 1950s, which were only really the 1950s on television.

Pronatalist pundits may have the ear of the Republican Party, but the arguments aimed directly at women are couched in pop psychology and guilt. In *Creating a Life* (published in the UK under the more revealing title *Baby Hunger*), the economist Sylvia Ann Hewlett warned educated women that by focusing on careers and self-development and fun in their twenties and early thirties they risked missing their chance at marriage and children and would end up living lives of emptiness and remorse. Lori Gottlieb's much-discussed bestselling book *Marry Him* urged women in their thirties to forget Mr. Right and settle for Mr. Good Enough before their eggs go bad. (How come books about the importance of landing a man never advise women to catch one by becoming a kinder, more generous, more interesting person? It's always the same thin gruel: Ask for less and be glad if you get it.) Conservative law professor Helen Alvaré, adviser to the US Conference of Catholic Bishops, makes the Vatican version of the argument: Contraception makes women unhappy. It's physically harmful and doesn't work very well, it promotes what she calls "sexualityism"—that is, sexual freedom—and it causes out-of-wedlock births.[22] (You read that right: Birth control causes births.) Restricting access to contraception is much better for women: It makes for sex that will "bond families and create children." I am trying to think of just one splashy, high-concept bestselling book promoting marriage, children, and chastity to men as essential to their health and happiness.

What these hand-wringing advisers to women leave out is what women themselves want. As they show by the choices they make, the majority of women prefer education, employment, and "sexualityism" to early marriage and a passel of kids. It's not just that the conditions of modern life have made having a small, carefully planned family the sensible choice for many more women than not. Children are wonderful and marriage can be delightful, but there's more to life than raising a family, and always has been.

Except for a few bumps—the postwar baby-boom years, for example—the American fertility rate (number of children per woman) has been declining since Thomas Jefferson was president. Way before urbanization, secularization, feminism, reliable birth control, and the other developments to which lowered fertility rates are usually attributed, couples were already striving to have fewer children than nature would send them, using whatever primitive methods they could think of, including abortion. Maybe given their druthers, which they rarely were, not many women ever really wanted to be married off in their teens and have a baby every year or two until their wombs fell out or they dropped dead of exhaustion. In any case, once women got their hands on reliable no-fuss contraception—the Pill—they took full advantage, and not just in wealthy industrialized nations either. With some notable exceptions—sub-Saharan Africa, for example—fertility rates are dropping through the floor all over the world. In 1960, women in Latin America had an average of almost six children. Today, they have an average of 2.3. In Brazil women have fewer children than in the United States—1.8 to our 1.9.[23] Which raises an interesting question: If fertility declines all over the world, where will those hardy philoprogenitive conquerors feared by pronatalists come from? The rest of the world will be as old and tired as we are.

Birth control has enabled women to invest in higher education and skills, join the workforce in greater numbers, and make more money over the course of their lifetimes. (This is the same phenomenon that is described by anti-feminists as "career women" being cold, materialistic, and man-hating.) Since opposing contraception sounds retrograde and bizarre, abortion takes the blame. Abortion opponents are always talking about the millions of workers and consumers who were killed in the womb. Some might reply that there are quite enough of us already, given the global ecological crisis: When God told Adam and Eve to be fruitful and multiply, the world's population consisted of two people. In any case, one can't assume that the 55 million abortions since *Roe* have meant 55 million fewer people (much less the 85 million some abortion opponents get by counting the nonexistent children of those nonexistent children). For one thing, a lot of those women would have been having abortions whether it was legal or not. For another, without legal abortion, fewer older women would chance having a baby at all, because of the greater risks of Down syndrome and other genetic problems. Moreover, having an abortion doesn't necessarily mean you end up having fewer children: It might mean you have the two children you want later. And if being a little older means you are better able to raise your children well, doesn't that increase the likelihood that they will become productive citizens?

Later marriage and smaller families means more female brainpower available for innovative thinking, creative work, entrepreneurship, and leadership. Oceans of talent were lost when our society was organized to channel women into marrying early, staying home with children, and working only casually, if at all. (Black women, of course, did not have that luxury.) Pronatalists forget about that when they bemoan declining fertility rates as an economic disaster. Funny too how they insist human ingenuity can outwit the depletion of natural resources caused by overpopulation (or, as they would prefer, "overpopulation") and overconsumption, but assume that same intelligence can't create a functioning society if women don't have more kids whether or not this is what women themselves want.

And what about the people here right now? Here is where we see the class and race bias of pronatalism. Our society ignores millions of poor, black, or brown young people. We don't educate them well or feed them well or house them well. We put far too many in prison. A "ghetto name" on a résumé is the kiss of death.[24] Some of these young people will enter middle age never having had a steady job or having acquired the skills to get one. Millions will never have a chance to develop and express their gifts. There is no immutable reason why this has to be the case, but pronatalists do not seem to be particularly concerned about it. These young people, and their mothers and fathers, not aborted fetuses, are our missing workforce. And our missing geniuses.

Abortion opponents love to talk about geniuses. Who knows what wonders some never-born person might have achieved had its mother not killed it in the womb? (If you really want to get metaphysical, what about all the geniuses that were never even conceived?) What if Beethoven's mother had aborted him? That's a question that pops up over and over in anti-abortion literature. (Oddly, no one asks what if Hitler's mother had aborted him or Beethoven's mother had kept Ludwig but aborted his troublesome brothers.) Nobody asks about

Beethoven's mother's own life—a fairly miserable round of pregnancy, childbirth, and child death. Was Maria Magdalena Keverich van Beethoven put on earth only to produce her wunderkind? Might she have had gifts of her own that she never got to offer the world?

Pronatalists are wasting their time trying to cajole, bully, or draft women into some sort of procreation army. Women didn't want to be baby machines a century ago, when Teddy Roosevelt was lecturing them about their demographic duties, and they certainly don't want to be ones now. Like men, women want to have as many children as they want to have, not more. And they want to have them when they are ready and able to care for them in the context of their actual lives, not before (or after). The widespread preference for small families is unlikely to change, especially given tough economic times. In fact, the trend is growing: Black women used to have more children than white women, a source of great concern to pronatalists, but today they have on average 2 children, which is not that far from white women's 1.8. Hispanic women currently have 2.4 children, but that's on the way down too. Even Mormons, often cited for their large families, are having fewer kids these days.

Pronatalists show little interest in dealing with these trends in a realistic way. They don't want to give women and families the economic and social supports that would let those women who want to have more children do so without major sacrifice: That would be socialism. And they don't want to do what would be needed to develop the potential of *all* the children (and adults) we already have; that would be socialism too. Disastrous as they claim the consequences of small families will be to our national glory, it would seem there are things even worse: universal affordable high-quality day care, income supports for poor families, paid parental leave, renewed government commitment to racial equality. Forget helping all families. "At the end of the day," says Jonathan Last, "there's only one good reason to go through the trouble a second time: Because you believe, in some sense, that God wants you to."[25] Last, at least, acknowledges that it's unlikely that restricting abortion would raise the fertility rate much, although he supports the effort anyway. But it is hard to find an American pronatalist who doesn't think having babies is what womanhood is all about, and it is hard to find one who doesn't support a return to conservative sexual and family mores for women.

It's almost as if that were the main idea all along.

Abortion is often discussed as a culture-war issue. That's another way of saying it isn't very important, like the question of whether a nativity scene can be placed in a public park. For years, a robust school of progressive thinking called women who were alarmed about the future of reproductive rights naïve. The Republican Party isn't serious about restricting abortion, they claimed, politicians just talk like that to keep the base motivated. As Thomas Frank put it in his book *What's the Matter with Kansas?*: "The trick never ages; the illusion never wears off. Vote to stop abortion; receive a rollback in capital gains taxes. Vote to make our country strong again; receive deindustrialization. Vote to screw those politically correct college professors; receive electricity deregulation."[26]

It's a little hard to make that claim today (and yes, those who maintained it are mostly men). But some progressives still argue that focusing on abortion rights distracts from the important issues, which are economic, and gets in the way of alliances with Catholics and evangelicals who are anti-abortion but liberal on some other issues. As I write, Pope Francis, *Time*'s Person of the Year, is being hailed across progressive media, including *The Nation*, where I am a columnist, as a force for economic and social equality—as if he can speak for equality as the head of a hierarchically organized church that bars women from the priesthood, and thereby from all authority; that deprives women of the right to control their fertility, even if that means grave injury and even death; that shames divorced people and denies marriage to gays and lesbians; and that has protected pedophile priests all over the world for decades and has yet to come to terms with the true extent of that crime.

Setting women off to one side, as if half of humanity were a footnote to something called society or politics or economics, is an old story. But reproductive rights are not a distraction from the important, economic issues. They *are* an economic issue: Without the ability to limit and to time their pregnancies, women will always be disadvantaged at work and subordinate to men. Much has been made of recent statistics suggesting that young women are closing the wage gap with young men. It's one of the statistics that Hanna Rosin cites in her book *The End of Men: And the Rise of Women* to show that women are poised to dominate the workplace, and indeed, everything else. To the extent that her claims have merit—we'll see what happens when those young women have kids—it's because women have access to good birth control, backed up by abortion. When those were unavailable, women didn't dominate anything but baby showers.

In the end, abortion is an issue of fundamental human rights. To force women to undergo pregnancy and childbirth against their will is to deprive them of the right to make basic decisions about their lives and well-being, and to give that power to the state. Moreover, the logic of the anti-abortion movement makes all pregnant women less than full citizens, including those who want to have a baby, because it places the supposed interests of the fetus ahead of the woman's own interests and deprives her of rights granted to everyone else: to make one's own medical decisions and to receive equal treatment under the law. It would be unthinkable for state law to require the harvesting of organs from the dead against their expressed will, even though such laws would save the lives of many born people. But Marlise Muñoz, who suffered a stroke when she was fourteen weeks pregnant, was kept on life support in a Texas hospital for seven weeks against her own previously expressed wish and the wishes of her family even though she was brain dead (that is, legally dead) and the fetus was very likely seriously damaged. Texas law denies pregnant women, even those in the earliest stages, the right to have their end-of-life wishes respected.[27] Muñoz's family had to go to court to force the hospital to turn off the machines. As Lynn Paltrow, head of National Advocates for Pregnant Women, put it, "What the Texas law is saying [to] women [is] . . . everybody else can decide what happens if you become unable to express your wishes about what treatment you do and don't want to have—except you."[28]

This is not about "life." It's about treating women as potting soil. It's about control.

FIVE

SIX MYTHS ABOUT ABORTION

1. THE BIBLE FORBIDS ABORTION

It shouldn't matter what the Bible says about abortion—or indeed anything else. The United States is not a theocracy. Still, given the certitude of abortion opponents that abortion violates God's Word, it might come as a surprise that neither the Old Testament nor the New mentions abortion—not one word. Abortion opponents have to extrapolate from passages about quite other things: prophecies of women eating their young, or massacres in which pregnant women are ripped apart, or someone wishes he had died in his mother's womb. God tells Jeremiah, "Before I formed you in the womb I knew you" (so Jeremiah existed before he was even conceived?).[1] The Psalmist tells God, "You knit [me] together in my mother's womb" (so at some point in the womb he had not been fully knitted and was more like a jumble of yarn?).[2] In Luke 1:41, pregnant Virgin Mary visits her pregnant cousin Elizabeth, whose "baby"—the future

John the Baptist—"leaped in her womb."[3] Passages like these are only relevant to abortion if you already think they are. The same is true, of course, of "Thou shalt not kill," better translated as "Thou shalt not murder," which, as applied to abortion, begs the question of whether or not the fertilized egg/embryo/fetus is a person, and if so, whether the commandment applies to it since many kinds of killing—war, self-defense, capital punishment—don't seem to count.

The Old Testament is a very long book, full of bans and pronouncements and detailed instructions about daily life—what to wear, what not to eat, how to harvest your crops. It condemns many activities: cursing your parents, witchcraft, blasphemy, all punishable by death. There are plenty of biblical characters whose sins, including their sexual sins, are vividly portrayed, and much excoriating of pretty girls for gadding about in fine clothes and inspiring lust in men. But there is no mention of abortion.

It's not that the Old Testament is reticent about women's bodies, either. Menstruation gets a lot of attention. So do childbirth, infertility, sexual desire, prostitution (death penalty), infidelity (more death penalty), and rape (if the woman is within earshot of others and doesn't cry out . . . death penalty). How can it be that the authors (or Author) set down what should happen to a woman who seeks to help her husband in a fight by grabbing the other man's testicles (her hand should be cut off) but did not feel abortion deserved so much as a word?[4] Given the penalties for nonmarital sex and being a rape victim, it's hard to believe that women never needed desperately to end a pregnancy, and that there was no folk knowledge of how to do so, as there was in other ancient cultures. Midwives would have known how to induce a miscarriage; those "witches" would have known herbs and potions.

A passage often cited by abortion opponents is Exodus 21:22–23:

> If people are fighting and hit a pregnant woman and she gives birth prematurely but there is no serious injury, the offender must be fined whatever the woman's husband demands and the court allows. But if there is serious injury, you are to take life for life . . . [5]

Contemporary abortion opponents interpret this passage as distinguishing between causing a premature birth (fine) versus causing a miscarriage (death penalty), which is indeed what most modern translations suggest. (Interestingly, the King James version renders the first alternative "so that her fruit depart from her," which is more ambiguous and closer to the Hebrew original.) Unfortunately for abortion opponents, at least one thousand years of rabbinical scholarship say the fine is for causing a miscarriage and the death penalty is for causing the death of the *pregnant woman.* If anti-abortion exegetes are only now finding in this rather obscure passage evidence for an absolute biblical ban on abortion, you have to wonder why no one read it that way before. The Talmud permits abortion under certain circumstances, in fact requires it if the woman's life is at stake.

The New Testament was a second chance for God to make himself clear about abortion. Jesus had some strong views of marriage and sex—he considered the Jewish divorce laws too lenient, disapproved of stoning adulteresses, and did not shrink from healing a woman who had "an issue" (vaginal bleeding of some sort) that had lasted twelve years and would have made her an outcast among Jews. But he said nothing about abortion. Neither did Saint Paul, or the other New Testament authors, or any of the later authors whose words were interpolated into the original texts.

2. WOMEN ARE COERCED INTO HAVING ABORTIONS

Abortion opponents claim girls and women are frequently forced or bullied into terminating wanted pregnancies. That 64 percent of women "feel pressured to abort" is a claim that shows up over and over in anti-abortion literature. In South Dakota, the need to prevent supposedly widespread coercion was cited in support of a 2011 law that required a seventy-two-hour waiting period and counseling at an anti-abortion crisis pregnancy center. As the journalist Robin Marty was the first to report, the 64 percent statistic comes from a 2004 article in *Medical Science Monitor*, "Induced Abortion and Traumatic Stress: A Preliminary Comparison of American and Russian Women" by Vincent M. Rue, Priscilla K. Coleman, James J. Rue, and David C. Reardon.[6] That may sound scientific, but don't be so sure. David Reardon is a major anti-abortion activist, tireless promoter of "post-abortion syndrome," a condition rejected by the American Psychological Association, and director of the anti-abortion Elliot Institute. (According to its Web site, the name was "picked from a baby names book" because it sounds both friendly and academic.) His PhD in biomedical ethics comes from Pacific Western University, an unaccredited correspondence school. *Medical Science Monitor*, an online journal, has published other spurious research, for example, papers defending the discredited vaccine-autism connection. In 2012 it was exposed as one of a circle of journals that agreed to inflate their citation rankings by citing one another. That its

Web site is littered with typos and grammatical errors does not inspire confidence.

There are a number of problems with the paper in question, which was actually not about coercion but a comparison of post-abortion trauma in American and Russian women. Its sample was tiny (217 Americans), self-selected, far more white and middle-class than the general population of women who've had abortions, plus the women were reporting on abortions a decade earlier. Half thought abortion was wrong; only 40 percent thought women should have a right to it. Thirty percent said they had "health complications" after the abortion, which could mean anything. (According to the Guttmacher Institute, only .05 percent of first trimester abortions have complications "that might require hospital care.") Interestingly, the American women, though not the Russian women, reported staggering amounts of violence and trauma in their lives before the abortion.

A woman who felt abortion was wrong, and believed she had suffered emotionally and physically from having one, might well be more likely, when asked about it ten years later, to blame her abortion on others. But what does it mean to feel pressured or coerced to abort? Abortion opponents cite lurid news stories of women threatened with guns or even murdered for rejecting abortion. That's coercion. But a parent who lays out in detail the hard life of a single mother is not forcing a daughter to terminate her pregnancy, nor is a boyfriend who says he's not up for marriage or ready to be a father, or a sister who says there's no room for another baby in a shared apartment. We have all felt pressured by others to choose this course of action or that, but that doesn't mean the decision isn't ultimately our own.

How common is it for a woman to be pushed into an abortion she doesn't want? In a 2005 Guttmacher Institute survey, 1,209 women were asked their reasons for choosing abortion. Fourteen percent cited "husband or partner wants me to have an abortion" and 6 percent cited "parents want me to have an abortion." (Interestingly, both these answers were down from a similar survey in 1987, when 24 percent of women mentioned the wishes of husbands/partners and 8 percent mentioned those of parents.) Not surprisingly, then, women did not choose abortion in a vacuum: Their relationships influenced their decisions, and, as with other decisions, probably not always in ways they were happy about. But when asked to name the single most important reason, less than 0.5 percent each cited the wishes of husband/partner or parents.[7] That argues strongly against the claim that women who have abortions typically want to continue the pregnancy but are pressured into terminating it by others, from whom the law needs to protect them.

3. ABORTION IS DANGEROUS

Anti-abortion literature is full of stories about women gravely injured or even killed in clinics, which are invariably described as filthy places staffed by incompetent "abortionists" and nasty employees. Such places exist: A woman died in Kermit Gosnell's Philadelphia clinic, some were injured, and all received inferior care. Steven Brigham, another rogue provider, has operated in different locations for years and has somehow managed to evade the law. Both these men stayed in business because they were cheap, they were in the neighborhood, they performed abortions later than the law allowed, and they zeroed in on low-income patients who, sadly, were used to being treated badly by people in authority.

No doubt there are other inferior clinics out there. Poor care, overpricing, and rude staffers can be found in every medical field. But you don't find people using examples of it to inveigh against an entire specialty—railing against the greed of orthopedic surgeons (average 2012 salary, $315,000) or calling for surprise inspections of dentists because every year a few people die from preventable errors during dental procedures.[8] Only in abortion care do the few bad providers taint all the others—and taint them so much that opponents can pass laws that would virtually shut down the entire field in the name of patient safety.

No medical procedure is without risk, and given that over a million abortions are performed every year, there are a lot of chances for something to go wrong. And yet, in contrast to the lurid claims of anti-abortion activists, abortion is remarkably safe. The CDC reports that for the seven years from 2003 to 2009, the most recent period for which it has figures, the national mortality rate was .67 deaths per 100,000 abortions. In 2009, a total of eight women died due to abortion.[9] Tragic as that is, compare it with fatal reactions to penicillin, which occur in 1 case per 50–100,000 courses.[10] And what about Viagra? According to the Association of Reproductive Health Professionals, it has a death rate of 5 per 100,000 prescriptions.[11] But you don't find legislators calling for a ban on Viagra, or suggesting that men are too emotional or dimwitted or brainwashed by the "culture of sex" to assess the risks and benefits for themselves.

Really, though, there is only one directly relevant comparison of risk with respect to abortion, and that is pregnancy and childbirth. The death rate for that is 8.8 women per 100,000.[12] As I've mentioned before, continuing a pregnancy is 12 to 14 times as potentially fatal as ending it. That means abortion is always potentially lifesaving for a pregnant woman. (And getting more so, because the maternal mortality rate is rising in the US even as it is falling around the world.) And it's not just a matter of the death rate. According to Amnesty International, in 2004 and 2005, more than 68,000 women nearly died in childbirth in the United States.[13] The risks of producing a baby include ectopic pregnancy, gestational diabetes, bacterial vaginosis, preeclampsia, anemia, urinary tract infections, placental abruption, hyperemesis gravidarum (the constant and severe nausea that killed Charlotte Brontë), depression, postpartum psychosis, and PTSD—to say nothing of morning sickness, heartburn, backache, stretch marks, episiotomy or cesarean scarring, decreased marital happiness, and lowered lifetime income.

Curiously, no one suggests that obstetricians be compelled to read pregnant women scripts about the dangers that lie ahead before sending them home for twenty-four hours to think about whether they wish to proceed.

4. THERE ARE TOO MANY ABORTIONS

People often say there's too much abortion, but how do they know what is the right amount? Doesn't that depend on what women's reasons are? If women are ending pregnancies because they don't have enough knowledge about sex or power in their relationships or good birth control and get pregnant when they don't want to be, that's definitely too many abortions. And if women are aborting wanted pregnancies because they are too poor to raise that child, or fear being shamed, or don't have enough support from family or partner, that's also too many. The same is true if a woman has an abortion she doesn't want because someone bullies her into it, although that one works both ways: Women are bullied into having babies too.

Sometimes what people mean when they say there are too many abortions is that we need to help girls and women take charge of their sexuality and have more options in life. According to the Guttmacher Institute, in 2011 abortion declined by 13 percent from 2008, mostly because of better access to birth control and to longer-acting birth control methods like the IUD.[14] That is very good news. But often what people mean is that women are too casual about sex and contraception. When Naomi Wolf writes about her friends' it-was-such-good-Chardonnay abortions, she is saying women get pregnant by accident because they are hedonistic and shallow. It is difficult to come down hard on abortion as immoral, to insist that the ideal number of abortions is zero, as Will Saletan of *Slate* maintains, without blaming the individual woman who got herself into a fix and now wants to do a bad thing to get out of it.[15] In this version, there are too many abortions because women are irresponsible and what they need is a good scolding. Because scolding always helps.

From another perspective, though, there is too *little* abortion. New York Archbishop Timothy Dolan laments that some 40 percent of pregnancies in New York City are terminated.[16] But what if that's not because there are exceptional numbers of unwanted pregnancies in the five boroughs, or because New York women are particularly heedless and selfish and fond of Chardonnay? Perhaps it reflects the fact that abortion is more common in cities, especially among poor people, people of color, and single women, all of which New York has in great numbers, and the fact that New York City has many abortion providers, good public transportation to reach them, and no major restrictions, plus New York State covers abortion on Medicaid. The extra expenses that can double the costs—transportation, child care, lost wages, overnight stays—rarely apply. Perhaps if it were as easy to get an abortion in Missouri or Mississippi, their rates would approach New York City's. A 2007 study found that in 2000, 83,000 women would have had abortions if abortion were covered by universal health insurance. In other words, the abortion rate would have been 6 percent higher.[17] A 2009 review of thirty-eight studies found that about one-fourth of women who would otherwise have had Medicaid abortions gave birth when that funding was unavailable.[18]

If abortion were free and every woman could easily get to a provider, how many would there be? In New York City, there are women who can only get an abortion because the New York Abortion Access Fund (NYAAF) helps them pay for it. They're not quite poor enough for Medicaid, or they're poor but don't qualify. NYAAF tries to help everyone who calls their hotline, although usually not with the full cost of the procedure. But NYAAF is a small, all-volunteer organization: What about women who don't know it exists? Reports that women in some communities take pills or herbs to self-abort suggests that even in the abortion capital of America, there's an unmet need.

5. ABORTION IS RACIST

In February 2011, a three-story-high billboard popped up in the fashionable SoHo neighborhood of New York City. Featuring an adorable little black girl in a sweet pink dress, it proclaimed, "The Most Dangerous Place for an African American Is in the Womb."[19] The previous year, billboards in Atlanta showed a little black boy with the slogan "Black Children Are an Endangered Species." The brainchild of Life Always, a Texas anti-abortion group, these signs, and similar ones around the country comparing abortion to slavery, aroused so much indignation from black women that they were quickly taken down. But the charge that abortion is racist is commonplace in the pro-life movement, for whom Planned Parenthood perpetrates genocide against people of color, and Margaret Sanger, its founder, was a eugenicist on a par with the Nazis.

If the womb is the most dangerous place for an African American, that makes black women, not those who profit from and perpetuate racism, the most dangerous people to their communities, and abortion a bigger threat than poverty, prisonification, AIDS, crumbling housing, inferior schools, poor health care, job discrimination, violence, maternal and infant mortality, and all the other ills besetting African Americans. It makes black women, the victims of racism, the real racists. Put like that it doesn't make much sense. But then it doesn't make much sense to compare abortion to slavery, either. Are pregnant black women slave owners who profit from the forced labor of their embryos and fetuses? Could they sell them to other black women slave owners who wanted to raise production on their uterine plantations? The metaphor ignores the subjectivity of black women; once again, a woman is a vessel, a place—in this case a hostile place.

Imagery of abortion as slavery or genocide allows abortion opponents to posture as anti-racists without having to learn anything about the lives of black women or lift a finger to rectify the enormous and ongoing legacy of slavery and segregation. Just shame black women into giving birth to more children than they feel they can safely bear or care for, and all will be well.

"They tell African American women that we are now responsible for the genocide of our own people," wrote Loretta Ross about the Genocide Awareness Project, a poster campaign focused on college campuses. "We are now accused of 'lynching' our children in our wombs and practicing white supremacy on ourselves. Black women are again blamed for the social conditions in our communities and demonized by those who claim they only want to save our souls (and the souls of our unborn children). This is what lies on steroids look like."[20] Ross, a key African American activist and thinker on reproductive justice and race, reminds us that black women have a long tradition of reproductive-rights activism and have long taken steps to control their fertility: "When methods of fertility control have been available and accessible, African American women have advocated for and used these strategies even more frequently than their white counterparts."[21] Black women have always had more abortions per capita than white women, including more dangerous and fatal illegal ones. Black women do not have a high abortion rate because they are bent on exterminating black children, however, but because they have less access to good birth control and health care and therefore have more unplanned pregnancies.

Was Margaret Sanger a racist? No. She shared the eugenicist views that were current among intellectuals, scientists, policymakers, and ordinary people in the 1920s and 1930s, including those opposed to birth control because it lowered the white fertility rate. But reprehensible as she sometimes sounds today, calling for the sterilization of "dysgenic types," she did not believe in white superiority or black inferiority. This was clear to her contemporaries, who understood, moreover, that what motivated her was the liberation of women from the burden of unwanted pregnancy, which was something women themselves, including poor ones and black ones, desperately sought. That is why Sanger and the organization she founded, which eventually became Planned Parenthood, had the support of such prominent black leaders as W.E.B. Dubois, the founder of the NAACP; Mary McLeod Bethune, the founder of the National Council of Negro Women; Rev. Adam Clayton Powell of Harlem's powerful Abyssinian Baptist Church; Martin Luther King Jr.; and Coretta Scott King. When Martin Luther King accepted Planned Parenthood's Margaret Sanger Award in 1966, he compared Sanger's fight for birth control to the civil rights movement: "She launched a movement which is obeying a higher law to preserve human life under humane conditions."[22]

Do you think Dr. King would have said that about someone who wanted to exterminate black people?

6. ABORTION OPPONENTS WOULD NEVER PUNISH WOMEN

That's what they always say: Women are abortion's "other victim." Only the providers should be charged with a crime. That view would come as news to the many countries where women are in prison for ending their pregnancies. If abortion opponents in El Salvador have no problem with a ban that has sent dozens of women to prison for up to thirty years for "aggravated homicide," as well as for miscarriages and stillbirths that are suspected of being caused by abortion, why would they object to similar laws in Louisiana? If Nicaragua can confine a twelve-year-old rape victim in a hospital "under state protection" until she gave birth, why couldn't that happen someday in South Dakota?[23]

Right now, putting women on trial for abortion sounds far-fetched, I admit. There's little heart for it in the ranks of the pro-life movement. But the groundwork is being laid. Women have been arrested for self-abortion in several states, although few have been convicted.[24] Hundreds have been arrested and some imprisoned for drug use or other behavior during pregnancy, even when no bad outcome occurred, and even when the law was clearly designed for some other purpose (to protect living children from meth labs, for example).[25] For decades the anti-abortion movement has striven to enshrine in law the view that the embryo and fetus are persons. They won passage of the federal Unborn Victims of Violence Act, which made causing the death of embryos and fetuses a separate crime from the harm caused to the pregnant woman, and versions of that law in many states. In the spring of 2014, despite strenuous objections from women's groups and medical organizations, the Tennessee state legislature passed with bipartisan support, and the moderate Republican governor signed, a bill that would subject to criminal penalties of up to fifteen years in prison drug-using women who had a poor pregnancy outcome.[26]

In 2007, sixteen-year-old Rennie Gibbs was charged with "depraved heart murder" in Mississippi, when she experienced a stillbirth at thirty-six weeks. There was no evidence linking her drug use with the baby's death (big clue: The umbilical cord was wrapped around its neck), and twenty-five years of research has failed to find evidence that cocaine use causes stillbirth. For seven years, Gibbs faced the prospect of life in prison, and when a judge finally dismissed the charges, the assistant district attorney in charge of the case told reporters he plans to try again, this time with manslaughter charges.[27]

As abortion becomes restricted, and the embryo and fetus are regarded as legal persons in more and more areas of the law, it becomes increasingly difficult to say why a pregnant woman's conduct during pregnancy should not be subject to legal scrutiny. Why it is permissible for a woman to end a pregnancy by going to a clinic when she can't do the same by self-aborting at home, and why it is legal to kill embryos and fetuses in abortion when killing them in domestic violence or a drunken driving accident is a major felony? A doctor performs an abortion; a boyfriend, upon request, beats a woman's belly till she miscarries. From the point of view of the embryo or fetus, what's the difference?

SIX

WHAT DO ABORTION OPPONENTS REALLY OPPOSE? (HINT: IT'S NOT JUST ABORTION)

In theory, perhaps, opposition to abortion need not be linked to anti-feminism, the shaming of sexually active girls and single women, fears of white demographic decline, conservative views of marriage and sexuality, or outright misogyny. But in the real world, such connections are hard to overlook. The anti-abortion movement is inescapably entangled with patriarchal religion: the Catholic Church, evangelical and fundamentalist Protestantism, Mormonism. That is where the opposition's organizational muscle, its funding, its political power and its grassroots support come from. As the movement has increasingly merged with the political right, it has helped move the whole political discussion far to the right on a wide range of issues related to sex, women, poverty, race, health care, and the role of government.

It looks like a single-issue movement—protect the unborn!—but a closer look shows it's about much more than that.

POLITICS

Until the early to mid-1980s, Republican voters were at least as likely as Democrats to support contraception and abortion rights—in some states more so, because ethnic working-class Catholics were strong Democrats.[1] It was Democratic state legislators who kept contraception illegal in Connecticut until 1965, when the Supreme Court finally struck down the law. That changed as the Republican Party mobilized religious conservatives as part of its strategy to win Catholics and the white South. Today the Republican Party is not only the political home of the anti-abortion movement but of opposition to just about everything on the women's rights to-do list: broad access to contraception; comprehensive sex education; equal pay legislation; same-sex marriage; the Violence Against Women Act; CEDAW, the international women's equality treaty; paid sick leave; raising the minimum wage; and of course the Affordable Care Act. Like all anti-feminists, they claim to revere motherhood, but what they seem to mean is stay-at-home married motherhood. Where is the outcry from Republicans on the lack of affordable child care, or on the many forms of job discrimination against pregnant women and mothers?

No wonder the party has a woman problem, even among its own office-holders. As of 2013, Republican women constitute only 23 percent of women in Congress, and one-third of women in state legislatures. (They do better in the governor's mansion: In 2013, four out of the five female state governors are Republicans.) While there are plenty of sexist Democrats, it's only Republican politicians who make outlandish public statements about rape, or claim that for the Affordable Care Act to cover birth control insults women as raging sluts dependent on the largesse of "Uncle Sugar."[2] Texas gubernatorial candidate Greg Abbott campaigned against abortion-rights heroine Wendy Davis with rock musician Ted Nugent, best known for obscene and sexist attacks on female politicians (he's called Hillary Clinton "a toxic cunt," "a two-bit whore," and a "worthless bitch"), and for calling President Obama a "subhuman mongrel."[3] Despite training sessions intended to teach Republican male politicians how not to offend women, they just can't help themselves.

Republicans seem fairly oblivious to the many contradictions in which opposition to abortion involves them. Thus, the party that claims to want less regulation passes regulations whose only purpose is to put abortion clinics out of business. The party that claims to care about babies cuts government programs that benefit pregnant women, infants, and children, including the seriously sick and disabled children they want to force women to bear. The party that claims people don't need government to tell them how to live thinks women cannot be trusted with the decision of whether or not to continue a pregnancy. And of course, the party that claims to care about "life" is tightly allied with the National Rifle Association. Guns don't kill people, pregnant women kill people.

BIRTH CONTROL AND SEX EDUCATION

Opponents love to compare abortion to the Holocaust, but if a pill could have prevented Auschwitz, who wouldn't take it?

According to the Guttmacher Institute, in 2010 publicly funded family planning services prevented 2.2 million unintended pregnancies, which would have otherwise led to 760,000 abortions.[4] (That's added on to the countless pregnancies prevented by birth control the woman pays for privately or through insurance.) Increased use of better contraception, not restrictions on abortion access, led to a 13 percent drop in abortions between 2008 and 2011.[5] Modern contraception works pretty well: The two-thirds of women who use it consistently account for only 5 percent of abortions.[6] And yet, not one major anti-abortion organization supports making birth control more available, much less educating young people in its use: not Feminists for Life, National Right to Life, or the Susan B. Anthony List; not American Life League, Americans for Life, or Pro-Life Action League, to say nothing of the US Council of Catholic Bishops, Priests for Life, and Sisters for Life. Anti-abortion organizations either openly oppose contraception, or are silent about it. Even Democrats for Life of America avoids the subject.

It is hard to find a public-health expert who will deny that the most effective way to prevent abortion is reliable contraception, but anti-abortion hardliners find ways to dispute this no-brainer. They argue that the Pill and emergency contraception are "abortifacients," "baby pesticide," and "killer pills," which prevent the implantation of fertilized eggs, no matter how many studies show that these drugs do not work this way. (By their math, the actual number of abortions is practically infinite—the millions of women on the Pill could be having "abortions" every month.) They argue that birth control is ineffective (so it doesn't kill babies after all?), but they also argue that the root problem is "the contraceptive mentality," the contemporary norm of sex for pleasure and intimacy without fear of pregnancy.

In other words, birth control does work—unfortunately. They argue that abortion, like our low fertility rate, is due to people hating children. (Does having a small family mean you don't like kids?) They argue that contraception puts women at men's mercy, because they have no acceptable reason to reject sex. (How about, "I don't want to have sex with you, Charlie"?) But they also argue that contraception unleashes women's libido.

It's true that people have sex without wanting to make a baby. This is hardly a modern innovation. Even when childbirth was often fatal, when startling numbers of unmarried women and poor couples abandoned their newborns to near certain death in foundling hospitals, when syphilis had no cure and unwed pregnancy could mean being turned into the streets or forced into a hated marriage, people had plenty of sex within and outside marriage. And given that people are not going to stop having sex, and are not going to start wanting to have ten children, the only way to lower the abortion rate is to blanket the nation in birth control. But that would mean accepting that modern life is here to stay.

Of course, it's not hard to find individual abortion opponents who support birth control—some surveys even suggest most people who think abortion is "morally wrong" think birth control is "morally acceptable."[7] The important evangelical ethicist David Gushee is outspoken in favor of public funding for contraception. Louisiana governor Bobby Jindal, an anti-abortion practicing Catholic, has called for putting birth-control pills over the counter. But given the leading role of the Catholic Church and right-wing Protestant denominations in the anti-abortion movement, these voices are not likely to alter the discourse. In 2012, the National Association of Evangelicals daringly listed "easier access to contraceptive information and services" among more familiar anti-abortion strategies like parental consent and waiting periods. The group was strenuously attacked by other Christian conservatives, and since then, it has concentrated on supporting the right of all employers to refuse to offer contraceptive coverage to their employees.[8]

In fact, as white evangelicals increasingly ally with the Catholic Church against abortion, some are turning against birth control, too. It isn't just oddballs like the Duggar family of *19 and Counting*, or Quiverfull families, who practice extreme wifely submission and produce as many children as possible to create more soldiers for Christ. "Can Christians Use Birth Control?" asks Albert Mohler, president of the Southern Baptist Theological Seminary. Besides the "contraceptive mentality" and the "raging debate" around the imaginary abortifacient nature of the Pill, there's cultural ruin:

> We should look closely at the Catholic moral argument as found in *Humanae Vitae*. Evangelicals will find themselves in surprising agreement with much of the encyclical's argument. As the Pope warned, widespread use of the Pill has led to "serious consequences" including marital infidelity and rampant sexual immorality. In reality, the Pill allowed a near-total abandonment of Christian sexual morality in the larger culture. Once the sex act was severed from the likelihood of childbearing, the traditional structure of sexual morality collapsed.[9]

Eventually Mohler decides the Catholic Church goes too far. Married couples may use birth control—as long as they avoid "abortifacients"—in other words, stick to the methods available in the 1950s. If the condom tears or the diaphragm slips, no Plan B for you.

If anti-abortion leaders were opposed only to abortion, why would they be so keen to stretch its definition to include the most effective and most popular methods of contraception? Why do they cling to the notion that the Pill causes abortion? Why don't they welcome recent studies showing that emergency contraception prevents ovulation, not implantation? The fact that they grasp at straws suggests what they really object to is sex without a significant threat of pregnancy and the social changes connected to that. You'll notice Mohler doesn't give contraception credit for anything good: more years of education for women, as well as better health, lower maternal mortality, and greater commitment to careers; fewer early, hasty marriages, less stress on couples (and better sex); more attention and resources for each child. For Mohler, the last fifty years have been one long moral catastrophe. Birth control makes people happier, healthier, better educated, and more prosperous. That's terrible!

Instead of joining pro-choicers in calling for expanded access to affordable birth control, abortion opponents use their considerable political clout to cut state and federal funds for family planning for low-income women, ban discussion of it in sex education classes (except with reference to failure rates), exempt even ordinary secular businesses from covering it under the Affordable Care Act if the owner objects, and pass legislation permitting pharmacists to refuse to fill prescriptions for it. In 2011 the GOP-led House of Representatives even voted 240–185 to wipe out funding for Title X, the once-noncontroversial family planning program that serves some 5 million low-income women and men per year.[10] Republicans claimed their opposition is based on the fact that roughly a quarter of the funds go to Planned Parenthood, which provides abortion care at some but not all of its clinics, even though the monies are barred by law from funding abortion services.[11] The Senate scotched the House plan, but the GOP hasn't given up. In 2014, the Republican-controlled House tried to cut Title X funding by $10 million. Meanwhile, having succeeded in excluding abortion coverage from the Affordable Care Act, Congress moved right on to trying to weaken coverage for contraception by demanding a so-called "conscience clause" be added to the law's preventive coverage mandate, a clause so broad it would cover virtually any employer.

When anti-abortion Republicans do come out for contraception, their proposals are unrealistic, if not disingenuous. "We pro-life advocates need to lead the Title X charge," urged Republican lobbyist Juleanna Glover in a rather desperate-sounding 2012 *New York Times* op-ed. Her suggestion—beef up Title X, but bar funds from "any group that performs abortions" (that is, Planned Parenthood)—may sound like a reasonable compromise, but it's a fantasy.[12] In the first place, there is no organized politically powerful anti-abortion force that is keen on birth control. The GOP of contraception enthusiasts like Nelson Rockefeller, Bob Packwood, the Richard Nixon who signed Title X, and the George H. W. Bush who was so keen on birth control as a congressman that he was nicknamed "Rubbers"? That party is gone, supplanted by one in thrall to the religious right and other ideological extremists, who consolidated their power in Tea Party election victories beginning in 2010. In the second place, there is no alternate network of actually existing clinics to replace those of Planned Parenthood. When Texas cut roughly forty Planned Parenthood clinics from its new Texas Woman's Health Program in 2011, reimbursement claims for birth control dropped by 38 percent for low-income women, while claims for wellness exams dropped by 23 percent.[13] By 2013, the *Austin Chronicle* reported, Republican lawmakers had cut two-thirds of the state's family-planning budget, and seventy-six family planning clinics (including non–Planned Parenthood ones) had closed. The number of women served was 77 percent fewer than in 2011.[14] It's hard to believe that conservatives proffering an olive branch to pro-choicers over contraception are making a genuine attempt at compromise rather than a cynical rhetorical gesture.

The same pattern holds for sex education. Abortion opponents promote abstinence-only education despite strong evidence that it has no long-term positive effects. It may delay sex for younger teens, but not by much, and when those kids do have sex they are less likely to use condoms or contraception.[15] Texas has the nation's third highest rate of teen pregnancy, but in 2011 anti-abortion stalwart Gov. Rick Perry prevented the Health Department from applying for millions of dollars in federal funds aimed at preventing teen pregnancy through birth control alongside abstinence education. In 2013, however, Texas spent $1.2 million of federal money on a Web site to promote abstinence before marriage.[16] (Yes, the federal government is still funding abstinence-only sex education, despite President Obama's stated opposition to sex education that doesn't include information about contraception.)[17] The Web site, "Our Town 4 Teens," contains no mention of birth control and no sexual health information. Moreover, since 1998, Texas has required parental permission for teenagers to get prescription birth control from state-funded clinics. (Utah is the only other state with such a regulation.)[18] Does this sound like a state that cares more about preventing abortions caused by unwanted pregnancy or one that uses fear of pregnancy in a vain attempt to keep girls and women from having sex and wants to punish them with childbirth if they do?

For the organized anti-choice movement, contraception and realistic sex education are not solutions to the problem of abortion. All three are aspects of the same moral and social disaster. As Susan B. Anthony List leader Marjorie Dannenfelser put it, "The bottom line is that to lose the connection between sex and having children leads to problems."[19]

And the biggest of these problems? Women having lots and lots of sex. Consider Rush Limbaugh's attacks on Sandra Fluke. After the Georgetown University law student was barred from an all-male congressional panel on mandated coverage of contraception in the Affordable Care Act in February 2012, she testified in favor of the measure to a Democratic congressional panel. Although her examples of particular people harmed by Georgetown's refusal to cover birth control were circumspect—a married couple, a lesbian who needed the Pill to control her polycystic ovarian syndrome, a rape victim—Limbaugh called her a slut and a prostitute:

> What does it say about the college coed Susan Fluke [sic], who goes before a congressional committee and essentially says that she must be paid to have sex? What does that make her? It makes her a slut, right? It makes her a prostitute. She wants to be paid to have sex.
>
> She's having so much sex she can't afford the contraception. She wants you and me and the taxpayers to pay her to have sex.[20]

Limbaugh, who's been married four times and has no children, is probably no stranger to birth control, yet he apparently thinks a woman needs to take a pill every time she has sex. (After attacking Fluke forty-six times in three days, he apologized for his "insulting word choices," while comparing birth-control coverage to taxpayer-funded sneakers for students who want to run to keep fit.)[21] His fantasies about the licentious behavior enabled by the Pill—at one point he insisted that Fluke post her sex tapes online—are in the same vein as his bizarre free association about abortion. When a caller asked how to stop abortion, Limbaugh's answer fused violence against errant women with the iconic symbol of masculine resistance to the nanny state: "require that each one occur with a gun."[22] He wasn't the only person making the connection. One of Texas Republican Congressman Steve Stockman's 2013 campaign bumper stickers read IF BABIES HAD GUNS THEY WOULDN'T BE ABORTED. VOTE PRO-LIFE! At the 2013 March for Life in Washington, DC, I saw this handmade sign: BABIES GESTATING IN UTERO MAY ENGAGE IN SELF-DEFENSE AND STAND THEIR GROUND CUS UTERI ARE THEIR RIGHTFUL HOMES FOR 9 MONTHS.

Mainstream commentators tend to roll their eyes at Limbaugh, but the views he expressed about contraception are not so rare, and not so ineffectual. In 2011, Planned Parenthood had to stop providing birth control to low-income New Hampshire women when the state's all-male executive council rejected around $1.8 million in state and federal funds. "I am opposed to abortion," said council member Raymond Wieczorek. "I am opposed to providing condoms to someone. If you want to have a party, have a party but don't ask me to pay for it."[23] The benefits of birth control to women's health, the economic costs of unwanted pregnancies, childbirth, and children, even the suffering of women who need the Pill to control disease, like Fluke's unfortunate friend—these sensible policy concerns were nothing compared to the chance to give the finger to women: Have sex on your own dime, tramps. (Needless to say, these attacks on sex-related drugs and devices for women never extend to Viagra.) Fluke herself continues to symbolize America's moral downfall. At the 2013 Values Voters Summit, Gary Bauer, then head of the Family Research Council, attacked President Obama for telephoning Fluke to congratulate her on her testimony:

> I still remember when presidents made personal phone calls to astronauts to tell them how proud they were of them, but of course the space program's in the trash can, thrown there by Barack Obama. . . . Now we live in an era where a president praises a promiscuous coed because she thinks *you* ought to buy her birth-control pills. That, my friends, is the definition of civilizational decline.[24]

Modernity used to mean brave men using science to conquer space; now it means trashy "coeds" using science—and your taxes—to satisfy their lust.

The proof that abortion opponents' objections to birth control go beyond protective feelings for zygotes is that they don't go out of their way to promote contraceptive methods that even they have to admit do nothing to block implantation: condoms, diaphragms, cervical caps, spermicidal sponges, tubal ligations, vasectomies, withdrawal. Imagine if the National Right to Life Committee endorsed Trojans and the Today sponge (*Safe for you . . . and your fertilized egg!*). Abortion opponents also condemn or are silent about the many kinds of sexual pleasure that do not involve ejaculating in the vagina, although these also can serve as birth control, and have done so for centuries. When Joycelyn Elders, US surgeon general during the Clinton administration, suggested that masturbation was "part of human sexuality, and . . . perhaps should be taught," she lost her job.[25] Why are abortion opponents so fixated on confining sex to penis-vagina intercourse—which not only causes unwanted pregnancies but is, for many women, not so satisfying?

If the movement against legal abortion were not fundamentally an expression of particular religious doctrines and particular attitudes toward women and sex, we would find anti-abortion politicians seeking votes by supporting contraception as common ground. After all, most people think birth control is a good thing. Almost all women who have ever had sex have used it at some time. By contrast, only 2 percent of Catholic women practice Natural Family Planning, the only birth-control method permitted by the Church, and no wonder: Besides the many days of no sex and the high failure rate, who wants to begin the day by examining one's cervical mucus?[26]

POVERTY

Logically, abortion opponents should care about poverty. The less punitive among them make much of the fact that almost three-quarters of women seeking abortion cite economic reasons for their decision.[27] I'm not so sure this statistic means that if they had more money, those same women would have those babies. Respondents to the question of why they were having an abortion were allowed to give multiple reasons, and poverty was rarely the only one cited. About the same percentage gave as their reason "having a baby would dramatically change my life" by interfering with education, work, or caregiving responsibilities. Almost half said they didn't want to be single mothers. It would be more accurate to say that poor women have more unplanned and ill-timed pregnancies. They have more abortions, but they also have more children.

So what are abortion opponents doing to make it possible for those low-income women to continue their pregnancies and raise those babies? Precious little. Indeed, there is an inverse relationship between support for abortion restrictions and support for programs that help low-income pregnant women, babies, and children. In the midst of the Republican-engineered government shutdown in the fall of 2013, the Women Infants and Children feeding program (WIC), which serves 8.9 million mothers and children under five, found itself in turmoil.[28] As its reserve funds ran out, some states refused new applicants or refused to print more vouchers. (Anti-abortion conservative pundit and Republican Party adviser Bill Kristol commented, "I don't think it's the end of the world.")[29] Contrast that with the special care shown during the shutdown to the Pentagon's civilian workers, most of whom were quickly called back from the furlough, or to the House gym, which stayed open.

Whether it's hunger, housing, social services, or education, if it benefits poor families, the anti-abortion party wants to cut it. Raise the minimum wage? That would hurt profits. Extend unemployment benefits? What, and let lazy people kick back in the safety net Paul Ryan claims is becoming a "hammock"?[30] Anti-abortion Republicans have been trying to get rid of the Affordable Care Act since the minute it was passed. As of early 2014, twenty-four states were refusing to expand their Medicaid rolls to cover those who make just a bit too much to qualify under the state's own rules ("too much" can be practically nothing—$11 a day in some states). Here was a big opportunity to make life a bit less precarious for millions of people, and cheaply, too: The expansion would be completely paid for by the federal government for three years, after which the state would have to foot only 10 percent of the bill at most. Two-thirds of the nation's uninsured single mothers and African Americans, and 60 percent of the uninsured working poor, live in these states—a perfect storm of race, class, and gender.[31] In every case, it was Republican governors and/or legislatures who rejected the expansion. So here's another thing more important than fetuses and babies and mothers: giving President Obama a poke in the eye with a sharp stick.

Anti-abortion conservatives cannot admit out loud that they have basically abandoned mothers and children. Churches and charities, they claim, will get them on their feet, with no red tape and no burden on the taxpayer. Meanwhile, let's close those clinics! But philanthropy cannot solve low-income women's fundamental problem—having a low income—any more than they can solve homelessness or hunger or drug addiction. Nor can the anti-abortion movement. The Nurturing Network, founded in 1985 by corporate executive turned homeschooling mother and anti-abortion activist Mary Cunningham Agee, claims that its network of tens of thousands of volunteers have helped 24,000 pregnant women in twenty-nine years, "in all fifty states and in thirty foreign countries," mostly middle-class college and working women. That's less than a thousand women a year, and the Nurturing Network is one of the bigger efforts of its kind.[32] To provide pregnant women and new mothers in need with real support and quality medical care would require considerable effort from the only entity with enough power and resources to do the job—state and federal government.

True, the Catholic Church lobbies Congress for social spending on behalf of the poor, as do some small liberal evangelical groups like Sojourners, and there are otherwise-liberal Democrats who oppose legal abortion, but the anti-choice movement as a whole has thrown in its lot with the most reactionary elements in the Republican Party, who want to slash already inadequate programs. In 2013, faced with a government shutdown that risked sending millions of families over the edge into poverty, the US Conference of Catholic Bishops (USCCB) prevailed on House Republicans to make expanding "conscience" objections to birth control a condition of keeping government open.[33] Result: shutdown. Nothing is more important than saving babies—except making it harder for women to get birth control. When Pope Francis publicly criticized the hierarchy for being "obsessed" with gays and abortion, the whole world cheered.[34]

MEN

Logically, abortion opponents should want to increase the burden of responsibility for men who impregnate women other than their wives or who abandon their wives when they are pregnant. After all, if the goal is to prevent abortion, it makes sense to give men a bigger stake in preventing unwanted pregnancy than they have at present. That holds whether the goal is to reduce unwanted pregnancy or to promote strict sexual mores. Women can't do this alone: Married or unmarried, men can just walk away, as they have done since history began. To be an effective deterrent, the consequences of pregnancy should hang over both partners. (In fact, since unwanted pregnancy and childbirth are themselves rather painful experiences, society should punish men more severely than women, to equalize their motivation.) But do abortion opponents call for boys to be expelled from Catholic schools and Christian academies like their pregnant girlfriends? Did they protest when San Diego Christian College fired Teri James for getting pregnant while unmarried—and then offered a job to her fiancé, who had impregnated her? (He said no thanks, and now they are married.)[35] Do they call on abstinence-only classes to compare boys who have sex to used chewing gum or dirty toothbrushes or much-handled Peppermint Patties? No, that humiliation is just for girls. Do they arrange elaborate Oedipal ceremonies in which boys pledge their virginity to their mothers, as girls pledge theirs to their fathers? Don't be silly. The anti-abortion movement may deplore all sex outside of marriage, but in practice its message is boys will be boys.

Why doesn't the movement use some of its famous political clout to pass laws compelling men who impregnate women to support them during pregnancy—housing, food, clothing, doctor bills? After all, abortion opponents are the ones who think it's a baby when it's only got one cell, so what is the justification for starting child support only after birth? The lack of interest in making men who impregnate women co-responsible for the care of the unborn—and the born—is another clue that abortion opponents' first concern is not to ensure the well-being of the embryo and fetus, but to control and punish the behavior of women, and only women.

VIOLENCE AGAINST WOMEN

Logically, abortion opponents should care *a lot* about domestic violence—after all, they claim women are routinely bullied by husbands, boyfriends, and pimps into having abortions they don't want. Pregnancy is a time when women are particularly likely to be attacked by their partners, but where were abortion opponents in the winter of 2012–13, when the Republicans were refusing to renew the Violence Against Women Act (VAWA) because it included protections for Native Americans, undocumented immigrants, and people who are lesbian, gay, bisexual, or transgender? Indeed, five important bishops, USCCB committee heads, came out against VAWA because it used the phrases "sexual orientation" and "gender identity" and did not include conscience protections exempting those who provide services to victims of sex trafficking from offering those victims emergency contraception and abortion.[36]

True, many Catholic individuals and congregations and agencies do much to help battered women. Catholic nuns do great work, despite the Vatican's investigation of the Leadership Conference of Women Religious, the largest organization of American nuns, for excessive independence and "radical feminism."[37] But violence against women is far too big a problem to be solved by local charities. Where are the calls for affordable housing and income supports or jobs or a vast network of shelters so that pregnant women and new mothers can escape their abusers? Instead, fetal-homicide laws, passed in the 1990s at the instigation of abortion opponents who said they wanted to protect pregnant women from violence, almost always at the hands of male partners, are being used against pregnant women themselves.

Catholic priests and evangelical pastors preach against abortion all the time—Respect Life Sunday is a regular feature on the Catholic calendar. There's no Respect Women Sunday, although violence against women, an ongoing feature of life for millions, surely happens more frequently than abortion, a rare event for most women. Indeed, since the Catholic Church challenges statistics suggesting that Catholic women are as likely to have abortions as non-Catholics by claiming that those women are not active churchgoers, one wonders why priests feel the need to lecture their parishioners so often about this.

Note too that the Catholic Church opposes divorce, as do some evangelicals. Bestselling author and megapastor Rick Warren, who preaches wifely submission, holds that the Bible permits divorce only for desertion and sexual infidelity; domestic violence doesn't count. (After the story hit the news when he was invited to give the invocation at President Obama's 2008 inauguration, relevant pages were removed from his church's Web site.) Warren is far from alone. In general, conservative evangelical/fundamentalist churches discourage women from divorcing abusive mates and instead advise pastoral counseling, which pressures women to stay in the marriage (perhaps they were not subservient enough?) and leaves them vulnerable to more abuse. Unsurprisingly, religious women are more likely to stay in abusive relationships, and to stay for longer than non-religious women, even when they do eventually leave. It would be hard to argue that anti-abortion Christians who oppose abortion have been as good a friend to women as they are to men and fertilized eggs.

MURDER

Logically, if abortion is really the murder of over 1 million children each year, no cause should be more important than the banning of abortion. In a way, Pope Francis was wrong to criticize the bishops for focusing so intently and harshly on abortion: The marvel is that so few Americans who say they think abortion is murder take any action to stop it. Imagine if over a million born children were killed by their parents every year (admittedly it is hard to picture the circumstances under which this annual slaughter would take place). Wouldn't stopping the killing be more important in deciding how to cast your ballot than highway financing or property taxes or whether or not a candidate had cheated on his wife?

Anti-abortion politicians, too, put all sorts of things higher on the list. In 2010 numerous anti-choice Republicans promised they would focus on jobs, jobs, jobs, not abortion—so luring corporations to their state with tax breaks was more important than the murder of children. When she ran for re-election in 2006, former Rep. Marilyn Musgrave, now Susan B. Anthony List vice-president of government affairs, told a crowd of supporters, "As we face the issues that we are facing today, I don't think there's anything more important out there than the marriage issue."[38] If outlawing abortion is less important than keeping Adam and Steve from the altar, abortion can't be all that terrible. In fact, in 2007 the Catholic bishops issued a statement permitting adherents to vote for pro-choice politicians as long as they did so for other, serious reasons.[39] What issue could possibly outweigh the annual legal murder of over a million children?

SELF-INTEREST

Logically, abortion opponents should not make arguments about the harm abortion supposedly does to women. Ending a pregnancy would be just as bad if it left women better off, as indeed it usually does—that is why opponents call it "selfish." Clinging to discredited claims that abortion will give a woman cancer, drive her insane, and ruin her life just makes abortion opponents look desperate and deceptive. If they were honest they would say, yes, obviously, abortion may give you a better life. It will let you have children when you're ready for them, and that goal, achieved some other way, would be wonderful. If you have that baby you may struggle for years, be stuck in a job that bores you silly, lose the respect of your community, be tied to a man you can't stand, perhaps never achieve the life you were hoping for—and let's not forget pregnancy and childbirth carry risks of their own. But difficult as your life may become, and maybe the lives of your loved ones as well, you can take comfort in the fact that you did the right thing.

The fact that abortion opponents try to persuade women that having accidental and unwanted babies is good for *them*— for their physical and mental well-being, their happiness, their relationships, their futures—when in fact, as we know from countries where abortion opponents make and enforce the laws, they would be just as opposed to ending a pregnancy that would leave a woman blind or paralyzed, shows that they understand deep down that abortion as murder is not persuasive, the way, say, murder as murder is. It has to be buttressed with appeals not just to ethics but self-interest: Abortion will hurt *you*. We don't make those kinds of arguments when urging people not to commit serious harm to others. (Don't beat your children—you'll be lonely in old age.)

ASSISTED REPRODUCTION TECHNOLOGY

Logically, abortion opponents should oppose in-vitro fertilization with the same passion they bring to abortion. "Babies" are killed all the time in fertility clinics. Extra embryos, and defective ones, are discarded; when too many implant in the womb, doctors may kill some to increase the chances of healthy development for the rest. Even if frozen, embryos may deteriorate over time or eventually be discarded at the parents' request. Why is it rare to see large groups of people praying the rosary in front of fertility clinics or shouting at women on their way in? Why don't fertility specialists have to wear bulletproof vests? Why don't hospitals deny them admitting privileges the way they do doctors who perform abortions? The difference between a petri dish and a womb isn't in the embryos, it's in the woman's perceived intention. The woman undergoing IVF is fulfilling her traditional motherly role, even if she kills a lot of embryos in the process; the woman undergoing abortion is seen as rejecting it, even if she already has six kids.

In *The Party of Death*, the conservative writer Ramesh Ponnuru argues that abortion opponents aren't hypocrites for overlooking fertility medicine: "prolife principles don't by themselves lead to a ban on IVF; they lead only to regulations that prevent fertility clinics from 'discarding excess embryos' or implanting several and then aborting some fetuses."[40] I like that "only"— who needs to look at what procedures work best, let's just wave our magic pundit wand! Under the influence of the Vatican, Italy passed a law in 2004 that Ponnuru might have usefully investigated. It banned donating eggs or sperm, freezing embryos, or screening them for defects and diseases, required that only three eggs at a time could be harvested, and that all the resultant embryos be implanted. The results were not good: Women could not refuse embryos that were likely to be unhealthy (paradoxically, they could abort them later, since abortion was legal) and the low number of eggs retrieved meant women had to undergo more cycles. The framers of these new rules don't seem to have thought much about the physical and emotional stress of the new rules on women, the actual patients. Rather than endure this cumbersome and humiliating regime, many couples went abroad for treatment, even after the law was modified, in 2009.[41] (In 2014, the constitutional court struck down the ban on sperm and egg donation, and the government admitted the law had basically collapsed.)[42]

Similar obstacles would face infertile couples here if abortion opponents got to design IVF protocols, but they're not trying. IVF is just too popular. And yet, these are the people who spent years preventing the marketing of emergency contraception on the specious grounds that it kept fertilized eggs from implanting, and when they lost that battle, spent many more years limiting its sale, and are still trying to do so. So, real or imaginary fertilized egg in a woman: baby. Fertilized egg in a petri dish: It's complicated.

RELIGION

It seems almost too obvious to mention that the religious denominations most energetically opposed to abortion rights also deny equality to women. With a few exceptions, they don't ordain women, and even when they do, leadership is firmly in the hands of men, as is the official interpretation of sacred texts and traditions. Perhaps unsurprisingly, given the Bible's obsession with prostitutes, adulteresses, seductresses, women who lie about rape, and disobedient women beginning with Eve, these faiths see female sexuality and female will as potentially polluting and dangerous, and place great emphasis on female virginity and chastity. When their leaders try to show empathy to women, it's as the Other: victims who need help, reprobates who need guidance, martyrs who sacrifice themselves for children or family, the occasional heroine or saint who manages to surmount or sidestep her constricted role while also fulfilling it, like the Virgin Mary or Teresa of Avila or, for that matter, many a pastor's energetic wife. Pope Francis recently suggested that the Church needed a "theology of the woman."[43] Men are just people—no special theology of the entire male sex required.

Religious hostility to feminism is not new. Today it's abortion, yesterday it was the Equal Rights Amendment, decades ago it was bobbed hair and women's suffrage. But today's antifeminist Christianity, like ultra-orthodox Judaism and fundamentalist Islam, is arguably more intense, because it's more obviously on the losing side of history. It's also more confused and cynical. Despite its general suspicion of working mothers, ambitious women, female leadership, and nontraditional gender roles, the Christian right was wildly enthusiastic when Sarah Palin, mother of five including a baby with Down syndrome, ran for vice president. Her value as a high-profile charismatic candidate—a woman, too, so take that, Democrats—was greater than anything to be gained by attacking her seemingly egalitarian marriage and man-size ambitions. Even Phyllis Schlafly, who has spent her whole life attacking working mothers despite having a very active and profitable career herself, had nothing bad to say about Palin. Imagine what she would have said had Palin been a Democrat!

Of course, there are secular people who completely oppose legal abortion. But they're not driving the movement. It's hard to square the conviction that a woman should be compelled to bear every child she conceives, no matter what, with the belief, to which most secular people at least pay lip service, that she should decide for herself the shape of her life. How is she supposed to do that while undergoing random pregnancies and childbirths and raising the results? Secular people may believe abortion is wrong, they may even think women who have abortions are sluts and worse, but they don't have a divinely approved worldview that officially defines women in terms of wifely, domestic, and maternal duties and makes abortion the key to modern downfall and depravity.

Perhaps this is a good place to point out that most mainstream Protestant denominations, as well as reform and conservative Judaism, are at least moderately pro-choice, although they hardly shout their position from the rooftops. Their quiet on the subject gives the misleading impression that "faith" itself is hostile to reproductive rights. Be that as it may, if you want to understand why there is so little significant organized resistance to legal abortion in France, Germany, Britain, and Scandinavia, the lower level of religiosity, and the much smaller role religion plays in national life, is much of the answer.

Among American states, there's a correlation between white religiosity, Republican Party power, restrictions on abortion, and the status of women. The ten states where women's status is highest (measured by economic security, leadership, and health) are strongly Democratic, with strong secular cultures (in order: Maryland, Hawaii, Vermont, California, Delaware, Connecticut, Colorado, New York, New Jersey, and Washington). The ten states where women's status is lowest are solidly Republican, with churches wielding a lot of political and cultural power (Georgia, Indiana, South Dakota, Arkansas, Texas, Mississippi, Alabama, Oklahoma, Utah, and Louisiana).[44]

If you compare states by the number of abortion restrictions, it's practically a topsy-turvy image: The top states for women's status, where religion plays a relatively small role in political life, have few abortion restrictions. The bottom states, where religion infuses politics, have many. As the political scientist Jean Reith Schroedel sums it up in her ingenious study, *Is the Fetus a Person?*, "Women's status is consistently lower in anti-abortion states than in pro-choice states, indicating that lawmakers in the former are more interested in attacking women's rights than protecting fetal life."[45] Schroedel also shows that anti-choice states do little to ensure the health and well-being of fetuses and babies (prenatal care, drug treatment, and other assistance to pregnant women), let alone children and families, and are down at the bottom when it comes to education, child care, access to food stamps, Medicaid, and welfare. Is it an accident that these states—hostile to abortion and women's rights, and providing little social support for families—are full of devout right-wing Christians?

If your goal is to protect fetuses, let alone the children they become, depriving women of the wherewithal to make a decent life for their children, and keeping millions in poverty or near it, makes no sense. It only makes sense if what you really care about is keeping women in the place ordained for them by the Christian right—relatively powerless but protected by their husbands and families if lucky and good, and just plain powerless, if not.

SEVEN

CAN THERE BE A COMPROMISE ON ABORTION?

Many people think it would be good to find a middle position on abortion. If only the whole business of unwanted pregnancy and fetuses and women with their complicated demands and needs would just go away! "Permit but discourage" is one middle-of-the-road suggestion, popularized by Roger Rosenblatt in his 1992 book *Life Itself: Abortion in the American Mind*, but like "safe, legal, and rare" it's less a policy prescription—more birth control? longer waiting periods? making women feel guiltier?— than an expression of discomfort. However many abortions there are and no matter who has them or why, I want there to be fewer! A political compromise wouldn't necessarily achieve civic peace, since it would infuriate the people who care the most: Abortion-rights opponents would continue to insist that anything short of a total ban was state-sanctioned murder, and abortion-rights supporters would continue to argue that increased restrictions violate women's right to self-determination. Still, might there be an agreement that marginalized both those groups? They would continue to protest and agitate, of course, but the majority would feel a good balance had been reached.

Let's look at some possibilities.

We could limit legal abortion by *reason*. Polls show majority support for legal abortion in situations that are clearly beyond the woman's control: criminal sex acts and significant medical problems for her or the fetus. After that, depending on the reason, a slim to decisive majority of Americans say they want the woman to pay the price for having done the deed. (It doesn't seem to register that others—her family, the baby itself—may pay the price too.) Why not limit legal abortion to situations where the majority approves of the woman's reason for terminating her pregnancy? If that seems too rigid, for particularly painful cases we could also bring back the hospital committees that used to decide whether a woman's circumstances were sufficiently horrific to deserve to be spared childbirth—sort of like the old television show *Queen for a Day*, with the women who can tell the most persuasive tales of woe winning abortions instead of washing machines.

The trouble is, taken together, those widely acceptable reasons apply to fewer than 10 percent of the 1.06 million abortions that took place in the United States in 2011, the most recent year for which we have figures.

And surely many of those women would have a hard time proving that they qualified. Who decides if a suicide threat is real or "just a bid for attention"? How inevitable does death or permanent injury have to be? How do you prove you were impregnated by your uncle, Rotarian of the Year, without a DNA test of the aborted fetus or born baby? Most rape victims don't report their rapes, and it's not as though police and prosecutors just take their word for it when they do. And what about pregnancy in the context of abusive relationships or birth-control sabotage by boyfriends? It might not be rape in the eyes of the law, but it's certainly coercive, and, as mentioned earlier, it's not as rare as you might think.

The vast majority of women who have abortions have them for social, economic, and personal reasons: They do not have the resources to mother a child well or at all. Thus, limiting abortion to the reasons supported by the majority would leave at least 900,000 women a year, most of them already mothers, most poor or low-income, and disproportionately women of color, unable to end their pregnancies legally. What would happen to them? As in the days before *Roe*, they would walk through fire to find clandestine providers or sympathetic doctors who would declare them sufficiently ill or mentally unbalanced to qualify for a legal procedure. Once again, women who could afford it would travel to places where abortion was legal, the way Irish women go to Great Britain and Polish women go to Ukraine. More women would try to self-abort, by buying pills over the Internet or at flea markets, or by using older methods: poisonous herbs, knitting needles, throwing themselves down stairs. Indeed, this is already happening as clinics close.

It would not take long for the inherent unfairness and clumsiness of this system, with its obvious racial, class, and social biases and its inevitable tragedies, to dismay ordinary citizens. The medical profession has been remarkably slow to defend abortion providers, but that might change as emergency rooms started seeing women with incomplete self-induced miscarriages, and as doctors fell afoul of the new rules, as interpreted by zealous anti-abortion prosecutors. Far from bringing social peace, the reasons compromise would simply start the abortion wars all over again.

Second idea: We could limit legal abortion by *time*. A majority of Americans think abortion should be legal in the first trimester, but support falls off quickly after that.[1] Abortion opponents have won points with the public by focusing on later abortions and portraying them as common and barbaric; that was the public-relations genius of the campaign against "partial-birth abortion." Pro-choicers correctly counter that abortions after twenty weeks are very rare (only 1.5 percent of all abortions) and often performed for grave reasons.[2] If late abortions are so upsetting, and also so rare, what if we permitted abortion on demand in the first trimester, and limited it after that to the most acceptable reasons, mentioned above? Almost 9 in 10 abortions would take place as they do now, in the first twelve weeks of pregnancy—maybe more, because women would struggle mightily to meet that sharp deadline and clinics would adapt to fit them in. Only a bit more than 1 in 10 would hit a roadblock, and of those, the ones with medical reasons would still be able to terminate their pregnancies. Sound fair?

We've already seen states pass near-total bans on abortions after twenty weeks on the claim that those fetuses can feel pain. In 2013 the House of Representatives passed the Pain-Capable Unborn Child Protection Act, a federal ban (it failed in the Senate); in 2014 Republican senators tried again, and are sure to push the law should the GOP take the Senate. This bill, it should be noted, sets prison terms of up to *five years* for doctors who fall afoul of its stringent terms. The only exceptions are for rape, incest, or to save the woman's life. Woe betide the doctor who errs on the side of protecting his patient: To be safe from prosecution, he really should wait until she has one foot in the grave, like Michelle Lee, or maybe two, like Savita Halappanavar. (Fetal defect doesn't count, by the way, even if it's a fatal one. Abortion opponents have decided that it is more "compassionate" to force a woman to stay pregnant, give birth, and watch her baby die in hospice care.) Most researchers agree that fetuses at that stage have not developed the necessary neurological wiring to feel pain, but polls suggest a plurality of Americans would approve of such a measure, depending on how the polling question is worded.[3] Given that common feeling, why not sacrifice the minority—1 in 10, 1 in 100, whatever works—in order to shore up the right of the vast majority to terminate their pregnancies in the early stages?

Such a bargain is not on the table, and never will be. For one thing, it would require overturning *Roe*, which forbids banning second-trimester abortion. People who propose these reasonable-sounding measures always leave that bit out. And once the Supreme Court reversed itself on *Roe*, throwing abortion back to the states, all bets would be off. Having won such a momentous victory, why would abortion opponents give 90 percent of it back for the sake of civic peace? Only liberals do that. Abortion opponents would keep doing exactly what they are doing now: fighting to ban abortion state by state and nationally, passing restrictions, closing clinics, harassing doctors and patients, scaring the public with lurid tales, insisting that the remotest taint of abortion be removed from public funding and health insurance. Even leaving *Roe* aside, in what imaginary state legislature would a proposal pass that restricted abortion on demand to the first trimester, while preserving and even expanding access to it so that women would not be unjustly barred from first-trimester abortions by poverty and geography? Where doctors who perform abortions are ostracized and threatened and occasionally even murdered, how would those permitted first-trimester abortions and carefully approved later abortions happen?

Pro-choicers wouldn't take defeat lying down, either. The 11 percent of abortions that occur after the first trimester include the saddest and most desperate cases: the young girls who didn't realize they were pregnant or couldn't bear to tell their parents; low-income women who went over into the second trimester while they were trying to put together the clinic fee; women whose partners deserted them upon learning of the pregnancy, leaving them with no way to support the kids they already have; and of course women whose fetuses have serious physical or mental defects, many of which cannot be discovered until around twenty weeks or even later. Quite a few women, moreover, won't even know they are pregnant until they have gone over the twelve-week limit.[4] A deadline tight enough to please those who are so appalled by second-trimester abortion that they would make it a crime to end a pregnancy at thirteen weeks or sixteen weeks or even twenty-four weeks would be a deadline that would punish the most needy and socially isolated women, and the earlier the cutoff was, the greater the number who would suffer.

Let me give you an example of a second-trimester abortion patient. Through a volunteer group called Haven, I hosted overnight in my spare room a woman who had come to New York for an abortion at nineteen or twenty weeks. "Janelle" was twenty five, African American, and lived in a housing project in a very poor neighborhood in another city. She was a nice person, friendly and warm. I liked her. She spoke eagerly and affectionately about her three children, and about her mother, who was caring for them while she was away. It seemed to me

Janelle had her hands full, but that was not why she was ending the pregnancy. The reason, she told me over spaghetti, was that the children's father had left her for another woman and cut off support for the family. Janelle had only worked briefly, as a file clerk in a temporary jobs program, but welfare reformers would be proud of her: She didn't want to go on public assistance. She wanted to pull herself together and earn a living. ("I don't just want a job," she told me proudly, "I want a career.") She didn't have money for an abortion, and neither did her mother. By the time she found her way to her city's abortion fund ("They were the only people who were kind to me," she said), she had gone over the time limit of her local clinics and needed the astronomical sum of $1,500 to get an abortion in New York City. Usually funds give only a few hundred dollars, but this one put up the whole amount, even including transportation.

It is hard to see how Janelle could have had her abortion much earlier, and it is hard to see how she could have coped with another baby. But would her very ordinary story persuade a committee or a judge that she deserved a dispensation from the first-trimester rule? You may not even feel much sympathy for her yourself. Three kids by twenty-five? Relying on a boyfriend for support? But why should women like Janelle have to lay bare the most intimate details of their lives to win the approval of a judge or a committee of worthies or a pair of psychiatrists or whomever the state would appoint to pass judgment upon her? There are thousands upon thousands of Janelles, women caught in complicated situations that outsiders can hardly understand (and that would hardly be improved by forcing them to have a baby). Besides being costly, complicated, unrealistic, and dehumanizing, a second-trimester ban would end up being another way of dividing women into good and bad, madonnas and whores.

As with limiting abortion by reason, if we compromised by restricting abortion by time, we would see more women like Janelle forced into deeper trouble or resorting to illegal abortion and self-abortion. And for what? Janelle's abortion was late because she had no money, but let's say she had also needed a few weeks to take stock of her situation. Is that so terrible? If it is patronizing to force women into waiting periods, as if they need to be compelled by law to think about what they are doing when they have already made up their mind, there is something cruel about forcing women into a quick decision, especially given the way we have built abortion up into an immense and fearful test of morality and self-worth. We claim to worry about abortion regret. Well, some women need time to decide what to do.

What if we took a different tack and in return for an earlier cutoff date for legal abortion we expanded *access to realistic sex education and contraception*? Polls suggest the majority might be happy with this, and so would many pundits. And indeed, if every woman got respectful reproductive health care, if she could see a doctor she trusted promptly when she needed to switch her brand of pill, if all the women who could benefit from the IUD could get it with no copay as the Affordable Care Act promises to many, if emergency contraception cost a dollar or two instead of $50, if teens (and grown-ups) were not so ignorant about their bodies—if, if, if!—we would definitely have fewer unwanted pregnancies, and therefore fewer abortions. But birth control isn't magic and people aren't so simple. Even if the no-copay birth-control provisions of the Affordable Care Act reduce unwanted pregnancy by half—a stupendous public health achievement—we would still have some 500,000 to 600,000 women wanting abortion, and unless abortion access were greatly expanded, the same proportion as now—around 11 percent—would miss a twelve-week cutoff. Janelle would still be out of luck.

I plucked these numbers out of the air, obviously, but it doesn't matter, because this compromise is not going to happen, no matter how many ordinary people or important commentators think it should. As with guns and the NRA, so with abortion and the organized movement against it: What matters is passion, strategy, money, and organization, not what boxes people check on a poll. As resistance to the birth-control provisions in the Affordable Care Act vividly demonstrates, to say nothing of the persistence of abstinence-only sex education despite its proven worthlessness, the struggle over abortion plays out over everything connected to sex and reproduction, and it would play out over this compromise too. There's no way the organized anti-abortion movement would turn around and embrace comprehensive sex education, let alone publicly provided birth control for young people, even though most people favor these measures.[5] And because state governments have great power in these areas, the states in which the anti-abortion movement is strong would reject them.

Well, then, why not accept reality and limit abortion by *geography*? Let New York be New York and Texas be Texas. Overturn *Roe*, let pro- and anti-choice forces hash it out in each state, and in Washington as well. That's democracy.

In effect, we're already well on our way in that direction. Supreme Court rulings permitting restrictions have allowed vastly uneven access to abortion from one state, or even one whole region, to another. Going forward, the court would not even need to overturn *Roe*. It could simply approve more and more restrictions, holding that they are not serious enough to violate *Planned Parenthood v. Casey*. (In that 1992 decision, a plurality of justices upheld *Roe* but permitted states to pass restrictions as long as they did not constitute an "undue burden" on a woman's choice. What makes a burden undue remains a mystery.) It could hold that new information about fetal development meant states could bar abortion after x number of weeks. It could decide that states had the right to regulate clinics even if the requirements forced most of them to close. It could find that if restrictions meant no doctors performed abortions in that state, doctors were making a free choice not to comply with reasonable requirements. *Roe* would still be the law of the land, but only in a formal, abstract sense. *Brown v. Board of Ed* is still law, after all, and it is hard to imagine that the Supreme Court will ever overturn it and permit explicit public-school segregation, but over the course of half a century, its scope has been so narrowed and the will to enforce it so weakened that public schools are as segregated today as they were sixty years ago.[6]

If abortion opponents ever became a majority on the Supreme Court, they might find it politically shrewder to hollow out *Roe* rather than overturn it outright. Allowing states to impose restrictions that raise the cost of the procedure so much that patients can't afford it, or that drive clinics out of business one by one, doesn't have the same national shock value or potential for political organizing as overturning *Roe* would have. As with other proposed compromises, the geographical solution would reinstate the exact situation *Roe* was intended to rectify: safe abortion for women who live in, or can travel to, places where it is legal, and underground procedures and self-abortion for the rest. In much of the country, we are already there. In 2008, Arizona had nineteen providers; now, after a law banning nurse practitioners from performing medication abortions, it has seven.[7] Because of new restrictions in Ohio, three abortion clinics closed in 2013, while more are in danger of following suit.[8] In 2011, Texas had forty-four clinics. By early 2014, after new restrictions passed, there were twenty-four. If the law is fully implemented, by the time you read this there may be only six.

The geographic compromise, in other words, is essentially happening now, and it's a disaster for women. Abortion is becoming less and less available not only in red states, where anti-abortion sentiment is strong, but also in some pinkish states, like Pennsylvania and Wisconsin. Mississippi, North Dakota, South Dakota, Arkansas, and Missouri have only one clinic each.[9] Wyoming has none, although it has three doctors or hospitals who do a few abortions. (In 2009, more than 90 percent of Wyoming women who had abortions had them out of state.)[10] The closing of two Montana clinics—one by retirement, the other by alleged anti-abortion vandalism—leaves the state with only two, and other closings in the region mean those two serve a swath of 1,200 miles that extends from the western border of Idaho to the eastern border of the Dakotas.[11] The blizzard of proposed restrictions does its work even when most bills fail. Abortion is further stigmatized, opponents are energized, and women who don't stay on top of the news may get the impression abortion has become illegal or unavailable.

Do we really want to repeat history? One might ask too why the right to an abortion should be remanded back to the states when other constitutionally protected rights are not, no matter how unpopular they are. The First Amendment still covers the whole country even though majorities in plenty of states would love to bring back public-school prayer, teach creationism in biology class, and, for all we know, decorate every courtroom with the Ten Commandments. In any case, the geographic compromise would backfire. Instead of peace and common sense, abortion politics would rage in fifty state legislatures and in Congress, and abortion laws would be subject to shifts with every election. Much like what is happening now, only more so.

We could always try the kinder, gentler faith-based compromise: Restrict—no, ban—abortion, but *ameliorate poverty*. Liberal anti-choice groups like Sojourners, the evangelical group headed by Jim Wallis, and Democrats for Life, as well as the USCCB and other Catholic organizations, acknowledge that women seeking abortion are often poor and struggling. Why not help them? Leaving aside for the moment how many poor women who have abortions would have those babies if they were a little less poor, we are definitely talking about a long-term project. In today's climate of outright hostility toward the poor, especially single mothers, especially black and Latina single mothers, it is hard to see where the political will is going to come from to seriously improve low-income women's lives— let alone to improve them so much that those who would have chosen abortion will feel they can manage an ill-timed extra baby. Programs that benefit low-income mothers and children have been slashed: welfare, funding for child care and after-school programs, housing subsidies, contracts with private agencies that help families in crisis. Even food stamps are on the chopping block.[12]

Abortion opponents who blame poverty for abortion are hardly putting forward bold proposals for change. In 2006, for example, Democrats for Life put forward their 95-10 Initiative, which they claimed would reduce the number of abortions by 95 percent in ten years. Only four proposals dealt with poverty. (The rest involve familiar anti-abortion measures like informed-consent requirements slanted to dissuade women from choosing abortion, making adoption easier, and yet more abstinence-only education.) They were: campus day-care centers for student mothers; health insurance for low-income pregnant women; beefing up the Women, Infants and Children's feeding program (WIC); and increasing funding for battered women's shelters and counseling programs.[13] (The bill based on 95-10, the Pregnant Women Support Act, died in committee in 2009, although Democrats for Life takes credit for the inclusion of a Pregnancy Assistance Fund in the Affordable Care Act.) I'm guessing, though, that it would take more than the prospect of some day care to persuade a reluctant college student to have a baby. She can't raise a child in her dorm room, after all. Similarly, more WIC coupons are all very well, but a woman poor enough to be eligible for them will still be poor once she has them. Back in the 1990s, proponents of welfare reform argued that benefits were so lavish they encouraged women to have babies just to get on the dole—you'll notice few abortion opponents are suggesting poverty be ameliorated *that* much.

Perhaps we could just *become western Europe*. When Wendy Davis's filibuster thrust Texas's proposed twenty-week time limit into the news, anti-choice conservatives were quick to point out that most liberal western European countries cut off abortion on demand much earlier than the United States. (They were forgetting Great Britain and the Netherlands, which permit abortion till twenty-four weeks. Canada, by the way, has no time limit at all.) In France, Germany, and Denmark it's twelve weeks after conception, in Sweden eighteen. Most have other restrictions too, like parental consent and waiting periods.[14] On paper, western Europe does indeed look strict.

In reality, though, not so much. In France, you can get an abortion at any public hospital and it's paid for by the government. In Germany, you can get one at a hospital or a doctor's office, and health plans cover the fee for low-income women. Mandated counseling is sympathetic and non-directive. In Sweden, abortion is free. Cost and access, the two things that push abortion later in pregnancy here, are not issues there.

Those time limits have exceptions too, for (depending on the country) mental and physical health, fetal anomaly, or rape. And the rules are, in practice, flexible. If a teenage girl shows up at a Swedish hospital twenty weeks pregnant and frantic, ways can be found to quietly help her. Moreover, should a German woman be denied a second-trimester abortion, she can probably get to the Netherlands, and a French one to London, more easily than a woman in the Mountain States or the Rio Grande Valley or much of the Deep South can travel to the nearest clinic hundreds of miles away.

The whole context of abortion is different. Schools teach realistic sex education, birth control is free and available, the health-care system covers everybody, and there is far less poverty. There is no powerful anti-abortion movement writing the laws and watching over doctors' shoulders. No one is going to thrust a bloody fetus photo in a woman's face or make her doctor tell her she'll get cancer.

If the United States were to adopt western European abortion restrictions, it should, in fairness, adopt its generous abortion access, progressive sexual-health policies, and secular welfare state as well. Taken together, these policies have meant far fewer unintended pregnancies, and therefore fewer abortions. The European way might be a compromise worth discussing. But how many conservatives promoting its tighter laws on later abortion are interested in doing so?

What about *adoption*? Everyone loves adoption. It's "winwin." A baby gets a family, would-be parents get a child, a woman gets to move on with her life. Abortion opponents have long promoted adoption as an alternative to abortion. In July 2013, Texas state senator Eddie Lucio, a Democrat, even proposed a bill requiring women seeking abortion to complete a three-hour webinar on adoption first. "It is my hope that, when presented with more information on adoption resources and services available, more pregnancies can be carried to term," he said.[15] (Note the garbled grammar, in which "pregnancies" are to be given information and can then "be carried to term"— by whom would that be?) Women seeking abortion in Texas are already required to undergo counseling, and to receive state materials that include information on adoption.

Pro-choicers like adoption too. Hillary Clinton has said more than once that facilitating adoption would help make abortion "rare."[16] Similarly, in his 2009 speech at Notre Dame, President Obama proposed lowering the number of abortions by "mak[ing] adoption more available."[17] Contrary to opponents' claim that abortion clinics are just out to make money killing babies, some clinics partner with adoption services to help patients who decide against abortion or who arrive after the deadline for abortion has passed.

There's a difference, though, between facilitating adoption for pregnant women who want it and making adoption easier as a way to cut the abortion rate, as if adoption is automatically a better choice, and the reason a woman would choose abortion is that adoption procedures pose too many obstacles for her (or, as Senator Lucio seems to think, she is too slow-witted to appreciate its merits and needs to be forced to study up). This is hardly the case. If a woman doesn't want to work with an adoption agency, she can contact one of the many couples jostling for her attention on the Internet. The would-be adoptive parents are the ones easier adoption would benefit: tax breaks, streamlined procedures, less time for the birth mother to change her mind, fewer rights for the birth father. Leaving aside the merits of such proposals, how would making procedures easier for *adopters* increase the number of women who wanted to bear children to give to them?

Adoption has never been popular with pregnant women. Even in the 1950s and 1960s, at the height of what's been called the Baby Scoop Era, when unmarried white girls faced intense family and community disapproval and maternity homes worked in tandem with social workers to isolate and pressure them to relinquish their babies, 4 in 5 kept theirs. (Only 1.5 percent of black girls relinquished their babies—both because their families and communities were more accepting of nonmarital childbearing and because black babies were less desirable to would-be adoptive parents, most of whom were white, so no organized pressure was placed on these mothers.) Once abortion became legal, along with less harsh judgment on single mothers, the number of single women surrendering their babies for adoption plummeted. By 1989 fewer than 2 percent of unmarried whites and practically 0 percent of blacks gave up their infants.[18] That is where it remains today.

There are probably many reasons why pregnant women resist adoption, but surely one of them is the sheer emotional pain of carrying a pregnancy for nine whole months, giving birth, and then relinquishing the newborn, perhaps never to see it again. Our society encourages women to place a very high value on maternity as an essential part of female identity, both a high moral calling and the deepest source of satisfaction on earth. It's not easy to redefine motherhood as handing your baby over to a stranger. Why wouldn't a woman feel, *If I'm going to go through nine months of pregnancy plus childbirth, I'm not giving that baby up?* In the Turnaway study, which looked at women who wanted abortions but missed local or state deadlines—women, in other words, who had not reconciled themselves to the pregnancy although they were, in some cases, six months along—the large majority ended up keeping their children, no matter how discouraging their circumstances were. Only 9 percent chose adoption.[19]

So the first problem with adoption as an alternative to abortion is that very few pregnant women go for it. In a typical year only about 14,000 newborns are placed for adoption. It's hard to imagine a scenario in which adoption became so commonplace that it would make a real dent in the abortion rate. Even if the percentage of births that led to adoption returned to pre-*Roe* levels, which is most unlikely given the profound social changes of the last half century, and even if *all* of them were the result of abortions that didn't take place, we are still only talking about 200,000 fewer abortions. There would still be around 800,000 abortions each year.

And who would take those babies? According to 2002 figures, about 18.5 million American women aged eighteen to forty-four had ever "considered" adoption—even Hillary Clinton told *Time* magazine she had thought about it—and about 2.6 million had actually taken steps to adopt.[20] But "taken steps" is an advocacy term that might mean merely making a phone call or sending an e-mail asking for information. As of 2002, only 614,000 women under forty-five had ever completed an adoption.[21] Moreover, only a minority of these adoptions involved American newborns going to unrelated families: The rest were children adopted from foster care or placed with relatives, stepparents adopting their spouse's children, and international adoptions. Right now there are surely more people who want to adopt than there are American newborns available. But even assuming they could all pass a home study, are suitable parents, and would accept a child of any race or level of disability, if adoption rates for all races went to the level of pre-*Roe* adoption for whites, it would not take long to exhaust the backlog of would-be adopters. And then what?

Since pregnant women so decisively reject adoption, and since there does not seem to be an unending stream of baby-hungry singles or couples out there, what is the point of proposing it as a way of dealing with abortion? It's political. Pro-choicers get to demonstrate that they love children, care about families, and are not "pro-abortion." Anti-choicers get to look like women's friends, offering them a way out of forced child-raising, while making them feel guiltier about terminating a pregnancy. It's only nine months, how selfish not to make some nice couple happy. This privileging of the fetus and the would-be adopters over the pregnant woman is called finding common ground. We minimize the woman's experience: Juno cries in her hospital bed after giving birth, but pretty soon she's biking over to her boyfriend's house with her guitar. In a 2009 bloggingheads.tv debate, Beliefnet editor Steven Waldman proposed to a somewhat creeped-out Will Saletan that pregnant women considering adoption be encouraged with compensation for lost wages and education and health risk. He thought $1,000 should about cover it.[22]

This belittling of the birth mother is all over adoption literature. Yet birth mothers' organizations are vocal about the pain many women suffer, and the manipulative methods some adoption services use to take their children. One study found that twelve to twenty years after the adoption three-quarters of birth mothers still felt grief and loss.[23] Curiously, no one is suggesting this long-lasting suffering means women need to be counseled out of it, much less that adoption should be banned. Dr. Susan Wicklund, a Montana abortion provider, told me she had patients who had abortions after giving up a baby, because they couldn't bear the thought of going through adoption again. "There are also women who maybe gave away a child when they were teenagers, and now she's married with two or three kids, and gets pregnant. She doesn't want another baby, but her kids are old enough to know what's going on. What is she supposed to tell them: I'm having a baby and I'm giving it away?" Perhaps we see adoption as win-win because it's convenient. "We"—policymakers, politicians, people in the media— are far more likely to be or know adoptive parents than to be or know birth mothers, who tend to be younger and poorer, and who often, because of stigma, are silent about their experience.

Adoption purports to be another way of helping women, and sometimes it is. Not every woman with an unwanted pregnancy wants an abortion, and not every one of those wants to raise a child. But if we really put the pregnant woman first, there might not be more babies available for adoption, but more abortion and more support for single mothers.

But wait. Have we overlooked something? Perhaps there already *is* an abortion compromise, hiding in plain sight. Indeed, there is: the original 1973 *Roe* decision. *Roe* lets every woman follow her conscience and do what she believes is best in a contentious area about which people strongly disagree and maybe always will. It respects the right of doctors to care for their patients without being second-guessed and micromanaged by politicians and prosecutors who don't know one end of a speculum from the other. It is realistic about life—for example, that sex often occurs. It doesn't elevate fertilized eggs or embryos into children, but it protects the viable fetus. The pure prochoice position, after all, would be to set no limits on abortion: A woman's body belongs to her throughout all nine months of pregnancy, and the state has no business interfering. *Roe* kept pregnancy under the aegis of the state and gave the fetus, not yet a person in the eyes of the law, certain rights at the expense of the woman.

Opponents treat *Roe* as a ghastly improvisation with no precedent since ancient Greeks and Romans put unwanted babies out to be eaten by wolves, but it's actually in tune with very old understandings of fetal development as a gradual process. Aristotle divided it into three stages: vegetable, animal, rational. Both Augustine and Aquinas believed that ensoulment took place well after conception. Rabbinic authorities considered the embryo to be "water" until the fortieth day. In colonial America and in most states until after the Civil War, abortion was permissible under common law until quickening, well into the second trimester. Abortion was legal when the Declaration of Independence declared that life, liberty, and the pursuit of happiness were inalienable rights endowed by the Creator, and when the Constitution was written, too.[24] If the Founding Fathers had wanted to ban abortion, they could have, but they did not. Until prohibited by the Comstock laws in 1873, abortifacients with euphemistic names like Uterine Regulator and the Samaritan's Gift for Females were advertised in newspapers and readily available in shops.

Roe places the dividing line later than quickening, at twenty-four weeks, but the idea is the same: A fetus's claim on life begins when it has some kind of existence as an independent being. Under *Roe*, a woman's power over her fetus is not absolute: She can lose her right to terminate her pregnancy if she waits too long, even if (as is usually the case) she could not have done otherwise. And the fetus's power over the woman is not absolute either. Unless she agrees, it can't kill her or blind her or paralyze her, or prevent her from getting crucial medical treatment, even if protecting her means ending the pregnancy in the third trimester.

If only the Supreme Court had left *Roe* alone. Instead, they've let legislators whittle it away—upholding the Hyde Amendment's ban on Medicaid abortion (sorry, low-income women), upholding parental notification and consent (sorry, teenagers), upholding a ban on "partial-birth abortion" without an exception for the woman's health (sorry, patients; sorry, doctors), and so on. As of 2013, only one state, Oregon, has added no restrictions to the original *Roe* decision.[25] The vague "undue burden" standard in *Planned Parenthood v. Casey* virtually invites state and federal legislators to pass restrictive laws, culminating in the tidal wave that followed the 2010 elections. Maybe the court will strike the worst of them down, and maybe not. Who knows what an undue burden is in the mind of Justice Anthony Kennedy?

Meanwhile, if you live in Oklahoma or Louisiana, or Mississippi or Michigan, or dozens of other states, start saving your money. You—or your daughter, your sister, your friend, your wife—might need to end a pregnancy one day, and the nearest clinic could be hundreds of miles distant.

We had a compromise, and we compromised it away.

EIGHT

REFRAMING MOTHERHOOD

People think of pregnant women as weak and vulnerable, but when I was pregnant with my daughter I felt as if I could put my hand in fire and it would only glow. I never felt alone: There were two of us, right there. I didn't think of my child as an embryo or a fetus—medical words that belonged in a textbook or an abortion debate. I thought of her first as a funny little sea creature of indeterminate sex, and later, yes, as a baby, even though she was only a baby in my thoughts. Like many couples, her father and I even had a pet name for her—Winky. I wasn't a mother yet, but I was preparing to be one long before she was born. Waiting for the amnio tests to come back, I spent a lot of time wondering what genetic anomalies (as we are taught to call them because "defects" sounds so judgmental) I could live with—that is, the baby could live with. Blind, fine, deaf, fine—but what about blind and deaf? Down syndrome? Fragile X? Turner syndrome? As it turned out, I was lucky: The tests showed nothing abnormal, and I did not have to decide. I did not even know about the most disastrous possibilities: anencephaly or organs growing outside the body like some strangling vine. Today, if I'd gotten test results like that and lived in a state that bans abortion after twenty weeks I might have to travel to a distant state. I would be able to afford it, but what about the women who can't? What happens to them now? Do they have to carry their doomed Winky until it dies inside them or go through childbirth for the sake of "life"?

We think we value mothers in America, but we don't. We may revere motherhood, the hazy abstraction, the cream-of-wheat-with-a-halo ideal, but a mother is just a kind of woman, after all, and women are trouble and not so valuable. Low-income mothers drag down the country—why'd they have kids if they couldn't support them? Middle-class mothers are boring frumps. Elite ones are obsessed sanctimommies: Don't they know how annoying they are, with their yoga, their catfights over diapers and breastfeeding, their designer strollers that take up half the sidewalk so that people with important places to go have to take several extra steps?

Motherhood is interesting to the larger culture to the extent it can be turned into a sexual fantasy—the MILF—or as a way to set women against one another or to make judgments about them, or as a rationale to limit women's ability to do anything else, or as a way to manufacture that debilitating fog of guilt and anxiety that saps so many women's vitality and confidence. But in itself, taking care of children is not of great interest to the world at large. The work of mothers is so unvalued that a judge in Nebraska, previously a lawyer for Operation Rescue, can deny a sixteen-year-old in foster care the abortion she wants on the grounds that she isn't mature enough to choose abortion—but apparently she is mature enough to go through pregnancy and childbirth and raise a child.[1] Anybody can do that.

Aristotle thought a woman was a deformed man. Something had gone wrong in conception: Perhaps the south wind was blowing, instead of the more vigorous north. And although we may not believe in women's inferiority consciously anymore, the burden is on the woman if she wishes to participate fully in life, which has been organized around the ideal of the male worker without significant responsibilities at home. The burden is also on her if she has children, voluntarily or not—and if she doesn't have children, because what kind of woman doesn't have children? Also if she has sex, voluntarily or not. She is the one who has to use contraception, and use it right or pay the price for its failure. Are men held up to public scorn for fumbling the condom, or not withdrawing in time or, for that matter, assuming that his partner has taken care of birth control already? She is the stupid one, the careless one, the one who forgot for two minutes how easily her body could betray her. It is as if a woman lugs her reproductive system around with her like a fur coat in July. She can't be expected to move about freely like a normal person in that hot, bulky garment. But she could take it off, couldn't she, if she really wanted to?

Under these conditions, the ability to end a pregnancy is deeper than a right: It is basic self-preservation. Maybe there could be a society in which women were legally compelled to bear every child they conceived and yet did not find themselves thereby hampered, impoverished, trapped, chained to a hated partner, consigned to a lesser life. But that society would look nothing like the one abortion opponents want to bring about, which is basically a more retrograde version of our own, with women tied for decades to raising children as dependent wives or struggling single mothers. Could there be a society in which having a baby in high school made no difference to a girl's bright future? In which motherhood was such a light role there was no reason not to go along with a random pregnancy, because, say, children were raised communally, as in the original Israeli kibbutzim, and fear of being legally connected to the wrong man was not a factor because the woman had complete control over whether he stayed in her life and the child's life? In which pregnancy outside marriage was regarded so benignly, and motherhood was so richly rewarded—with scholarships, housing, job opportunities, government subsidies, social prestige and more—that a woman had nothing to lose and much to gain by bearing an accidental baby? It's all starting to sound like some sort of socialist matriarchy, which isn't at all what abortion opponents have in mind.

To them, motherhood is more about hatching a baby, less about what comes after. *When the little one comes, you'll love it and everything will work out. Meanwhile, here are some second-hand baby clothes.* The trouble with this view is not just that a woman can't return to the crisis pregnancy center and get help with groceries for her five-year-old or go back to medical school when her baby starts kindergarten. It's that it presents having a child as no big deal. Any woman can do it, even a twelve-year-old, and either just get on with her life or give the baby up. Once she gives birth, her job is practically done.

This cavalier attitude about childbearing and childrearing is an exaggerated version of the way motherhood is valued (or undervalued) by society generally. The whole world runs on women's unpaid or grossly underpaid labor, and it always has. When that work is an extension of female domestic roles—caring for children or the elderly, preparing food, cleaning houses—it is ill paid, insecure, low skilled, and low status. But when it is done within the family, it is so deeply mystified and romanticized, so wrapped in religion, morality, tradition, and ideas about what's natural that it looks like something else—a free gift of love, a personal preference, a private arrangement that stands outside the marketplace and cannot be judged by outsiders. And yet, if women rejected labor within the family, society would have to pay enormous sums to replace it. At least eldercare is generally recognized to be a personal sacrifice; some states will even pay relatives a small sum through Medicaid to keep an elderly person out of a nursing home.[2] The social value of motherhood is much more hidden. In fact, it is so obscured that in 2009 Sen. Jon Kyl (R-AZ) tried to strike pregnancy and childbirth from the list of conditions employers had to include in their health plans under the Affordable Care Act. "I don't need maternity care," Kyl argued. "I think your mom probably did," Sen. Debbie Stabenow (D-MI) tartly replied. But Kyl continued: "So requiring that on my insurance policy is something that I don't need and will make the policy more expensive."[3]

The Harvard economist Greg Mankiw also objects to the community rating of maternity care. "The goal is to spread the risk of childbirth among the larger community," he wrote on his blog. "But having children is more a choice than a random act of nature. People who drive a new Porsche pay more for car insurance than those who drive an old Chevy. We consider that fair because which car you drive is a choice. Why isn't having children viewed in the same way?"[4]

Leaving aside the fact that not all childbearing is so voluntary, is a baby like a luxury car? The social value of Porsches is very low. If nobody bought them (or yachts, or diamond-encrusted

Rolexes, or Jackson Pollocks), the world would go on much the same. But children are immensely important to everyone, including people who don't have any or want any. They have value both as the children they are, giving meaning and purpose and joy not just to their parents but grandparents, aunts, uncles, family friends (to say nothing of providing employment for millions of teachers, caregivers, pediatricians, nurses, toymakers, and so on), and as the adults they become. They are the future, after all: If women stopped having babies, the human race would end and Mankiw would have no students in his Econ 101 class. And if women stopped raising babies to adulthood, usually quite competently despite the cost to themselves and without anything remotely like enough support from the community whose costs Mankiw is so worried about, who would do that work?

Mankiw trivializes motherhood as a socially useless individual choice. Abortion opponents, who glorify motherhood in the abstract, trivialize it more subtly, by making it a question of no choice, of one-size-fits-all biological fate. They deny its physical risks, its social and economic costs, and its enormous personal consequences. They disregard the individual circumstances and inner life of the pregnant woman. They equate the value of a grown woman with that of a zygote. They entwine childbearing with the very different issues of chastity and sexual continence and use the threat of pregnancy to enforce their own repressive sexual mores. But whether a baby is a free personal choice or what you get for being a slut or God's beautiful gift to rape victims, the practical result is the same: Whatever difficulties motherhood entails are the problem of individual mothers.

What if we respected pregnancy and childbirth as major

physical, psychological, and economic events—as work? There's a reason they call childbirth labor. Making a healthy baby takes effort: It requires foresight and self-denial and courage. It's expensive and demanding and tiring. You have to learn new things, change many habits, possibly deal with complicated medical situations, make difficult decisions, and undergo stressful ordeals. I had a wisdom tooth pulled without Novocaine while I was pregnant—it hurt a lot and seemed to go on forever. The kindness of the very young dental assistant, holding back my hair as I spat blood into a bowl, will stay with me for the rest of my life. Pregnant women do such things, and much harder things, all the time. For example, they give birth, which is somewhere on the scale between painful and excruciating. Or they have a cesarean, as I did, which is major surgery. None of this is without risk of death or damage or trauma, including psychological trauma. To force girls and women to undergo all this against their will is to annihilate their humanity. When they undertake it by choice, we should all be grateful. That there is no way to equalize men's contribution to reproduction is all the more reason to honor women for volunteering to go through it on their behalf. "The world must be peopled," Benedick says in *Much Ado About Nothing*. But the only time we recognize the social value of childbearing is when we are blaming (middle-class white) women for not doing enough of it.

To a far greater degree than most other Western nations, we have decided that women should individually bear most of the consequences of becoming a parent. The sexual puritanism of conservative Christianity meets the conservative libertarianism of Greg Mankiw: Why should I pay for your birth control, or your abortion—or your baby? Get a husband! The results are all around us: in the highest rates by far of teen pregnancy and teen childbearing in the West, struggling single mothers, downwardly mobile families, child poverty. That this is degrading to women is obvious. But it is also degrading to motherhood. It turns what should be a source of strength and power and recognition into something that renders women weak and dependent, blocks them from full participation in life, undermines their economic standing, and leaves too many poor in old age, if not before. Perhaps that is the point. When you consider the way restrictions on abortion go hand in hand with cutbacks in social programs and stymied gender equality it is hard not to suspect that the aim is to put women and children back under male control by making it impossible for them to survive outside it.

How much do Americans really value mothering, the actual work, and mothers, the actual female humans? Not much. The United States is the most expensive country in the world in which to have a baby: A couple can expect to pay thousands in medical bills for pregnancy and delivery. The cost of delivery has tripled since 1996; the average total price charged for pregnancy and newborn care is now $30,000 for a vaginal delivery and $50,000 for a C-section.[5] Despite laws against pregnancy discrimination, more than 3,541 pregnancy discrimination charges were filed in 2013.[6] Pregnant women are routinely denied simple temporary job modifications, like not having to do heavy lifting or climb high ladders and being allowed to sit down occasionally and take more bathroom breaks.[7] Employers who are willing to accommodate disabled workers draw the line at pregnant ones. Guadalupe Hernandez, a line cook at a Mexican fast-food restaurant in Washington, DC, told the National Women's Law Center:

My boss said that from now on I'd need to get his permission whenever I wanted to use the bathroom and also tell all my coworkers. So several times a day I'd have to track him down and then let my coworkers know. I felt so humiliated. My boss sometimes said that I couldn't go to the bathroom. All of my coworkers were allowed to go to the bathroom as often as they wanted without ever asking for permission. I never had to ask permission to go to the bathroom before I got pregnant either, so I felt that I was being singled out and punished just because I was pregnant.

Many humiliations and petty tyrannies later, Hernandez was fired:

This incident devastated me. Now I wouldn't be able to bring any money into the family. For the first time in my life, I had to ask for government assistance (food stamps and unemployment benefits). I tried to look for other work, but every time I went to a potential employer, they looked at my belly and said "no." My husband, who was not working at the time, my older child, and my baby paid the price.[8]

Hernandez has filed a charge with the Equal Employment Opportunity Commission, claiming that she was fired because of her pregnancy, which is illegal. She is far from alone: Thousands of pregnant women are pushed out of jobs that they are perfectly capable of performing.[9]

Should a woman manage to hold on to her job till delivery, the law certainly won't help her keep it afterward. Unlike every other high-income country in the Organization for Economic Cooperation and Development, the United States does not offer mothers, much less fathers, a few months of paid leave.[10] The government will not provide day care so she can go back to work—she and her partner must find and pay for that themselves. On average, child care consumes some 49.5 percent of a low-income household's monthly expenses.[11]

Even the income tax code is stacked against her: Because the incomes of two married people are treated like a single income, and a mother typically earns less than her spouse, her income, stacked on top of his, may push the couple into a higher bracket, even if it is not much money. If you add up all the costs of working after having a baby (child care, transportation, clothing, taxes), it may indeed "not make sense" for her to stay on the job in the short term, although in the long term she may be hurting herself by staying home. (Actually, the costs of child care should be thought of as coming out of both parents' pay: Raising children is just as much his responsibility as hers. But in almost all coverage of the issue, it's the woman's paycheck that is balanced against the child-care bill, and that is how many couples tend to perceive it.)

It gets worse. As the noted sociologist Arlie Hochschild showed in *The Second Shift*, most married working mothers do the bulk of cleaning, cooking, household management, and child care, even when they earn the larger income—it's exhausting.[12] But if a wife gives up work and stays home, she becomes dependent on her husband for economic survival—what if he dies, gets sick, loses his job, divorces her, becomes an addict or alcoholic or an abuser? What if she wants to get a divorce herself? (Curiously, that possibility rarely comes up in discussions of the pros and cons of paid employment.) Even if she takes just a few years out of the workforce while her child is small, which might sound ideal in the abstract, she will likely find she can't get back in at anything like her former pay and level of responsibility. Of those women who return to the workforce but to a different job, almost 44 percent report that they worked fewer hours than before their first childbirth, not necessarily by choice.[13] Other studies have found that for every two years a woman is out of the workforce, her earnings fall by 10 percent.[14] And yet other studies find that the jobs mothers get when they do reenter the workforce pay on average 16 percent less.[15] The longer she stays home, the harder it will be for her to find a job when she decides she wants one. Not many employers will pick a fifty-year-old who's been out of work for fifteen or twenty years over a childless thirty-year-old with shiny new skills and boundless energy. It would feel, as one Salon.com commenter put it, "like hiring my grandmother."[16]

These conditions are always said to be about to change. When my daughter was a baby, the solution was going to be day care in the workplace: Employers wouldn't want to lose those splendid women they had trained and promoted and invested in. Then it was going to be flex time, and working from home and going part-time, which either was or was not the so-called mommy track, on which mothers would give up promotion in return for a shorter workweek. Some even argued that mothers quitting their jobs was a feminist power play—it would force employers to alter the workplace to lure them back. The media encouraged women to believe they could get back into the game whenever they wanted. It was as if there would be no new younger, cheaper, less encumbered people pouring into the pipeline, and as if sexism itself were dead.

Low-income women fare even worse. Thanks to welfare reform, fifteen states deprive the poorest women, the ones on welfare, of even a paltry increase in benefits if they have a baby conceived on the dole. These "family caps" have not achieved their goal of discouraging childbearing among the poor. They may even have increased it, because deep poverty increases teen pregnancy. Why is the government pursuing policies that further impoverish poor women and their children? It's for the same reason our society has refused to adjust to working mothers, even to the extent of longer school days and afterschool programs, let alone publicly funded high-quality child care. Mothers are supposed to be supported by husbands, and not bother employers or taxpayers with their whiny demands for equality and inclusion. We have engineered a society in which the timing of pregnancy can determine the rest of a woman's life. But when women respond logically to these constraints by limiting their childbearing and by using abortion to plan their pregnancies for when they will do the least damage, they are scorned as—how did Teddy Roosevelt put it?—vicious, cold, shallow-hearted, and self-indulgent.

At least married mothers get a pat on the head for upholding family values. As the Right tells it (and not just the Right), single mothers are the human pathogens of contemporary America. While there is some tolerance now for educated, adult, and prosperous "single mothers by choice," low-income single mothers, especially if they're women of color, are blamed for social ills from child abuse and crime to poor grades, low SAT scores, drug addiction, and poverty itself. (There was apparently no poverty back when most children were born within marriage.) And since women have babies outside of marriage willfully and intentionally and all by themselves, God forbid they should get a bit of help from the government: Then they become welfare queens and food-stamp fraudsters who eat up everyone else's taxes and have more babies to get more benefits. These babies grow up into enormous teenagers: criminals and layabouts if male, the next generation of welfare mothers if female. So heedless are these women in their procreation, so rapacious in their demands for sustenance, they seem hardly human at all: In the House debate over welfare reform in 1995, John L. Mica (R-FL) compared them to alligators and Barbara Cubin (R-WY) compared them to wolves.[17] The racial subtext to welfare reform hardly needed to be openly stated, but it was, repeatedly. Although most welfare recipients were white, most of the ones interviewed by the media in the run-up to reform were black or Latina; and though most recipients had no more children than the national average, coverage focused on the subset of mothers who had many, reinforcing the stereotype of women of color as promiscuous and irresponsible. The climax, perhaps, was a *New Republic* cover, bannered "Day of Reckoning" and "Sign the Welfare Bill Now" and illustrated with a photo of a young black woman smoking a cigarette and looking away from the baby she is bottle-feeding. (Fact: White women are almost twice as likely as black women to smoke during pregnancy.)[18]

Black or white, these powerless women have so much power, conservative British pundits say they caused the fiery London riots of 2011, although no one actually knows how many of the young people involved were raised by single mothers.[19] And in 2012, Republican presidential candidate Mitt Romney blamed them for America's staggering rates of gun violence, despite most guns being owned and used by adult men. This was his answer in the second presidential debate to a question about restricting assault weapons (don't be fooled by his gender-neutral language; it's only women who "have babies"):

> But let me mention another thing. And that is parents. We
> need moms and dads, helping to raise kids. Wherever possible
> the—the benefit of having two parents in the home, and that's
> not always possible. A lot of great single moms, single dads.
> But gosh to tell our kids that before they have babies, they
> ought to think about getting married to someone, that's a
> great idea.[20]

In addition to all their other faults, apparently single mothers are so stupid it simply never occurred to them to marry one of the many worthy suitors who, in this conservative fantasy, are vying for their hand. Getting pregnant, then birthing and raising children by themselves, is their own conscious choice. Might the shaming of female sexuality and the demonization of abortion promulgated by many Christian churches in low-income communities (and not only there) have something to do with women having kids too soon and too alone?

That a single mother is unfit by virtue of being unmarried is never far from the surface. She's unfit not just because she doesn't have a husband now to bring stability and order into the home, but because she didn't nail one down in the beginning, when she had the sex that produced the future criminals. A divorced mother gets credit for trying; a widowed mother is stalwart and heroic. These women also are raising children alone, with all the stresses and financial problems and potentially problematic boyfriends. The difference is they had their kids within marriage. The original intention is what matters, not the actual circumstances of child-raising. Of course, many single mothers had their babies expecting that marriage would follow eventually, but that just shows how foolish they were. Why should a man buy a cow—and a calf—when he's already drunk all the milk he wanted?

There is one mode of discourse, though, in which unmarried mothers are seen quite differently, and that is the anti-abortion one. If that same pregnant girl or woman decides the rigors of single motherhood are indeed too great and seeks an abortion, the whole picture changes. Now anti-choicers—including many of the same politicians who attack women who have kids out of wedlock as greedy idlers and who fund abstinence classes where girls are warned that losing their virginity will soil them for marriage and ruin their lives—eagerly present single motherhood as just a small bump in the Yellow Brick Road to happiness. Rightly seen, it's a challenge, a joy. The unwed pregnant woman who chooses to have her baby is not a moocher or a one-woman crime scene or a threat to America's greatness, she's doing the right thing, atoning for her "mistake." Of course, the best way to atone would be to let the baby be adopted by a Christian married couple. Many crisis pregnancy centers pressure young women to give up their babies, and many states force clinics to bring up adoption to women seeking abortion. "A single mother who keeps her baby is quite often denying that baby the father that God wants for that baby, and every baby, to have," writes the evangelical leader Rev. Richard D. Land, who not-so-subtly references the biblical story of King Solomon and the baby fought over by "two harlots."[21]

After birth, the frame shifts back to the evils of single motherhood and, for Republicans, the objective becomes cutting every single program that would help low-income babies grow up healthy. But until then, the woman is a hero. No matter how poor or troubled or ill equipped for parenthood she is, that baby is a wonderful gift from God—redemption itself.

Meanwhile, you might ask, where is Dad? In the first scenario, the one in which women "choose" to have kids without marriage, Dad is crucial. The absence of a father, not just his income and love and the added pair of hands but the special manly qualities he brings to parenting, dooms child and country. During the 1992 presidential campaign, Dan Quayle specifically attacked the beloved sitcom character Murphy Brown for "ignoring the importance of fathers by birthing a child alone."[22] But imagine if Murphy had decided to terminate the pregnancy. Then she would have found herself whisked into the anti-abortion frame, in which the man is more or less irrelevant, except to Reverend Land. Whatever they may say about the evils of single mothers and welfare and licentious sex when they are wearing their conservative anti-tax, Christian-right, family-values hats, when they are talking about abortion, abortion opponents are pro-Mom. They may pressure teenage girls to give up their babies for adoption, but they don't usually say an adult woman can't raise a child right on her own. They will say, all she needs is a little bit of help and she'll be fine.

Feminists for Life puts out a cheery handbook called "Raising Kids on a Shoestring." It's full of suggestions for stretching a dollar: Use coupons wisely, grow herbs on your windowsill, get information at the library, invest in cloth diapers, buy clothes at thrift stores, apply for food stamps. With a cover featuring a pretty young white woman in superhero goggles and cape, the message is that you can do this and have fun, too. It's a little hard to imagine to whom exactly the booklet's suggestions will come as news (pick up toys cheaply at yard sales? Who knew that was even possible!), but they reinforce the idea that the difficulties of single motherhood have been exaggerated. Advice about caring for a special-needs child and the number of the suicide hotline fit seamlessly into advice about weather-caulking your windows and buying unprocessed food. Except for the silence about sex and contraception, the can-do spirit is not so different from that of *Hip Mama* magazine. Abortion just doesn't come up. Instead difficulties are soft-pedaled: "Countless parents like me are raising kids on a shoe-string," says the superhero mom, "but we don't do it alone. Our real strength is in knowing how to get support."[23]

Sometimes, when she's one of their own, conservatives give the single-mom bashing a rest. After all, for them, single moth-erhood is the comparatively moral choice as long as the mother has a toe in the social-conservative Christian camp and does not present herself openly as a tramp and proud of it. Interest-ingly, in her book *Not Afraid of Life: My Journey So Far*, Bristol Palin describes her first sexual encounter with Levi Johnston in what sounded to some feminist commentators like date rape.[24] (She wrote that Levi "stole" her virginity on a camping trip while she was drunk on wine coolers.) In interviews, she re-jected that interpretation, presenting herself as having made "a foolish decision."[25] Fifty years ago, a woman like Bristol might have had a clandestine abortion or been quietly sent off to a maternity home to have her baby and give it up for adoption, or been pushed into a shotgun marriage. Nowadays, because abortion is legal, she gets credit for stepping up to the plate. When her pregnancy became known during the campaign, there was no pressure from the Christian right—or, it would seem, her parents—for her to marry Johnston, and no attack on Sarah Palin for being a bad mother and producing this way-ward daughter. At least Bristol wasn't one of those girls who kill their babies! (As for fatherhood, it would be hard to argue that Levi was going to model responsibility and authority and de-voted breadwinning for his son.) Bristol had her baby, made a lot of money lecturing teens on abstinence, and told *Good Morning America*, "I hope that other women with jerk boyfriends can read the book and be like, 'You know what? I don't have to be with this guy.'"

GIVING MOTHERS THEIR DUE

What would the United States be like if we really valued motherhood? Not in a sentimental, flattering sort of way, as when we say motherhood is the most important, hardest job in the world. That's obviously false. Plenty of work is harder—try mining coal or working in a sweatshop. And some is more important. Would the sum of human happiness be greater if Emily Dickinson had produced babies instead of poems? Those would have had to be some phenomenal children. Nobody says being a father, or a nanny, is the most important, hardest job in the world, after all. Only mothers get this particular pat on the head, which simultaneously acknowledges women do most of the work of "parenting" and belittles them for doing it.

If we really valued motherhood, we would make sure every young person had excellent sex education, and every girl and woman had access to birth control and abortion. At present around half of all pregnancies are accidental. "Unplanned" doesn't necessarily mean unwanted, but given how much hangs on childbearing, we should help women have kids because they've thought it through and are ready, not just because they happened to conceive at some arbitrary moment. Few contemporary Americans would say a woman should marry a man just because she slept with him, so why should she have a baby just because she slept with him? That's a rather whimsical way to make such a big life-changing decision with such a major effect on so many people.

We would make sure no woman is sidelined from work or public life because she has a baby, or for that matter several babies. We are a rich country, and motherhood is socially valuable work. It's not the only kind that women can do, of course; I'm not saying women should be made to feel they must have children to be happy or useful or truly female. But having kids is, in some sense, a service to the future of the community, and it should not mean poverty or a life of struggle to escape it, or the end of a woman's education or professional training, or having to stay in a bad relationship, or work that is less challenging and rewarding than she would otherwise be doing.

We would make child-raising the equal day-to-day responsibility of both parents, beginning with paid parental leave for both mothers and fathers, and moving on to flexible hours at work, with day care provided by employers and by government. Having children should not mean that women, as a class, have less social and economic and political power than men, but as long as women do the bulk of the work in the home, and make the bulk of the sacrifices on behalf of the family, they will be the second sex in the world at large—and as long as the expectation is that women will step aside at work and in public life when they have kids, the more rational it looks not to advance them too far beforehand or let them back in when they come knocking at the door.

We would see all women and all children as valuable, not just those who are white and fortunate. Families should not have to live in a slum, or a single room in a homeless shelter. They should have good health care, good food, good schools, safe neighborhoods—all the things that let human beings flourish. By some measures, the United States is one of the most unequal countries in the world. On child poverty, it ranks between Bulgaria and Romania—not a good place to be.[26] Many of the social issues we tend to see as having to do with sexual morality—teen pregnancy, unwanted pregnancy, unintended single motherhood, high rates of abortion—are strongly related to poverty and what comes with it: ramshackle health care, poor education, chronic unemployment, domestic violence, communities abandoned by the larger society, and a general feeling of hopelessness. Instead of seeing a low-income mother as a burden on society to whom government grudgingly doles out dribs and drabs of "services" that are never enough to lift her out of poverty or change her children's prospects, we need to flip the equation: What does this woman, and the millions like her, require to raise her children to be decent, healthy, well-educated, productive, happy adults—and to be one herself?

Finally, as supporters of reproductive rights, we would recognize that sex education, birth control, and abortion are not enough. It's not enough to say you have the right to avoid a harsh life by not having a child. That's only an inspiring message for a woman who thinks that if she waits a bit, her life will improve: She'll have a degree, a job, a partner, a future. But what if she has good reason to believe that conditions are not going to improve for her? What if she looks around her and sees that the choice is being a woman with children and a minimum-wage job and a woman with no children and a minimum-wage job? What if having a baby feels like a positive step, and indeed *is* a positive step? Not all pregnant teens and women in very discouraging circumstances are doing something they'll regret. For some it means taking charge of their life, and in a good way.

If the pro-choice movement's only focus is on helping women not have unwanted children, instead of also on making a fairer, more just society, then reproductive rights can feel like reproductive deprivation, as if motherhood is reserved for the prosperous. In the debate over welfare reform, a central paradox was that poor mothers were expected to work, no matter how ill paid and grueling and dead-end their jobs, while middle-class mothers were being urged to abandon promising careers to stay home. The best day care money could buy risked damaging Zach and Emily's cognitive and social development; but Keisha and Luis were better off watching TV all day with the lady down the hall than being cared for by their own mother. The missing piece—the right to mother, as well as the right not to mother—is one reason why the pro-choice movement looks so white and so middle-class, even though women of color and poor women have far more abortions per capita and less ability to travel to distant clinics as nearer ones are forced to close.[27]

TOWARD A STRONGER PRO-CHOICE MOVEMENT

For far too long the pro-choice movement was either complacent or defensive. It relied on brilliant lawyers and sympathetic judges, while abortion opponents built a grassroots movement and took over political offices from zoning boards and school boards to the legislature itself. It sold itself too cheaply to the Democratic Party, even when the Democrats were seeking out anti-abortion and anti-feminist candidates to run in conservative districts. It let its mostly white leadership age in place, pursuing their tired Beltway-focused strategies, and then wondered why young women and working-class women and women of color didn't connect with its organizations. There are good reasons for each of those approaches—abortion rights are a matter of law, for example, so obviously winning in legislatures and courts is important—but the result was a movement that was not very creative, and that didn't give ordinary people much to do beyond signing e-mail petitions and making donations.

If I wanted to get involved with reproductive rights in the small Connecticut town where I live part of the year, I would have no idea where to begin: whom to contact, what the needs and local concerns are. Do patients need a ride to the clinic or help paying for care or a place to stay overnight? Do clinics need escorts? And where are those clinics, anyway? When I checked it in the spring of 2014, the Web site of the NARAL state affiliate had not been updated since before the 2012 election. My e-mails to the two top officials listed went unanswered, although I did get an invitation to a statewide fundraising brunch. On the other hand, if I wanted to work *against* abortion rights, I'd head straight to St. Mary's Catholic Church, outside which stands a tombstone-like block of granite inscribed LIFE BEGINS AT CONCEPTION PRAY FOR THE UNBORN, or drop in at the Birthright storefront next to the nail salon. A few years ago a crisis pregnancy center even put up an eye-catching billboard on the road into town. I've never seen a billboard in the area with contact information for birth control or abortion.

Now, maybe Connecticut is all set: It's a blue state with no major laws limiting access, and only 5 percent of women live in a county without abortion services.[28] But that's no reason to rest on one's laurels. Couldn't its pro-choice energies be mobilized against the onslaught of anti-abortion legislation coming down in Congress, to say nothing of less fortunate states? In fact, if abortion rights are safe in Hartford, that's all the more reason for local pro-choicers to turn their attention to racism, poverty, violence, sexuality, and other issues that shape women's reproductive lives and choices, in Connecticut as elsewhere.

For far too long, the pro-choice movement has tailored its arguments, its goals, and its vision to avert immediate losses to its much more aggressive opponents. In his illuminating and provocative *Bearing Right: How Conservatives Won the Abortion Wars*, Will Saletan describes how the pro-choice movement conceded on the issue of public funding in the 1970s—with deep regret, but it did it—and won libertarian voters at the expense of poor women and the marginalization of abortion from the rest of health care.[29] Pro-choice organizations avoid talking directly about sex and sexual freedom, making narrow and expedient points against each new proposed restriction: Parental notification and consent laws are wrong because some families are violent and dysfunctional, twenty-week bans are wrong because of fetuses with extreme deformities; women need birth-control coverage in the Affordable Care Act because the Pill has other medical uses. In the early 1990s there were calls to allow the importation of mifepristone, then known as RU-486 and strictly banned from our shores, in order to use it in breast-cancer research. The refusal of abortion opponents to permit even small amounts into the country as a possible treatment for a deadly disease showed yet again their preference for embryos over women, but there was something a bit convenient in the alacrity with which pro-choicers seized on RU-486's curative potential: *Whew, never mind abortion, let's talk about breast cancer.*

Finally, that's beginning to change, and not a moment too

soon. New leaders are coming to the fore. Young pro-choicers are starting to take back the momentum that has belonged to opponents for decades. In 2013, forty-three-year-old Ilyse Hogue, who has broad experience in social-change work and online organizing, became the new head of NARAL. The explosion of young-feminist online media has raised awareness of the threat to reproductive rights and made it much easier for young women to find out how to connect with the pro-choice movement and one another. Young women are pouring into the established organizations, starting and staffing abortion funds, volunteering as clinic escorts, training as "abortion doulas" to give comfort and support to patients. There's a new outspokenness and an eagerness to challenge abortion stigma: Women are posting their abortion stories on the 1 in 3 Campaign Web site and elsewhere in the blogosphere. Jennifer Baumgardner's stereotype-blasting documentary, *I Had an Abortion*, has been shown all over the country. Angie Jackson, a young Florida activist who blogs as Angie the Anti-Theist, even live-tweeted her early medication abortion "to demystify abortions for other women." As I finish writing this chapter, Emily Letts, a twenty-five-year old counselor at the Cherry Hill Woman's Center in New Jersey, is making headlines with a video of her own procedure that has gone viral online. She looks calm and not in pain. The place is clean and bright. The procedure takes about three minutes. How many women didn't know that's what having an abortion was like?

Along with this new activism comes a broader vision of reproductive rights: reproductive justice. Pioneered in the early 1990s by the black feminist organization SisterSong, the concept of reproductive justice places the right to birth control and abortion within a women's human rights and social justice

framework. What do women need to mother as well as to decide when and if to have a child? How does the state interfere
with those rights, and to what ends? Answering those questions
brings in a host of issues—from racism and poverty and sexual
identity to the rights of immigrants and prisoners and women
workers—and a need to understand how they affect different
women differently. Reproductive justice connects the right to
no-copay contraception in your health insurance and the right
of prisoners to give birth unshackled and the targeting of black
and Latina mothers by the foster-care system. It connects the
right to choose abortion with the right to choose how to give
birth. Reproductive-justice organizing can claim important
victories. It lay behind the defeat of the Albuquerque twenty-
week abortion ban mentioned earlier, with women of color
leading a coalition of community groups. It shapes the work of
National Advocates for Pregnant Women, which fights the criminalization of pregnant women for conduct that supposedly
harms the fetus, whether it's drug use or attempted suicide or
refusing a cesarean.

There's pushback on the legislative front as well. In 2013,
California passed the nation's only law that year to expand
abortion access: Nurses and some other health professionals
(midwives, nurse practitioners, and physician assistants) are
now permitted to perform first-trimester nonsurgical abortions.[30] (This is what can happen when a state is controlled by
Democrats.) By early 2014, fifty-one pieces of pro-choice legislation had been introduced in fourteen states, the most since
the early 1990s.[31] Most of these measures will fail, but the as-
sertiveness they signal is important for its own sake. They provide a way to educate and mobilize and command attention, to
put legislators on notice and build support for the future. It's

about time: If pro-choicers don't turn the tide soon, it will be too late.

For those who are troubled by America's high abortion rate, the good news is that we already know what will lower it: more feminism. More justice. More equality. More freedom. More respect. Women should have what they need both to avoid unwanted pregnancy and childbirth and to have wanted children. For motherhood to truly be part of human flourishing, it has to be voluntary, and raising children—by both parents—has to be supported by society as necessary human work. Motherhood should add to a woman's ability to lead a full life, not leave her on the sidelines, wondering how she got there.

For this to happen, the old paradigms have to go: pregnancy as the punishment for sex, and women as endurers of fate or God's will, biologically destined to a lesser life and needing a man to survive. But even in feminist heaven, there will be abortion, as there is in even the most prosperous, enlightened countries in the world. Because life will always be complicated, there is no perfect contraception, and there are no perfect people, either. We need to be able to say that is all right.

AFTERWORD
TO THE 2015 EDITION

Pro was published just before the 2014 elections, and I wish I could report that to the vast surprise of pundits and pollsters, candidates dedicated to reproductive rights swept the land. That did not happen: Republicans took the Senate, raised their majority in the House to the biggest since the Second World War[1] and increased their hold on state governments. Pro-choicers took comfort where they could: Colorado voters rejected a personhood amendment, even as they elected to the Senate a congressman who had supported a federal version of the amendment and now claimed he hadn't understood what it meant; North Dakotans rejected a personhood amendment, even as they kept the state politicians who had almost pushed it into law. It would seem that the sleeping giant of pro-choice voters has yet to awaken, to say nothing of the people I call the muddled middle, who disapprove of abortion but don't want to see it criminalized.

On the one hand, the *Roe v. Wade* decision legalizing abortion is more popular than ever: 7 out of 10 Americans support it, according to a *Wall Street Journal*/NBC News poll in 2013. On the other, legislators elected by those same Americans (or, what amounts to the same Americans, because so many don't vote at all), are committed to passing laws that flagrantly violate *Roe* and are intended to push the Supreme Court to revisit *Roe* and overturn it. Result? More restrictions, more closed clinics, more laws and regulations that are just bizarre: In Alabama, a fetus can now have its own lawyer. And it's not just happening in red states, either. According to the Guttmacher Institute, 57 percent of women now live in states that are hostile to abortion rights. That percentage is sure to grow.

Elections may give the impression that abortion opponents have captured the majority, but are they really swimming in the mainstream? In my column in *The Nation*, I invited victorious abortion opponents to answer some questions about their views. The few dozen answers I got were a tiny sample, but they were still fascinating and I am grateful to my respondents for sharing their thoughts with me. Put bluntly, my respondents had some rather unusual ideas. For example, they did not see sex as an ongoing, normal part of life, even within marriage. They saw each act of sex as a separate decision, entailing a kind of contract to see a pregnancy through to birth. Even one of the few respondents who favored birth control thought celibacy was the way to go when you didn't want to have a baby: "This policy is actually GREAT for women, and spares them the whole 'sitting on the bathroom floor moment wondering what they are going to do.'" They saw no danger to women in criminalizing abortion: If they couldn't get legal abortions, women would simply keep the pregnancy—look how few abortions per capita there are in Mississippi, where there's only one clinic, or in Ireland, where abortion is illegal. (Irish women go abroad for abortion, of course—and do we really want the rest of the United States to emulate Mississippi, which comes in at the bottom on just about every indicator of women's status?) They refused to accept that having a baby could ever make a woman's life impossibly difficult, or harm her health, or dash her hopes and dreams. Somehow it would all work out. Poverty was a problem, sure, but the solution was marriage or charity or, for the more liberal among them, a very modest increase in government services. No one responded to my question about why the Republican Party, home of the anti-abortion movement, was busy cutting every thread of the safety net for women and children. As for that grand political compromise pundits keep hoping for, good luck: One person did mention concern for poverty when I asked if they felt there were any good arguments on the pro-choice side but she was the only person who thought pro-choicers had anything to offer.

I don't think my respondents represent what most Americans think by a long shot. But because of the political power and determination of the pro-life movement, and its strong connection with the Republican Party, the powerful Catholic Church, and some evangelical/fundamentalist denominations, their views have outsize weight in the political discourse on everything related to sex. When I debated abortion rights on the radio with Teresa Collett, a law professor at the University of St. Thomas, she announced that the reason women have abortions is that people lack "self-control." That is, they have too much sex. When I pointed out that married people are *supposed* to have sex with each other, she claimed married women didn't have abortions (three women immediately called the station to say they had had abortions as wives). That view of sex sounds stuffy and out of touch and even a bit weird when put so baldly, but it helps explain not just why abortion is so vulnerable but why abstinence-only sex education still flourishes despite its proven lack of efficacy, and why public funding for birth control—birth control!—is such a heavy lift.

You would think, after all, that abortion opponents would be keen on birth control. It's just common sense, backed up by study after study, that contraception prevents accidental pregnancy and thus prevents abortions. In her new book *Generation Unbound: Drifting into Sex and Parenthood Without Marriage*, Isabel Sawhill vividly documents the relation between accidental pregnancy, too-early parenthood, and poverty. She calls for wide dissemination of long-acting reversible contraception like the IUD and implants, which are much more effective than the Pill or condoms. Indeed, in Colorado, a privately funded program begun in 2009 provided 30,000 low-income girls and women with IUDs and implants, and the teen birthrate dropped by an astonishing 40 percent. The abortion rate dropped by 34 percent.[2] You'd think anti-choicers would rejoice. But no, as I write, the state legislature is debating whether to provide funding to keep the program going. Do IUDs prevent the implantation of fertilized eggs? That is the question now.

In *Pro* I argue that very few Americans really believe a fertilized egg, embryo, or even fetus is a person with a right to life; at bottom, the hostility to abortion is really about women and sex. Misogyny and sexual stigma are what keep us from thinking about abortion clearly. We talk about it as if it were an extreme action taken by irresponsible, selfish, promiscuous women—or, more kindly, "desperate" and "confused" women—when actually it is a normal part of women's reproductive life: One in three women will have had an abortion by menopause, and 6 in 10 women who end their pregnancies are already mothers.

The real enemy of reproductive rights is not just the powerful anti-abortion movement and the politicians who do its bidding. (And seriously, how many of those politicians are true believers?) It's the stigma and shame the issue evokes in the rest of us. That is what keeps the one in three women who've had abortions—and the husbands, boyfriends, parents, relatives, and friends who helped them—from standing up and saying, Enough already! That's what keeps many people quiet about their pro-choice convictions. Stigma produces silence, and silence produces political inertia. How much easier just to avoid the bad news, to tell yourself you or your loved ones won't ever need an abortion, or that when the dust settles it will still be available. You can always take a quick trip to New York if it comes to that, can't you?

After I read from *Pro* at a book fair, a lovely, literary, middle-aged woman who was volunteering came up to me. "I had an abortion," she said, "and I've never told anyone. Not even my best friend. You're the first." I asked her what she thought would happen if she did tell her friend. She said, "She'd probably tell me she had had one too." The great poet Muriel Rukeyser famously wrote if one woman told the truth about her life, the world would split open. It's going to take a lot more than one woman, but more than ever, that truth is what we need.

March 2015

ACKNOWLEDGMENTS

My deepest thanks to the many people who helped with the making of this book. Anna deVries was a fantastic editor, the hands-on kind who aren't supposed to exist anymore. Melanie Jackson, as always, was a wonderful agent.

Betsy Reed was the closest of readers and found many a thread that I had dropped. Hannah Gold was an indefatigable fact-checker. Rich Yeselson, Carole Joffe, Rebecca Traister, Richard Kim, and Ann Snitow generously took time to read and comment on chapters. For information and exchange of ideas, I'm grateful to Dan Maguire, Frances Kissling, Dr. Warren Hern, Merle Hoffman, David Karol, Ira Katznelson, Jonathan Zasloff, Christine Gudoff, Dr. Susan Wicklund, Meg Wolitzer, Reva Siegel, Robin Marty, Jodi Jacobson, Steph Herold, Irin Carmon, the members of the Women, Action and Media listserv and the ACN Talk listserv, and to Pat Thorpe, who came up with the title before I even had the idea of the book.

My sincerest thanks goes to the Puffin Foundation, for its generous support during the writing of this book.

As always my deepest gratitude is to Steven Lukes, for his love, encouragement, and patience, who listened to endless versions of practically every page, and always asked the right questions, even when I didn't want to admit it.

FURTHER READING

Brodie, Janet Farrell. *Contraception and Abortion in 19th Century America*. Ithaca and London: Cornell University Press, 1994.

Cannold, Leslie. *The Abortion Myth; Feminism, Morality, and the Hard Choices Women Make*. Middletown, CT: Wesleyan University Press, 1998.

Chesler, Ellen. *Woman of Valor: Margaret Sanger and the Birth Control Movement in America*. New York: Simon & Schuster Paperbacks, 2007.

Dubow, Sara. *Ourselves Unborn: A History of the Fetus in Modern America*. New York: Oxford University Press, 2010.

Erdreich, Sarah. *Generation Roe: Inside the Future of the Pro-Choice Movement*. New York: Seven Stories Press, 2013.

Fessler, Ann. *The Girls Who Went Away: The Hidden History of Women Who Surrendered Children for Adoption in the Decades Before Roe v Wade*. New York: Penguin, 2006.

Garrow, David. *Liberty and Sexuality: The Right to Privacy and the Making of Roe v. Wade*. New York: Macmillan, 1994.

Goldberg, Michelle. *The Means of Reproduction: Sex, Power, and the Future of the World*. New York: Penguin Press, 2009.

Gordon, Linda. *The Moral Property of Women: A History of Birth Control Politics in America*. Bloomington, IL: University of Illinois Press, 2007.

Greenhouse, Linda, and Reva B. Siegel. *Before Roe v. Wade: Voices That Shaped the Abortion Debate Before the Supreme Court's Ruling*. New York: Kaplan Publishing, 2010.

Joffe, Carole. *Doctors of Conscience: The Struggle to Provide Abortion Before and After Roe v. Wade*. Boston: Beacon Press 1995.

Joyce, Kathryn. *The Child Catchers: Rescue, Trafficking, and the New Gospel of Adoption*. New York: Public Affairs, 2013.

———. *Quiverfull: Inside the Christian Patriarchy Movement*. Boston: Beacon Press, 2009.

Kertzer, David. *Sacrificed for Honor: Italian Infant Adoption and the Politics of Reproductive Control*. Boston: Beacon Press, 1993.

Maguire, Daniel C., ed. *Sacred Rights: The Case for Contraception and Abortion in World Religions*. New York: Oxford University Press, 2003.

Marty, Robin, and Jessica Mason Pieklo. *Crow After Roe: How "Separate but Equal" Has Become the New Standard in Women's Health Care and How We Can Change That*. Brooklyn, NY: Ig Publishing, 2013.

Page, Cristina. *How the Pro-Choice Movement Saved America: Freedom, Politics, and the War on Sex*. New York: Basic Books, 2006.

Reagan, Leslie. *Dangerous Pregnancies: Mothers, Disabilities, and Abortion in Modern America*, Berkeley: University of California Press, 2009.

———. *When Abortion Was a Crime: Women, Medicine, and Law in the United States, 1967–1973*. Berkeley: University of California Press, 1998.

Roberts, Dorothy. *Killing the Black Body: Race, Reproduction, and the Meaning of Liberty*. New York: Pantheon, 1997.

Solinger, Rickie. *The Abortionist: A Woman Against the Law*. Berkeley: University of California Press, 1996.

Solinger, Rickie, ed. *Abortion Wars: A Half Century of Struggle, 1950–2000*. Berkeley: University of California Press, 1998.

Wicklund, Susan, and Alex Kesselheim. *This Common Secret: My Journey as an Abortion Doctor*. New York: PublicAffairs, 2007.

NOTES

INTRODUCTION

1 Amanda Marcotte, "Kansas Moves to Defund Planned Parenthood and Force Doctors to Report Every Miscarriage," *Slate*, March 26, 2014, slate.com/blogs/xx_factor/2014/03/26/kansas_moves_to_defund_planned_parenthood_and_force_doctors_to_report_every.html.

2 Jamaica Kincaid, "Commentary: President Obama Supports Women's Rights to Choose," BET, September 26, 2012, bet.com/news/features/vote-2012/news/politics/2012/09/26/commentary-president-obama-supports-women-s-rights-to-choose.html.

3 CNN, "Anti-Abortion Activist Can't Use 'Necessity Defense' in Slaying," December 22, 2009, cnn.com/2009/CRIME/12/22/kansas.doctor.killed/.

4 Lucinda Cisler, "Abortion Law Repeal (Sort Of): A Warning to Women," in *Notes from the Second Year*, eds.

Shulamith Firestone and Anne Koedt (New York: Radical Feminism, 1970), available at fair-use.org/lucinda-cisler/a bortion-law-repeal-(sort-of).

5   Ellen Willis, "Abortion: Is a Woman a Person?," in *The Essential Ellen Willis*, ed. Nona Willis Aronowitz (Minneapolis: University of Minnesota Press, 2014), 91.

6   Reva B. Siegel, "Abortion as a Sex Equality Right: Its Basis in Feminist Theory," in *Mothers in Law: Feminist Theory and the Legal Regulation of Motherhood*, eds. Martha Albertson Fineman and Isabel Karpin (New York: Columbia University Press, 1995), 44–72.

1. RECLAIMING ABORTION

1   Claudia Goldin and Lawrence F. Katz, "The Power of the Pill: Oral Contraceptives and Women's Career and Marriage Decisions," *Journal of Political Economy* 110 (2002): 730–70.

2   Centers for Disease Control and Prevention, "Achievements in Public Health, 1900–1999: Family Planning," December 3, 1999, cdc.gov/mmwr/preview/mmwrhtml /mm4847a1.htm.

3   Gretchen Livingston and D'Vera Cohn, "Childlessness Up Among All Women; Down Among Women with Advanced Degrees," Pew Research Center, June 25, 2010, pewsocialtrends.org/2010/06/25/childlessness-up-among-a ll-women-down-among-women-with-advanced-degrees/.

4   Lindsay E. Clark et al, "Reproductive Coercion and Co-Occurring Intimate Partner Violence in Obstetrics and Gynecology Patients," *American Journal of Obstetrics and Gynecology* 210, no. 1 (2014): 42.e1–e8.

5   Guttmacher Institute, "Induced Abortion in the United States," February 2014, guttmacher.org/pubs/fb_induced _abortion.html.

6   *American Experience*, "Timeline: The Pill," PBS, 1999–2002, pbs.org/wgbh/amex/pill/timeline/timeline2.html.

7   Rachel Benson Gold, "Lessons from Before Roe: Will Past Be Prologue?" *The Guttmacher Report on Public Policy* 6, no. 1 (2003): 8–11.

8   Linda Greenhouse and Reva B. Siegel, *Before Roe v. Wade: Voices That Shaped the Abortion Debate Before the Supreme Court's Ruling* (Kaplan Publishing, 2010), 267.

9   Gold, "Lessons from Before," 10.

10   Linda Greenhouse, "A Never-Ending Story," *The New York Times*, September 5, 2012, opinionator.blogs.nytimes .com/2012/09/05/a-never-ending-story/.

11   Gold, "Lessons from Before," 10.

12   Humphrey Taylor, "Attitudes to Abortion and Roe vs. Wade Are Now Almost Identical to Attitudes in 2005 and 2006," Harris Interactive, 2009, harrisinteractive.com /vault/Harris-Interactive-Poll-Research-Abortion-2009-08 .pdf.

13   Carole E. Joffe, *Doctors of Conscience: The Struggle to Provide Abortion Before and After Roe v. Wade* (Boston: Beacon Press, 1995), 212.

14   Brady Dennis, "Abortion Doctor Kermit Gosnell Convicted of Murder in Deaths of Three Infants," *The Washington Post*, May 13, 2013.

15   Elizabeth Nash et al, "Laws Affecting Reproductive Health and Rights: 2013 State Policy Review," Guttmacher Institute, January 2, 2014, guttmacher.org/statecenter /updates/2013/statetrends42013.html.

16   Sheila Bapat, "Ohio Diverts TANF Dollars to CPCs,

Revealing Connection Between Reproductive, Economic Justice," RH Reality Check, July 22, 2013, rhrealitycheck .org/article/2013/07/22/ohio-diverts-tanf-dollars-to-cpcs -revealing-connection-between-reproductive-economic -justice/.

17   Esmé E. Deprez, "The Vanishing Abortion Clinic," *Businessweek*, November 27, 2013.

18   Rachel Benson Gold and Elizabeth Nash, "Troubling Trend: More States Hostile to Abortion Rights as Middle Ground Shrinks," *Guttmacher Policy Review* 15, no. 1 (2012): 14–19.

19   Elizabeth G. Raymond and David A. Grimes, "The Comparative Safety of Legal Induced Abortion and Childbirth in the United States," *Obstetrics & Gynecology* 119, no. 2 (February, 2012): 215–19.

20   Guttmacher Institute, "Induced Abortion."

21   American Psychological Association, "Mental Health and Abortion," apa.org/pi/women/programs/abortion/.

22   Patrick D. Healy, "Clinton Seeking Shared Ground over Abortions," *The New York Times*, January 25, 2005.

23   Pew Research, "Roe v. Wade at 40: Most Oppose Over-turning Abortion Decision," Pew Research Center, January 16, 2013, pewforum.org/2013/01/16/roe-v-wade-at-40/.

24   Planned Parenthood, "'Alarmed and Saddened' by Komen Foundation Succumbing to Political Pressure, Planned Parenthood Launches Fund for Breast Cancer Services," January 31, 2012, plannedparenthood.org/about-us/news room/press-releases/alarmed-saddened-komen-foundati on-succumbing-political-pressure-planned-parenthood-launches-fun-38629.htm.

25   Pam Belluck, "Pregnancy Centers Gain Influence in

Anti-Abortion Arena," *The New York Times*, January 4, 2013.

26   NARAL, "Virginia Department of Health Referring Women to Crisis Pregnancy Centers That Shame, Mislead," Press release, July 1, 2013, naralva.org/media /press/20130701.shtml.

27   Pew Research Center, "Public Opinion on Abortion: Current Breakdown of Views, 2012–2013," July, 2013, features.pewforum.org/abortion-slideshow/slide2.php.

28   Dana Milbank, "Roe v. Wade's Greedy Offspring," *Washington Post*, January 17, 2012.

29   Naomi Wolff, "Our Bodies, Our Souls," *The New Republic*, October 16, 1995.

30   Andrew Sullivan, "Life Lesson," *The New Republic*, February 7, 2005.

31   P. C. Arck et al, "Stress and Immune Mediators in Miscarriage," *Human Reproduction* 16, no. 7 (2001): 1505–511.

2. WHAT DO AMERICANS THINK ABOUT ABORTION?

1   Center for Reproductive Rights, "Center for Reproductive Rights Files Case Revealing the Horrifying Reality of El Salvador's Ban on Abortion," Press release, March 21, 2012, reproductiverights.org/en/press-room/center-for -reproductive-rights-files-case-revealing-the-horrifying-re ality-of-el-salvador.

2   Douglas Dalby, "Inquiry Sought in Death in Ireland After Abortion Was Denied," *The New York Times*, November 22, 2012.

3   Geoff Garin and Molly O'Rourke, "A Deeper Look at Voters' Opinion on 20-Week Abortion Bans," Hart Research Association, August 28, 2013, plannedparent hood.org/files/PPFA/FINAL_20_week_bans_polling _memo2.pdf.

4   Drew Griffin and Kira Kay, "Doctor Flies into South Dakota to Perform Abortions," CNN.com, March 31, 2006, cnn.com/2006/US/03/31/griffin.abortion/.

5   Fernanda Santos, "Albuquerque Voters Defeat Anti-Abortion Measure," *The New York Times*, November 20, 2013.

6   Lydia Saad, "Public Opinion About Abortion—An In-Depth Review," Gallup, January 22, 2002, gallup.com /poll/9904/public-opinion-about-abortion-indepth -review.aspx.

7   Tom W. Smith and Jaesok Son, "Trends in Public Attitudes Towards Abortion," The National Opinion Research Center, May 2013, norc.org/PDFs/GSS%20Reports /Trends%20in%20Attitudes%20About%20Abortion_Final .pdf.

8   Quinnipiac University, "U.S. Catholics Back Pope on Changing Church Focus, Quinnipiac University National Poll Finds; Catholics Support Gay Marriage, Women Priests 2–1," Poll, October 4, 2013, quinnipiac.edu/news -and-events/quinnipiac-university-poll/national/release -detail?ReleaseID=1961.

9   CBS News, "Views of Economy Remain Negative, More Optimism About Housing Than Job Market," Poll, July 24, 2013, realclearpolitics.com/docs/2013/CBS _National_0724b.pdf.

10 Rachel K. Jones and Jenna Jerman, "Abortion Incidence and Service Availability in the United States, 2011," *Per-*

spectives on Sexual and Reproductive Health 46, no. 1 (2014): 3–14.

11   Lawrence B. Finer et al, "Reasons U.S. Women Have Abortions: Quantitative and Qualitative Perspectives," *Perspectives on Sexual and Reproductive Health* 37, no. 3 (2005): 110–18.

12   Washington Post Editorial Board, "Woman with Weak Heart to Have Abortion Today / Struggle Has Stirred National Debate." SFGate, October 20, 1998, sfgate .com/health/article/Woman-With-Weak-Heart-To-Have -Abortion-Today-2984322.php.

13   ACLU, "Tamesha Means v. United States Conference of Catholic Bishops," December 2, 2013, aclu.org/reproductive -freedom-womens-rights/tamesha-means-v-united-states -conference-catholic-bishops.

14   Saad, "Americans' Abortion Views Steady Amid Gosnell Trial," Gallup, 2013, http://www.gallup.com/poll /162374/americans-abortion-views-steady-amid-gosnell -trial.aspx.

15   TMZ Staff, "Mitt Romney's Son Signed 'Abortion' Clause in Surrogate Birth Contract," TMZ, September 21, 2012, tmz.com/2012/09/20/mitt-romney-son-tagg-abortion-claus e-surrogate-birth-agreement-contract-bill-handel/.

16   Rick Pearson and Duaa Eldeib, "Walsh, Duckworth Clash on Medicare, Abortion," *Chicago Tribune*, October 18, 2012.

17   AtCenterNetwork, "Libertyville Abortion Demonstration," July 30, 2007, youtube.com/watch?v=Uk6t_tdOkwo.

18   Associated Press, "Bush: Debate 'Went Great'; Abortion Reply Clarified," *Los Angeles Times*, September 26, 1988.

19   Lydia Saad, "Majority of Americans Still Support Roe v. Wade Decision," Gallup, January 22, 2013, gallup.com

/poll/160058/majority-americans-support-roe-wade -decision.aspx.

20   Gallup, "Abortion," Poll, 2014, gallup.com/poll/1576 /abortion.aspx#1.

21   Rachel Benson Gold and Elizabeth Nash, "State Abortion Counseling Policies and the Fundamental Principles of Informed Consent," *Guttmacher Policy Review* 10, no. 4 (Fall 2007): 6–13.

22   Pew Research Center, "Public Opinion Supports Alito on Spousal Notification Even as it Favors *Roe v. Wade*," Pew Research Center Pollwatch, November 2, 2005, people -press.org/2005/11/02/public-opinion-supports-alito-on-sp ousal-notification-even-as-it-favors-iroe-v-wadei/.

23   Charlotte Lozier Institute, "Staff: Michael J. New," lozierinstitute.org/about/staff/.

24   Sofia Resnick, "Anti-Abortion Scholar: Restrictions Should Be Designed to Raise Costs for Women," *Mother Jones*, September 21, 2012.

25   Lawrence B. Finer et al, "Timing of Steps and Reasons for Delays in Obtaining Abortions in the United States," *Contraception* 74 (2006): 334–44.

26   Ramesh Ponnuru, *The Party of Death: The Democrats, the Media, the Courts, and the Disregard for Human Life* (Washington, DC: Regnery Publishing, 2006), 17–20.

27   Amelia Thomson-Deveaux, "The Last of the Late-Term Abortion Providers," *American Prospect*, September 20, 2013.

28   Saad, "Public Opinion About Abortion."

29   Smith and Son, "Trends in Public Attitudes Towards Abortion."

30   Pew Research, "Roe v. Wade at 40: Most Oppose Overturning Abortion Decision," Pew Research Center, Janu-

ary 16, 2013, pewforum.org/2013/01/16/roe-v-wade-at-40/; image courtesy of Polling Report, pollingreport.com /abortion.htm.

31 Ibid.

32 Karen Pazol et al, "Abortion Surveillance—United States, 2010," *Morbidity and Mortality Weekly Report* 62, no. ss08 (2013): 1–44.

33 Rachel K. Jones, Ushma D. Upadhyay, and Tracy A. Weitz, "At What Cost?: Payment for Abortion Care by U.S. Women," *Women's Health Issues* 23, no. 3 (May 2013): e173–78.

34 NARAL, "Abortion Bans at 20 Weeks: A Dangerous Restriction for Women," January 1, 2014, prochoiceamerica .org/media/fact-sheets/abortion-bans-at-20-weeks.pdf.

35 University of Pennsylvania, "Firearm Injury in the U.S." Firearm & Injury Center at Penn, 2011, uphs.upenn.edu /ficap/resourcebook/pdf/monograph.pdf.

36 Public Policy Polling, "MS GOP: Bryant for Gov., Barbour or Huckabee for Pres," Poll, April 7, 2011, publicpol icypolling.com/pdf/PPP_Release_MS_0407915.pdf.

3. WHAT IS A PERSON?

1 G. Noe et al, "Contraceptive Efficacy of Emergency Contraception with Levonorgestrel Given Before or After Ovulation," *Contraception* 81, no. 5 (May 2010): 414–20; Gillian Dean, MD, et al, eds., *Contraceptive Technology: Twentieth Revised Edition* (New York: Ardent Media, 2011), 147–91.

2 Reed Abelson, "Catholic Hospitals Expand, Religious Strings Attached," *The New York Times*, February 20, 2012.

3   Platform Staff, "Republican Platform 2012," August 2012, gop.com/wp-content/uploads/2012/08/2012GOPPlatform .pdf.

4   Ann Coulter, "Don't Blame Romney," *Human Events*, November 7, 2012, humanevents.com/2012/11/07/ann -coulter-dont-blame-romney/.

5   Joel Feinberg, "Abortion," in *Matters of Life and Death*, ed. Tom Regan (Philadelphia: Temple University Press, 1980), 37–75.

6   UCSF Medical Center, "Conception: How It Works," ucsfhealth.org/education/conception_how_it_works/.

7   Rachel Benson Gold, "The Implications of Defining When a Woman Is Pregnant," *The Guttmacher Report on Public Policy* 8, no. 2 (May, 2005): 7–10.

8   Christine Gudorf, "Contraception and Abortion in Ro-man Catholicism," in *Sacred Rights: The Case for Con-traception and Abortion in World Religions*, ed. Daniel Maguire (New York: Oxford University Press, 2003), 69.

9   Robert George and Christopher Tollefsen, *Embryo: A Defense of Human Life*, Second Edition (Princeton: The Witherspoon Institute, 2011), 20.

10   Ibid., 12.

11   Ibid., 22.

12   Ibid., 20.

13   Kim Masters, "In 'Horton' Movie, Abortion Foes Hear an Ally," NPR, March 14, 2008, npr.org/templates/story /story.php?storyId=88189147.

14   C-SPAN, "Todd Akin Denounces Stem Cell Research," C-SPAN, May 24, 2005, c-span.org/video/?c4001028/todd -akin-denounces-stem-cell-research.

15   Aeschylus, *The Oresteia*, trans. Douglas Young (Norman, OK: University of Oklahoma, 1974), 122.

16   Ibid.

17   Ibid.

18   Ibid., 125.

19   Miriam Lichtheim, ed. *Ancient Egyptian Literature; A Book of Readings* (Berkeley: University of California Press, 1973), http://www.humanistictexts.org/ptahhotep.htm.

20   M.A.S. Abdel Haleem, ed. *The Qur'an* (New York: Oxford University Press, 2004), Sura 2:223.

21   Gudorf, "Contraception and Abortion," 63.

22   Ellen Willis, "Abortion: Is a Woman a Person?," in *The Essential Ellen Willis*, ed. Nona Willis Aronowitz (Minneapolis: University of Minnesota Press, 2014), 92.

23   Ronald Dworkin. *Life's Dominion: An Argument About Abortion, Euthanasia, and Individual Freedom* (New York: Knopf, 1994), 13.

24   Center for Reproductive Rights, "The World's Abortion Laws 2011," September 2011, http://reproductiverights .org/sites/crr.civicactions.net/files/documents/Abortion Map_2011.pdf.

25   Dworkin, *Life's Dominion*, 13.

26   George and Tollefsen, *Embryo*, 138.

27   Washington Post Editorial Board, "Rick Santorum Shows He's the Wrong Man to Be President," *Washington Post*, February 27, 2012.

28   Kaiser Health News, "VP Debate: How Faith Informs the Candidates on Abortion," October 12, 2012, kaiserhealth news.org/multimedia/2012/october/danville-debate-biden -ryan-abortion.aspx.

29   The Diane Rehm Show, "States and the Debate Over Abortion Rights," Transcript, *The Diane Rehm Show*, April 8, 2013, thedianerehmshow.org/shows/2013-04-08 /states-and-debate-over-abortion-rights/transcript.

30   Sheryl Gay Stolberg, "The Nation; Shifting Certainties in the Abortion War," *The New York Times*, January 11, 1998.

31   Guttmacher Institute, "Requirements for Ultrasound," State Policies in Brief, May 1, 2014, guttmacher.org/state center/spibs/spib_RFU.pdf.

32   Emily Ramshaw, "In Texas and Va., Different Reactions to Sonogram Bills," *Texas Tribune*, February 23, 2012.

33   Associated Press, "Senate Approves Bill on 'Wrongful Births,'" *Arizona Capitol Times*, March 6, 2012.

34   Erin Matson, "How Virginia's 'Conscience Clause' for Genetic Counselors Could Set a National Precedent," RH Reality Check, April 8, 2014, http://rhrealitycheck .org/article/2014/04/08/virginias-conscience-clause -genetic-counselors-set-national-precedent/.

35   Guttmacher Institute, "Counseling and Waiting Periods for Abortion," State Policies in Brief, May 1, 2014, gutt macher.org/statecenter/spibs/spib_MWPA.pdf.

36   Tracy Weitz, "What We Are Missing in the Trans-vaginal Ultrasound Debate," RH Reality Check, March 1, 2013, rhrealitycheck.org/article/2013/03/01/challenges-in-the-tr ans-vaginal-ultrasound-debate/.

37   Sarah Terzo, "78% of Pregnant Women Seeing an Ultra-sound Reject Abortions," *Life News*, February 7, 2013.

38   Focus on the Family, "Focus on the Family Clarifies Op-tion Ultrasound Numbers," October 18, 2011, focusonthe-family.com/about_us/news_room/news-releases/2011/2011 1018-focus-on-the-family-clarifies-option-ultrasound-num bers.aspx.

39   Jeanne Monahan, "Ultrasound Policy," FRC, July 2010, http://www.frc.org/onepagers/ultrasound-policy.

40   Politifact, "More Than 90% of Women Change Their

Minds About Having an Abortion After Seeing an Ultrasound, Rachel Campos-Duffy Says," July 12, 2013, politifact
.com/wisconsin/statements/2013/jul/12/rachel-campos
-duffy/more-90-women-change-their-minds-about
having-abor/.

41 Mary Gatter et al, "Relationship Between Ultrasound
Viewing and Proceeding to Abortion," *Obstetrics &
Gynecology* 123, no. 1 (2014): 81–87.

42 Abigail Pesta, "Personhood USA's Keith Mason Eyes
Election Day 2012," *Newsweek*, June 25, 2012, mag
.newsweek.com/2012/06/24/personhood-usa-s-keith
-mason-eyes-election-day-2012.html.

43 Denise Grady, "Medical Nuances Drove 'No' Vote in
Mississippi," *The New York Times*, November 14, 2011.

44 Julie Rovner, "Abortion Foes Push to Redefine Personhood," NPR, June 1, 2011, npr.org/2011/06/01/136850622/.

45 Personhood USA, "About Us," personhoodusa.com/about
-us/our-mission/.

46 Robin Marty, "Mississippi Personhood: They're Baaaacccck-
kkk!" RH Reality Check, March 5, 2013, rhrealitycheck.org
/article/2013/03/05/mississippi-personhood-theyre-baa
aacccckkkk/.

47 Irin Carmon, "Personhood's Mississippi Moment of
Truth," *Salon*, November 8, 2011, salon.com/2011/11/08
/personhoods_mississippi_moment_of_truth/.

48 Irin Carmon, "The Next Front in the Abortion Wars: Birth
Control," *Salon*, October 26, 2011, salon.com/2011/10/26/
the_next_front_in_the_abortion_wars_birth_control/.

49 Grace Wyler, "Personhood Movement Continues to Divide Pro-Life Activists," *Time*, July 24, 2013; Phyllis
Schlafly, "The Personhood Amendment Is a Mistake,"

Eagle Forum, May 6, 2010, eagleforum.org/topics/life/2010/personhood-5-06-2010.pdf.

50   Mississippi Public Broadcasting. "State of the State 2013," January 23, 2013, youtube.com/watch?v=VbOb_UHkoa0&feature=youtu.be.

51   Erik Eckholm, "Push for 'Personhood' Amendment Represents New Tack in Abortion Fight," *The New York Times*, October 26, 2011; Carmon, "Personhood's Mississippi Moment of Truth"; Tim Murphy, "Mississippi Dem Unsure What Personhood Does, Still Supports It," *Mother Jones*, October 26, 2011, motherjones.com/mojo/2011/10/mississippi-gubernatial-candidates-unsure-what-personhood-does-supports-it.

52   Mike Celizic, "Octuplet Mom Defends Her 'Unconventional' Choices," *Today*, February 6, 2009, today.com/id/29038814/ns/today-parenting_and_family/t/octuplet-mom-defends-her-unconventional-choices/#.Uzgmua1dX2A.

53   Congregation for the Doctrine of the Faith, "Instruction *Dignitas Personae*," June 20, 2008, vatican.va/roman_curia/congregations/cfaith/documents/rc_con_cfaith_doc_20081208_dignitas-personae_en.html.

54   Sarah Elizabeth Richards, "Get Used to Embryo Adoption," *Time*, August 24, 2013, ideas.time.com/2013/08/24/get-used-to-embryo-adoption/.

55   Washington Times, "Embryo Adoption Becoming the Rage," *The Washington Times*, April 19, 2009.

56   US Department of Health & Human Services, "Embryo Adoption," 2013, hhs.gov/opa/about-opa-and-initiatives/embryo-adoption/index.html.

57   Richard Perez-Pena, "'70 Abortion Law: New York Said Yes, Stunning the Nation," *The New York Times*, April 20, 2000.

58 Kay Johnson et al, "Recommendations to Improve Pre-conception Health and Health Care—United States," *Morbidity and Mortality Weekly Report* 55, no. 4 (April 21, 2006): 1–23.

59 January W. Payne, "Forever Pregnant," *Washington Post*, May 16, 2006, washingtonpost.com/wp-dyn/content/article/2006/05/15/AR2006051500875.html; Kay Johnson et al, "A Report of the CDC/ATSDR Preconception Care Work Group and Select Panel on Preconception Care," Centers for Disease Control, April 21, 2006, cdc.gov/mmwr/preview/mmwrhtml/rr5506a1.htm.

60 Payne, "Forever Pregnant."

61 Centers for Disease Control and Prevention, "Contra-ception: How Effective Are Birth Control Methods?," August 28, 2013, cdc.gov/reproductivehealth/UnintendedPregnancy/Contraception.htm.

62 Jane E. Brody, "Switching Contraceptives Effectively," *The New York Times*, September 17, 2012, well.blogs.nytimes.com/2012/09/17/switching-contraceptives-effectively/; National Health Service, "How Long Does It Usually Take to Get Pregnant?" NHS Choices, November 21, 2013, nhs.uk/chq/Pages/2295.aspx?CategoryID=54&SubCategoryID=127.

63 Amelia Thomson-DeVeaux, "Arizona Woman Fights Her Hospital on Forced Cesarean Section," Care2, October 5, 2009, care2.com/causes/arizona-woman-fights-cesarean.html; ACLU, "Coercive and Punitive Governmental Responses to Women's Conduct During Pregnancy," September 30, 1997, aclu.org/reproductive-freedom/coercive-and-punitive-governmental-responses-womens-conduct-during-pregnancy.

64 Lynn M. Paltrow and Jeanne Flavin, "Arrests of and

Forced Interventions on Pregnant Women in the United States, 1973–2005: Implications for Women's Legal Status and Public Health," *Journal of Health Politics, Policy and Law* 38, no. 2 (2013): 299–343.

65 Amie Newman, "Pregnant? Don't Fall Down the Stairs," RH Reality Check, February 15, 2010, rhrealitycheck.org/article/2010/02/15/pregnant-dont-fall-down-stairs/.

66 Ed Pilkington, "Indiana Prosecuting Chinese Woman for Suicide Attempt That Killed Her Foetus," *The Guardian*, May 30, 2012.

67 Mayo Clinic Staff, "Miscarriage," Mayo Foundation, mayoclinic.org/diseases-conditions/pregnancy-loss-miscarriage/basics/definition/con-20033827.

68 Karlyn Bowman and Jennifer K. Marsico, "Attitudes About Abortion," American Enterprise Institute, January 16, 2014, aei.org/papers/politics-and-public-opinion/polls/attitudes-about-abortion-an-aei-public-opinion-study/.

69 Edward Walsh, "Queries Get Personal, McCain Gets Irritable," *Washington Post*, January 27, 2000.

4. ARE WOMEN PEOPLE?

1 Sarah K. Cowan, "Secrets and Social Influence" (PhD diss., University of California, Berkeley, 2013).

2 Centers for Disease Control and Prevention, "Unintended Pregnancy Prevention: Female Sterilization," December 7, 2000, cdc.gov/reproductivehealth/unintendedpregnancy/Sterilization.htm.

3 John Eligon and Michael Schwirtz, "Senate Candidate Provokes Ire with 'Legitimate Rape' Comment," *The New York Times*, August 19, 2012.

4   Public Broadcasting System, "South Dakota Law Bans Most Types of Abortion," PBS NewsHour, March 3, 2006, pbs.org/newshour/bb/law-jan-june06-abortion_3-03/.

5   Susan A. Cohen, "Abortion and Mental Health: Myths and Realities," *Guttmacher Policy Review* 9, no. 3 (2006): 8–16.

6   Justice Kennedy, "*Gonzoles v. Cahart*," Cornell University Law School, April 18, 2007, law.cornell.edu/supct /pdf/05-380P.ZO.

7   Ross Douthat, "The Daughter Theory," *The New York Times*, December 14, 2013.

8   Claudia Goldin and Lawrence F. Katz, "The Power of the Pill: Oral Contraceptives and Women's Career and Marriage Decisions," *Journal of Political Economy* 110, no. 4 730–70. See also Martha J. Bailey, "More Power to the Pill: The Impact of Contraceptive Freedom on Women's Life Cycle Labor Supply," *The Quarterly Journal of Economics* 121, no. 1 (2006): 289–319.

9   Caitlin Knowles Myers, "Power of the Pill or Power of Abortion? Re-Examining the Effects of Young Women's Access to Reproductive Control," Institute for the Study of Labor discussion paper No. 6661, www.sole-jole .org/12100.pdf.

10   Russell Shorto, "Contra-Contraception," *The New York Times*, May 7, 2006.

11   Jacki Calmes and Gardiner Harris, "Obama Endorses Decision to Limit Morning-After Pill," *The New York Times*, December 8, 2011.

12   Amy H. Herring et al, "Like a Virgin (Mother): Analysis of Data from a Longitudinal, U.S. Population Representative Sample Survey," *British Medical Journal* 347 (2013).

13   Stephanie Mencimer, "Holding Birth Control Hostage," *Mother Jones*, April 30, 2012.

14   The American College of Obstetricians and Gynecologists, "Committee Opinion: Over-the-Counter Access to Oral Contraceptives," December 2012, acog.org /Resources_And_Publications/Committee_Opinions /Committee_on_Gynecologic_Practice/Over-the -Counter_Access_to_Oral_Contraceptives.

15   Shauna R. Prewitt, "Giving Birth to a 'Rapist's Child': A Discussion and Analysis of the Limited Legal Protections Afforded to Women Who Become Mothers Through Rape," *Georgetown Law Journal* 98 (2010): 827–62.

16   Michael Kimmel, "Fired for Being Beautiful." *The New York Times*, July 16, 2013.

17   Maureen Dowd, "Dressed to Distract." *The New York Times*, June 5, 2010.

18   Jonathan V. Last, *What to Expect When No One's Expecting: America's Coming Demographic Disaster* (New York: Encounter Books, 2013), 18.

19   David Goldman (writing under the name Spengler), "The Peacekeepers of Penzance," *Asia Times*, August 22, 2006, www.atimes.com/atimes/Middle_East/HH22Ak02 .html.

20   Theodore Roosevelt, "On American Motherhood," Speech given before National Congress of Mothers, March 13, 1905, Washington, DC, nationalcenter.org/TRoosevelt Motherhood.html.

21   Jan M. Hoem, "Why Does Sweden Have Such High Fertility?" Max Planck Institute for Demographic Research, April 6, 2005, demogr.mpg.de/papers/working /wp-2005-009.pdf.

22   Helen Alvaré, "The White House and Sexualityism,"

The Witherspoon Institute, July 16, 2012, thepublicdis
course.com/2012/07/5757/.

23   United Nations Population Division, "World Population
2012," 2012, http://www.un.org/en/development/desa/pop
ulation/publications/pdf/trends/WPP2012_Wallchart.pdf.

24   Marianne Bertrand and Sendhil Mullainathan, "Are
Emily and Greg More Employable Than Lakisha and
Jamal? A Field Experiment on Labor Market Discrimination," National Bureau of Economic Research, July
2003, nber.org/papers/w9873.

25   Last, *What to Expect*, 170.

26   Thomas Frank, *What's the Matter with Kansas?: How
Conservatives Won the Heart of America* (New York: Henry
Holt, 2005): 7.

27   Manny Fernandez, "Texas Woman Is Taken Off Life Support After Order," *The New York Times*, January 26, 2014.

28   Bill Hoffmann, "Lynn Paltrow on Pregnant Woman on
Life Support: Change Law," Newsmax TV, December 30,
2013, newsmax.com/NewsmaxTv/pregnant-woman-life
-support/2013/12/30/id/544453/.

5. SIX MYTHS ABOUT ABORTION

1   *The Holy Bible, New International Version* (Grand Rap-
ids: Zondervan House, 1984), Jeremiah 1:5.

2   Ibid., Psalm 139:13.

3   Ibid., Luke 1:41.

4   Ibid., Deuteronomy 25:11–12.

5   Ibid., Exodus 21:22–23.

6   Robin Marty, "No Evidence for Claim that Sixty-Four
Percent of Women Were Coerced to Do So," RH Reality

Check, March 22, 2011, rhrealitycheck.org/article/2011
/03/22/percent-women-getting-abortions-coerced
-explained/; Vincent M. Rue et al, "Induced Abortion
and Traumatic Stress: A Preliminary Comparison of
American and Russian Women," *Medical Science Monitor* 10, no. 10 (2004), SR5–SR16.

7   Lawrence B. Finer et al, "Reasons U.S. Women Have
Abortions: Quantitative and Qualitative Perspectives,"
Perspectives on Sexual and Reproductive Health 37, no. 3,
(September 2005): 110–118.

8   Alexandra Sifferlin, "Doctors' Salaries: Who Earns the
Most and the Least?" *Time*, April 27, 2012.

9   Karen Pazol et al, "Abortion Surveillance—United States,
2010," *Morbidity and Mortality Weekly Report* 62, no.
ss08 (2013): 1–44.

10   Marcio A. da Fonesca, "Adverse Reaction to Amoxicillin:
A Case Report," *American Academy of Pediatric Dentistry*
22, no. 5 (2000): 401–04.

11   Association of Reproductive Health Professionals, "Mifepristone Safety Overview," Clinical fact sheet, April 2008,
arhp.org/publications-and-resources/clinical-fact-sheets
/mifepristone-safety-overview.

12   E. G. Raymond and D. A. Grimes, "The Comparative
Safety of Legal Induced Abortion and Childbirth in
the United States," *Obstetrics & Gynecology* 119, no. 6
1271–272.

13   Amnesty International, *Deadly Delivery: The Maternal
Health Care Crisis in the USA* (London: Amnesty International, 2010), 3.

14   Rebecca Wind, "U.S. Abortion Rate Hits Lowest Level
Since 1973," Guttmacher Institute, February 3, 2014.

15   William Saletan, "Safe, Legal, and Never," *Slate*, January 26, 2005, slate.com/articles/health_and_science/human _nature/2005/01/safe_legal_and_never.html.

16   Paul Vitello, "Religious Leaders Call for New Efforts to Lower the City's 'Chilling' Abortion Rate," *The New York Times*, January 6, 2011.

17   Stanley K. Henshaw and Rachel K. Jones, "Unmet Need for Abortion in the United States," Guttmacher Institute, September 20, 2007, paa2008.princeton.edu/papers/80673.

18   Stanley K. Henshaw et al, "Restrictions on Medicaid Funding for Abortions: A Literature Review," Guttmacher Institute, June 2009, guttmacher.org/pubs/Medic aidLitReview.pdf.

19   Akiba Solomon, "9 Reasons to Hate Anti-Abortion Billboards That Target Black Women," Color Lines, Feburary 25, 2011, colorlines.com/archives/2011/02/nine_reasons _to_hate_anti-abortion_billboards_that_target_black _women—and_one_reason_to_feel_the_lo.html.

20   Loretta Ross, "Re-enslaving African American Women," *On the Issues*, November 24, 2008, ontheissuesmagazine .com/2008fall/cafe2/article/22.

21   Loretta Ross, "African-American Women and Abortion," in *Abortion Wars: A Half Century of Struggle 1950–2000*, ed. Rickie Solinger (Berkeley: University of California Press, 1998), 161.

22   Michelle Goldberg, "Awakenings: On Margaret Sanger," *The Nation*, February 27 2012.

23   Andrea Barron, "Nicaragua's Anti-Abortion Law and US Extremists," *The Nicaragua Dispatch*, November 27, 2013.

24   Lynn M. Paltrow and Jeanne Flavin, "Arrests of and Forced Interventions on Pregnant Women in the United

States, 1973–2005: Implications for Women's Legal Status and Public Health," *Journal of Health Politics, Policy and Law* 28, no. 2 (January 15, 2012): 299–343.

25   Ada Calhoun, "The Criminalization of Bad Mothers," *The New York Times*, April 25, 2012.

26   Blake Farmer, "Tennessee Bill Could Send Addicted Moms to Jail," NPR, April 21, 2014, npr.org/blogs/health/2014/04/17/304173789/tennessee-bill-could-send-addicted-moms-to-jail.

27   Nina Martin, "A Stillborn Child, a Charge of Murder, and the Disputed Case Law on 'Fetal Harm,'" ProPublica, March 18, 2004, propublica.org/article/stillborn-child-charge-of-murder-and-disputed-case-law-on-fetal-harm. See also Laura Huss, "Mississippi Murder Charge Against Pregnant Teen Dismissed," National Advocates for Pregnant Women, April 4, 2014, advocatesforpregnantwomen.org/blog/2014/04/mississippi_murder_charge_agai.php.

6. WHAT DO ABORTION OPPONENTS REALLY OPPOSE?

1   Lydia Saad, "Republicans', Dems' Abortion Views Grow More Polarized," Gallup, March 8, 2010, gallup.com/poll/126374/republicans-dems-abortion-views-grow-polarized.aspx.

2   Aaron Blake, "Huckabee: Dems Think Women Can't Control Their Libido," *Washington Post*, "Post Politics," January 23, 2014, washingtonpost.com/blogs/post-politics/wp/2014/01/23/huckabee-dems-think-women-cant-control-their-libido/.

3   Adele M. Stan, "Why Wendy Davis' Opponent Is Stumping with Misogynist Ted Nugent," RH Reality Check,

February 19, 2014, rhrealitycheck.org/article/2014/02/19 /wendy-davis-opponent-stumping-misogynist-ted-nugent/.

4   Jennifer J. Frost, Mia R. Zolna, and Lori Frohwirth, "Contraceptive Needs and Services: 2010," Guttmacher Institute, July 2013, guttmacher.org/pubs/win/contrace ptive-needs-2010.pdf.

5   Rebecca Wind, "U.S. Abortion Rate Hits Lowest Level Since 1973," Guttmacher Institute, February 3, 2014, guttmacher.org/media/nr/2014/02/03/index.html?utm _source=feedburner&utm_medium=feed&utm_campa ign=Feed%3A+Guttmacher+(New+from+the+Guttmac her+Institute).

6   Frost, Zolna, and Frohwirth, "Contraceptive Needs."

7   Frank Newport, "Americans, Including Catholics, Say Birth Control Is Morally OK," Gallup, May 22, 2012, gallup.com/poll/154799/americans-including-catholics -say-birth-control-morally.aspx.

8   Robert Pear, "Obama Reaffirms Insurers Must Cover Contraception," *The New York Times*, January 20, 2012.

9   Albert Mohler, "Can Christians Use Birth Control?" albertmohler.com, May 8, 2006, albertmohler.com /2006/05/08/can-christians-use-birth-control/.

10   David Nather and Kate Nocera, "House votes to defund Planned Parenthood," Politico, February 18, 2011, http:// www.politico.com/news/stories/0211/49830.html.

11   Aimee Miles, "A Guide to GOP Proposals on Family Planning Funds," *Kaiser Health News*, March 9, 2011, kaiserhealthnews.org/stories/2011/february/18/planned -parenthood-title-10.aspx.

12   Juleanna Glover, "Republicans Must Support Public Financing for Contraception," *The New York Times*, December 27, 2012.

13   Becca Aaronson, "Claims Drop Under State-Run Women's Health Program," *Texas Tribune*, December 13, 2013.

14   Jordan Smith, "Texas Family Planning (Still) Costs More, Serves Fewer Women," *Austin Chronicle*, November 19, 2013.

15   Guttmacher Institute, "Facts on American Teens' Sources of Information About Sex," February 2012, guttmacher .org/pubs/FB-Teen-Sex-Ed.html.

16   Carolyn Jones, "State Health Department Spends $1.2 Million on Abstinence-Only Project," *Texas Observer*, September 25, 2013.

17   National Abstinence Education Association, "HHS Releases List of Successful Grantees for New Competitive Education Program," October 1, 2012, abstinenceworks. org/news/109-hhs-releases-list-of-successful-grantees-for-new-competitive-abstinence-education-program; Sarah Kliff, "Under Obama Administration, Abstinence-Only Education Finds Surprising New Foothold," *Washington Post*, May 8, 2012, washingtonpost.com/blogs/wonkblog /post/under-obama-administration-abstinence-only-educ ation-finds-surprising-new-foothold/2012/05/08/gIQA8fc wAU_blog.html.

18   Heather Boonstra and Elizabeth Nash. "Minors and the Right to Consent to Health Care," *The Guttmacher Report on Public Policy* 3, no. 4 (2000), 4–8.

19   Nick Sementelli, "Logical Fallacies and Radical Policies," Faith in Public Life, June 8, 2011, faithinpubliclife .org/blog/logical_fallacies_and_radical/.

20   Bob Garfield, "Rush Limbaugh, You Elite Liberal Feminist!" *The Guardian*, March 3, 2012.

21   Rush Limbaugh, "A Statement From Rush." RushLim

baugh.com, March 3, 2012, rushlimbaugh.com/daily /2012/03/03/a_statement_from_rush.

22   Conor Friedersdorf, "Rush Limbaugh: 'You Know How to Stop Abortion? Require That Each One Occur with a Gun,'" *The Atlantic*, January 17, 2013.

23   Jason McLure, "New Hampshire Planned Parenthood Stops Providing Birth Control," Reuters, July 8, 2011, reuters.com/article/2011/07/08/us-planned-parenthood -new-hampshire-idUSTRE7675Z820110708.

24   RWW Blog, "Bauer: Praising a 'Promiscuous Co-Ed' Like Sandra Fluke Is a Sign of 'Civilization Decline,'" October 11, 2013, youtube.com/watch?v=pT_N0yF5goY.

25   Paul Richter and Marlene Cimons, "Clinton Fires Surgeon General over New Flap," *Los Angeles Times*, December 10, 1994.

26   Rachel K. Jones and Joerg Dreweke, "Countering Conventional Wisdom: New Evidence on Religion and Contraceptive Use," Guttmacher Institute, April 2011, guttmacher .org/pubs/Religion-and-Contraceptive-Use.pdf.

27   Lawrence B. Finer et al, "Reasons U.S. Women Have Abortions: Quantitative and Qualitative Perspectives," *Perspectives on Sexual and Reproductive Health* 37, no. 3 (2005): 110–18.

28   Clare O'Conner, "Government Shutdown: 9 Million Moms and Babies at Risk as WIC Program Halts," *Forbes*, October 2, 2013.

29   Alex Pyke, "Top Conservative: Not 'The End of the World' for Women and Infants Losing Food During Shutdown," *Think Progress*, October 2, 2013, think progress.org/economy/2013/10/02/2716921/bill-kristol -shutdown-wic/.

30 Paul Krugman, "The Hammock Fallacy," *The New York Times*, March 6, 2014.

31 Sabrina Tavernise and Robert Gebeloff, "Millions of Poor Are Left Uncovered by Health Laws," *The New York Times*, October 2, 2013.

32 The Nurturing Network, "About Us," nurturingnetwork .org/aboutus.html.

33 Adele M. Stan, "At Any Cost: How Catholic Bishops Pushed for a Shutdown—and Even a Default—Over Birth Control," RH Reality Check, October 6, 2013, rhreality check.org/article/2013/10/06/at-any-cost-how-catholic-bis hops-pushed-for-a-shutdown-and-even-a-default-over -birth-control/.

34 Laurie Goodstein, "Pope Says Church Is 'Obsessed' with Gays, Abortion and Birth Control," *The New York Times*, September 19, 2013.

35 Katherine Bindley, "Teri James, Pregnant Woman Allegedly Fired for Premarital Sex, Sues Christian School," *Huffington Post*, March 1, 2013, huffingtonpost.com /2013/03/01/teri-james-pregnant-woman-fired-premarital -sex-christian-school_n_2790085.html.

36 Lauren Markoe, "Catholic Bishops Oppose Violence Against Women Act over Sexual Orientation Provisions," Sojourners, March 8, 2013, sojo.net/blogs/2013/03/08/cat holic-bishops-oppose-violence-against-women-act-over -sexual-orientation-provisio.

37 Michelle Boorstein and Elizabeth Tenety, "American Nuns Stunned by Vatican Accusation of 'Radical Feminism,' Crackdown," *Washington Post*, August 24, 2011.

38 Greg Giroux, "Musgrave's Priorities at Issue in Increas-

ingly Close Colo. 4 Race," *The New York Times*, September 28, 2006.

39 United States Conference of Catholic Bishops, "Forming Consciences for Faithful Citizenship," usccb.org/issues -and-action/faithful-citizenship/upload/forming-conscie nces-for-faithful-citizenship.pdf.

40 Ramesh Ponnuru, *The Party of Death: The Democrats, the Media, the Courts, and the Disregard for Human Life* (Washington, DC: Regnery Publishing, 2006), 156.

41 Paolo Setti, Emanuele Levi, and Pasquale Patrizio, "The Italian Experience of a Restrictive IVF Law: A Review," *Journal of Fertilization In Vitro* 2, no. 109.

42 Associated Press, "Italy Court Overturns Ban on Egg or Sperm Donation," *Washington Times*, April 9, 2014.

43 S. J. Antonio Spardo, "A Big Heart Open to God," *America Magazine*, September 30, 2013.

44 Anna Chu and Charles Posner, "Mapping the State of Women in America," Center for American Progress, September 25, 2013, americanprogress.org/issues/women /news/2013/09/25/75188/mapping-the-state-of-women-in -america/

45 Jean Reith Schroedel, *Is the Fetus a Person? A Comparison of Policies Across the Fifty States* (Ithaca, NY: Cornell University Press, 2000), 157.

7. CAN THERE BE A COMPROMISE ON ABORTION?

1 Lydia Saad, "Majority of Americans Still Support Roe v. Wade Decision," Gallup, January 22, 2013, gallup

.com/poll/160058/majority-americans-support-roe-wade-decision.aspx.

2 Guttmacher Institute, "Induced Abortion in the United States," February 2014, guttmacher.org/pubs/fb_induced_abortion.html.

3 William Saletan, "The Politics of Pain," *Slate*, July 26, 2013, slate.com/articles/news_and_politics/frame_game/2013/07/polls_and_fetal_pain_do_americans_support_a_ban_on_abortion_at_20_weeks.html.

4 A. Jenkins, S. Millar, and J. Robins, "Denial of Pregnancy: A Literature Review and Discussion of Ethical and Legal Issues," *Journal of the Royal Society of Medicine* 7, no. 104 (2011): 286–91.

5 Associated Press, "Birth Control at School? Most Say It's OK," CBS News, November 1, 2007, cbsnews.com/news/birth-control-at-school-most-say-its-ok/.

6 Richard Rothstein, "For Public Schools, Segregation Then, Segregation Since," Economic Policy Institute, August 27, 2013, epi.org/publication/unfinished-march-public-school-segregation/.

7 Esmé E. Deprez, "Abortion Clinics Close at Record Pace After States Tighten Rules," Bloomberg, September 3, 2013, bloomberg.com/news/2013-09-03/abortion-clinics-close-at-record-pace-after-states-tighten-rules.html.

8 Teddy Wilson, "Following Ohio Clinic Closures, Michigan Sees Influx of Ohio Patients Seeking Abortions," RH Reality Check, October 30, 2013, rhrealitycheck.org/article/2013/10/30/following-ohio-clinic-closures-michigan-sees-influx-of-ohio-patients-seeking-abortions/.

9 Austin Ruse, "Missouri Joins Five States with Only One Abortion Clinic," Breitbart, March 25, 2014, breitbart

.com/Big-Government/2014/03/23/Missouri-Joins-Five-Sta
tes-with-Only-One-Abortion-Clinic.

10   Niraj Chokshi, "State Abortion Rates Were Dropping
Even Before the Recent Surge in Restrictions," *Washington Post*, February 3, 2014.

11   Robin Marty, "America's Abortion-Free Zone Grows,"
The Daily Beast, April 14, 2014, thedailybeast.com/arti
cles/2014/04/14/america-s-abortion-free-zone-grows
.html.

12   National Center for Law and Economic Justice, "Poverty
in the United States: A Snapshot," nclej.org, September
2013, nclej.org/poverty-in-the-us.php.

13   Democrats for Life of America, "The 95-10 Initiative,"
April 21, 2005, democratsforlife.org/documents_etc/95-10
/95-10%20Document%20_TCB_.pdf.

14   Pew Research, "Abortion Laws Around the World," Re
ligion and Public Life Project, Pew Research Center,
September 30, 2008, pewforum.org/2008/09/30/abortion
-laws-around-the-world/.

15   Kolten Parker, "Lucio Files Bill to Require Pre-
Abortion Adoption Course," *San Antonio Express*, July
30, 2013.

16   Patrick D. Healy, "Clinton Seeking Shared Ground over
Abortion," *The New York Times*, January 25, 2005.

17   Michael D. Shear, "Obama Addresses Abortion Protests
in Commencement Speech at Notre Dame," *Washington Post*, May 18, 2009.

18   Anjani Chandra et al, "Adoption, Adoption Seeking, and
Relinquishment for Adoption in the United States," *US
Department of Health and Human Services* 306 (1999):
1–16.

19 Joshua Lang, "What Happens to Women Who Are Denied Abortions?" *The New York Times*, June 12, 2013.

20 US Department of Health & Human Services, "Adoption Experiences of Women and Men and Demand for Children to Adopt by Women 18–44 Years of Age in the United States, 2002," *Vital and Health Statistics* 23, no. 27 (2002): 1–36.

21 Ibid., 7.

22 bloggingheads.tv., "Steven Waldman (Beliefnet, *Founding Faith*) and William Saletan (*Slate, Bearing Right*)," June 26, 2009, bloggingheads.tv/videos/2151.

23 Susan M. Henney et al, "Evolution and Resolution: Birthmothers' Experience of Grief and Loss at Different Levels of Adoption Openness," *Journal of Social and Personal Relationships* 24, no. 6 (2007): 875–89.

24 Ranana Dine, "Scarlet Letters: Getting the History of Abortion and Contraception Right," Center for American Progress, August 8, 2013, americanprogress.org/issues/religion/news/2013/08/08/71893/scarlet-letters-getting-the-history-of-abortion-and-contraception-right/.

25 Sarah Kliff, "All States Except Oregon Now Limit Abortion Access," *Washington Post*, January 31, 2013.

8. REFRAMING MOTHERHOOD

1 Jessica Mason Pieklo, "In Denying a 16-Year-old Judicial Bypass, Nebraska Supreme Court Creates Ban on Abortions for Minors in State Custody," RH Reality Check, October 6, 2013, rhrealitycheck.org/article/2013/10/06/in-denying-a-16-year-old-judicial-bypass-nebraska-supr

eme-court-creates-ban-on-abortions-for-minors-in-state
-custody/.

2   US Department of Health & Human Services, "Using
        Medicaid to Cover Services for Elderly Persons in Resi-
        dential Care Settings: State Policy Maker and Stakeholder
        Views in Six States," HHS, 2002, hhs.gov/daltcp/reports
        /med4rcsb.htm.

3   Rachel Slajda, "Kyl: 'I Don't Need Maternity Care.'
        Stabenow: 'Your Mom Probably Did,'" *Talking Points
        Memo*, September 25, 2009, talkingpointsmemo.com/dc
        /kyl-i-don-t-need-maternity-care-stabenow-your-mom
        -probably-did.

4   Greg Mankiw, "Is Community Rating Fair?" Greg
        Mankiw's Blog, November 11, 2013, gregmankiw.blogspot
        .com/2013/11/is-community-rating-fair.html.

5   Elisabeth Rosenthal, "American Way of Birth, Costliest
        in the World," *The New York Times*, June 20, 2013.

6   US Equal Employment Opportunity Commission, "Preg-
        nancy Discrimination Charges FY 2010-FY 2013," EEOC,
        February 5, 2014, eeoc.gov/eeoc/statistics/enforcement
        /pregnancy_new.cfm.

7   Crystal Thomas, "Treating Pregnant Workers Right,"
        Chicago Sun-Times, April 16, 2014.

8   National Women's Law Center, "Fair Treatment for Preg-
        nant Workers: Guadalupe Hernandez's Story," NWLC,
        June 18, 2013, nwlc.org/resource/fair-treatment-pregnant
        -workers-guadalupe-hernandezs-story.

9   Dina Baskt, "Pregnant, and Pushed Out of a Job," *The
        New York Times*, January 30, 2012.

10   Sarah Jane Glynn and Jane Farrell, "The United States
        Needs to Guarantee Paid Maternity Leave," Center for

American Progress, March 8, 2013, americanprogress.org /issues/labor/news/2013/03/08/55683/the-united-states-ne eds-to-guarantee-paid-maternity-leave/.

11   Sarah Jane Glynn, "Fact Sheet: Child Care," Center for American Progress, August 16, 2012, americanprogress .org/issues/labor/news/2012/08/16/11978/fact-sheet-child -care/.

12   Arlie Russel Hochschild, *The Second Shift: Working Parents and the Revolution at Home* (New York: Viking, 1989). See also Richard H. Thaler, "Breadwinning Wives and Nervous Husbands," *The New York Times*, June 1, 2013.

13   Catalyst, "Women Leaving and Re-Entering the Workforce," Catalyst, March 18, 2013, catalyst.org/knowledge /women-leaving-and-re-entering-workforce.

14   Steve Greenhouse, "Recession Drives Women Back to the Work Force," *The New York Times*, September 18, 2009.

15   Judith Warner, "The Opt-Out Generation Wants Back In," *The New York Times*, August 7, 2013.

16   Tira Harpaz, "Can Women Over 50 'Lean In'?" *Salon*, March 23, 2013, salon.com/2013/03/23/is_leaning_in _an_option_for_women_over_50_partner/.

17   Vanessa Gallman, "Debate in House Is Emotional and Nasty. Those on Welfare Were Likened to Animals. Rhetoric Was Abrasive," *Philadelphia Inquirer*, March 25, 1995.

18   American Lung Association, "Women and Tobacco Use," American Lung Association, 2009, lung.org /stop-smoking/about-smoking/facts-figures/women-and -tobacco-use.html.

19   Tanya Gold, "The Right Has Chosen Its Scapegoat— The Single Mum. And She Will Bleed," *The Guardian*, August 19, 2011.

20   *Mother Jones*, "Mitt Romney Points Finger at Single Moms on Gun Violence," YouTube, October 17, 2012, youtube.com/watch?v=jIUyGrvMpVg.

21   Dr. Richard D. Land, "Adoption: The Best Option," *Christian Post*, November 23, 2013

22   Leslie Bennetts, "Summer of the Single Mom," *Daily Beast*, September 1, 2010, thedailybeast.com/articles /2010/09/01/jennifer-aniston-doesnt-deserve-bill-oreillys -scorn.html.

23   Feminists for Life of America, "Raising Kids on a Shoe-string," *The American Feminist*, 2009, http://feministsfor life.org/-taf/2009/Fall09.pdf.

24   Stephen Lowman, "Review of Bristol Palin's Memoir, 'Not Afraid of Life,'" *Washington Post*, June 22, 2011, articles .washingtonpost.com/2011-06-22/entertainment/3523 4814_1_bristol-palin-levi-johnston-memoir.

25   Katie Kindelan, "Bristol Palin Cites 'Foolish Decision' on Virginity and 'Not Accusing Levi of Date Rape,'" ABC News, June 27, 2011, abcnews.go.com/Politics/bri stol-palin-absolutely-mom-sarah-palin-run-president /story?id=13937099.

26   Fisher, "Map: How 35 Countries Compare."

27   Susan A. Cohen, "Abortion and Women of Color: The Bigger Picture," *Guttmacher Policy Review* 11, no. 3 (Spring, 2008): 2–12.

28   Guttmacher Institute, "State Facts About Abortion: Connecticut," Guttmacher Institute, 2014, guttmacher.org /pubs/sfaa/connecticut.html.

29   William Saletan, *Bearing Right: How Conservatives Won the Abortion War* (Berkeley: University of California Press, 2003).

30   Ian Lovett, "California Expands Availability of Abortions,"
      The New York Times, October 9, 2013.

31   Esmé E. Deprez, "Abortion-Rights Backers on Offense
      After 3-Year Drubbing," Bloomberg News, February 24,
      2014, bloomberg.com/news/2014-02-24/abortion-rights
      -backers-on-offense-after-3-year-drubbing.html.

AFTERWORD TO THE 2015 EDITION

1   Stephen Collinson, "Republicans Seize Senate, Gaining
      Full Control of Congress," CNN.com, November 5, 2014,
      cnn.com/2014/11/04/politics/election-day-story/.

2   Gail Sullivan, "How Colorado's Teen Birthrate Dropped
      40% in Four Years," *The Washington Post*, August 12, 2014,
      http://www.washingtonpost.com/news/morning-mix
      /wp/2014/08/12/how-colorados-teen-birthrate-dropped
      -40-in-four-years/.